Range

David Epstein is the author of the *New York Times* bestseller *The Sports Gene*. He has master's degrees in environmental science and journalism and has worked as an investigative reporter for *ProPublica* and a senior writer for *Sports Illustrated*. He lives in Washington, D.C.

ALSO BY DAVID EPSTEIN

The Sports Gene

Praise for *Range*

'David Epstein manages to make me thoroughly enjoy the experience of being told that everything I thought about something was wrong. I loved *Range*'   Malcolm Gladwell, author of *Outliers*

'An urgent and important book, an essential read for bosses, parents, coaches and anyone who cares about improving performance'
                    Daniel H. Pink, author of *Drive* and *To Sell is Human*

'It's a joy to spend hours in the company of a writer as gifted as David Epstein. And the joy is all the greater when that writer shares so much crucial and revelatory information about performance, success and education'   Susan Cain, author of *Quiet*

'A captivating read that will leave you questioning the next steps in your career – and the way you raise your children'
                    Adam Grant, author of *Originals* and co-author of *Option B*

'Extraordinary'   *Guardian*

'A goldmine of surprising insights. Makes you smarter with every page'
                    James Clear, author of *Atomic Habits*

'Brilliant, timely and utterly impossible to put down. If you care about improving skill, innovation and performance, you need to read this book'   Daniel Coyle, author of *The Talent Code*

'I want to give *Range* to . . . everyone who wants humans to thrive in an age of robots. *Range* is full of surprises and hope, a twenty-first-century survival guide'
                    Amanda Ripley, author of *The Smartest Kids in the World*

'Masterful. Perfect holiday reading'
                    Dr Adam Rutherford, author of *A Brief History of Everyone Who Ever Lived*

'Anyone contemplating a change of career late in life will find *Range* immensely reassuring. If you calculate that you don't have 10,000 hours left in which you can reasonably practise, you can use your range to connect ideas and use your varied experience'
                    Daniel Finkelstein, *The Times*

'The storytelling is so dramatic, the wielding of data so deft and the lessons so strikingly framed [it's] a pleasure to read . . . *Range* offers such a wealth of thought-provoking material'

New York Times Books Review

'Fabulous . . . If you are interested in champions' journeys, this is for you'

Judy Murray on Twitter

'As David Epstein shows us, cultivating range prepares us for the wickedly unanticipated . . . a well-supported and smoothly written case on behalf of breadth and late starts'

Wall Street Journal

'*Range* elevates Epstein to one of the very best science writers at work today. The scope of the book – and the implications – are breathtaking'

Sebastian Junger, filmmaker and author of *The Perfect Storm*

'One of the most thought-provoking and enlightening books I've read'

Maria Konnikova, poker player and author of *The Confidence Game*

'A fresh, brisk look at creativity, learning and the meaning of achievement'

Kirkus Reviews

'An assiduously researched and accessible argument for being a jack of all trades'

O Magazine, Best Nonfiction Books of 2019

'*Range* is a convincing, engaging survey of research and anecdotes that confirm a thoughtful, collaborative world is also a better and more innovative one'

NPR

'A clear and unfussy writer . . . this book is likely to resonate strongly with most teachers'

Tes

Range

How Generalists Triumph in a Specialized World

David Epstein

PAN BOOKS

First published 2019 by Riverhead Books
an imprint of Penguin Random House

First published in the UK in paperback 2019 by Macmillan

This edition published 2020 by Pan Books
an imprint of Pan Macmillan
The Smithson, 6 Briset Street, London EC1M 5NR
EU representative: Macmillan Publishers Ireland Ltd, 1st Floor,
The Liffey Trust Centre, 117-126 Sheriff Street Upper,
Dublin 1, DO1 YC43
Associated companies throughout the world
www.panmacmillan.com

ISBN 978-1-5098-4352-7

20

A CIP catalogue record for this book is available from the British Library.

Printed and bound by CPI Group (UK) Ltd, Croydon, CR0 4YY

For Elizabeth,
this one and any other one

Contents

And he refused to specialize in anything, preferring to keep an eye on *the overall estate* rather than any of its parts. . . . And Nikolay's management produced the most brilliant results.

—Leo Tolstoy, *War and Peace*

No tool is omnicompetent. There is no such thing as a master-key that will unlock *all* doors.

—Arnold Toynbee, *A Study of History*

Range

Roger vs. Tiger

LET'S START WITH a couple of stories from the world of sports. This first one, you probably know.

The boy's father could tell something was different. At six months old, the boy could balance on his father's palm as he walked through their home. At seven months, his father gave him a putter to fool around with, and the boy dragged it everywhere he went in his little circular baby walker. At ten months, he climbed down from his high chair, trundled over to a golf club that had been cut down to size for him, and imitated the swing he'd been watching in the garage. Because the father couldn't yet talk with his son, he drew pictures to show the boy how to place his hands on the club. "It is very difficult to communicate how to putt when the child is too young to talk," he would later note.

At two—an age when the Centers for Disease Control and Prevention list physical developmental milestones like "kicks a ball" and "stands on tiptoe"—he went on national television and used a club tall enough to reach his shoulder to drive a ball past an admiring Bob Hope. That same year, he entered his first tournament, and won the ten-and-under division.

There was no time to waste. By three, the boy was learning how to play out of a "sand twap," and his father was mapping out his destiny. He knew his son had been chosen for this, and that it was his duty to guide him. Think about it: if you felt that certain about the path ahead, maybe you too would start prepping your three-year-old to handle the inevitable and insatiable media that would come. He quizzed the boy, playing reporter, teaching him how to give curt answers, never to offer more than precisely what was asked. That year, the boy shot 48, eleven over par, for nine holes at a course in California.

When the boy was four, his father could drop him off at a golf course at nine in the morning and pick him up eight hours later, sometimes with the money he'd won from those foolish enough to doubt.

At eight, the son beat his father for the first time. The father didn't mind, because he was convinced that his boy was singularly talented, and that he was uniquely equipped to help him. He had been an outstanding athlete himself, and against enormous odds. He played baseball in college when he was the only black player in the entire conference. He understood people, and discipline; a sociology major, he served in Vietnam as a member of the Army's elite Green Berets, and later taught psychological warfare to future officers. He knew he hadn't done his best with three kids from a previous marriage, but now he could see that he'd been given a second chance to do the right thing with number four. And it was all going according to plan.

The boy was already famous by the time he reached Stanford, and soon his father opened up about his importance. His son would have a larger impact than Nelson Mandela, than Gandhi, than Buddha, he insisted. "He has a larger forum than any of them," he said. "He's the bridge between the East and the West. There is no limit because he has the guidance. I don't know yet exactly what form this will take. But he is the Chosen One."

———

This second story, you also probably know. You might not recognize it at first.

His mom was a coach, but she never coached him. He would kick a ball around with her when he learned to walk. As a boy, he played squash with his father on Sundays. He dabbled in skiing, wrestling, swimming, and skateboarding. He played basketball, handball, tennis, table tennis, badminton over his neighbor's fence, and soccer at school. He would later give credit to the wide range of sports he played for helping him develop his athleticism and hand-eye coordination.

He found that the sport really didn't matter much, so long as it included a ball. "I was always very much more interested if a ball was involved," he would remember. He was a kid who loved to play. His parents had no particular athletic aspirations for him. "We had no plan A, no plan B," his mother would later say. She and the boy's father encouraged him to sample a wide array of sports. In fact, it was essential. The boy "became unbearable," his mother said, if he had to stay still for too long.

Though his mother taught tennis, she decided against working with him. "He would have just upset me anyway," she said. "He tried out every strange stroke and certainly never returned a ball normally. That is simply no fun for a mother." Rather than pushy, a *Sports Illustrated* writer would observe that his parents were, if anything, "pully." Nearing his teens, the boy began to gravitate more toward tennis, and "if they nudged him at all, it was to stop taking tennis so seriously." When he played matches, his mother often wandered away to chat with friends. His father had only one rule: "Just don't cheat." He didn't, and he started getting really good.

As a teenager, he was good enough to warrant an interview with the local newspaper. His mother was appalled to read that, when asked what he would buy with a hypothetical first paycheck from playing tennis, her son answered, "a Mercedes." She was relieved when the reporter let her listen to a recording of the interview and they realized there'd been a mistake: the boy had said "*Mehr CDs*," in Swiss German. He simply wanted "more CDs."

The boy was competitive, no doubt. But when his tennis instructors decided to move him up to a group with older players, he asked to move back so he could stay with his friends. After all, part of the fun was hanging around after his lessons to gab about music, or pro wrestling, or soccer.

By the time he finally gave up other sports—soccer, most notably—to focus on tennis, other kids had long since been working with strength coaches, sports psychologists, and nutritionists. But it didn't seem to hamper his development in the long run. In his midthirties, an age by which even legendary tennis players are typically retired, he would still be ranked number one in the world.

———

In 2006, Tiger Woods and Roger Federer met for the first time, when both were at the apex of their powers. Tiger flew in on his private jet to watch the final of the U.S. Open. It made Federer especially nervous, but he still won, for the third year in a row. Woods joined him in the locker room for a champagne celebration. They connected as only they could. "I've never spoken with anybody who was so familiar with the feeling of being invincible," Federer would later describe it. They quickly became friends, as well as focal points of a debate over who was the most dominant athlete in the world.

Still, the contrast was not lost on Federer. "His story is completely different from mine," he told a biographer in 2006. "Even as a kid his goal was to break the record for winning the most majors. I was just dreaming of just once meeting Boris Becker or being able to play at Wimbledon some time."

It seems pretty unusual for a child with "pully" parents, and who first took his sport lightly, to grow into a man who dominates it like no one before him. Unlike Tiger, thousands of kids, at least, had a head start on Roger. Tiger's incredible upbringing has been at the heart of a batch of bestselling books on the development of expertise, one of which was a parenting manual written by Tiger's father, Earl. Tiger was not merely playing golf. He was engaging in "deliberate practice," the only kind that counts in the now-ubiquitous ten-thousand-hours rule to expertise. The "rule" represents the idea that the number of accumulated hours of highly specialized training is the sole factor in skill development, no matter the domain. Deliberate practice, according to the study of thirty violinists that spawned the rule, occurs when learners are "given explicit instructions about the best method," individually supervised by an instructor, supplied with "immediate informative feedback and knowledge of the results of their performance," and "repeatedly perform the same or similar tasks." Reams of work on expertise development shows that elite athletes spend more time in highly technical, deliberate practice each week than those who plateau at lower levels:

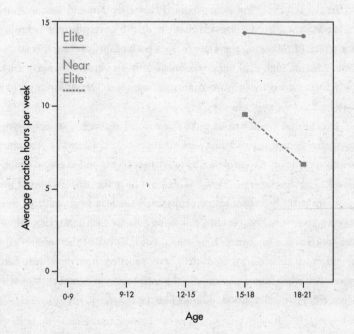

Tiger has come to symbolize the idea that the quantity of deliberate practice determines success—and its corollary, that the practice must start as early as possible.

The push to focus early and narrowly extends well beyond sports. We are often taught that the more competitive and complicated the world gets, the more specialized we all must become (and the earlier we must start) to navigate it. Our best-known icons of success are elevated for their precocity and their head starts—Mozart at the keyboard, Facebook CEO Mark Zuckerberg at the other kind of keyboard. The response, in every field, to a ballooning library of human knowledge and an interconnected world has been to exalt increasingly narrow focus. Oncologists no longer specialize in cancer, but rather in cancer related to a single organ, and the trend advances each year. Surgeon and writer Atul Gawande pointed out that when doctors joke about left ear surgeons, "we have to check to be sure they don't exist."

In the ten-thousand-hours-themed bestseller *Bounce*, British journalist Matthew Syed suggested that the British government was failing for a lack of following the Tiger Woods path of unwavering specialization. Moving high-ranking government officials between departments, he wrote, "is no less absurd than rotating Tiger Woods from golf to baseball to football to hockey."

Except that Great Britain's massive success at recent Summer Olympics, after decades of middling performances, was bolstered by programs set up specifically to recruit adults to try new sports and to create a pipeline for late developers—"slow bakers," as one of the officials behind the program described them to me. Apparently the idea of an athlete, even one who wants to become elite, following a Roger path and trying different sports is not so absurd. Elite athletes at the peak of their abilities do spend more time on focused, deliberate practice than their near-elite peers. But when scientists examine the entire developmental path of athletes, from early childhood, it looks like this:

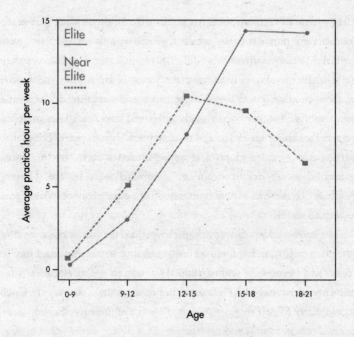

Eventual elites typically devote *less* time early on to deliberate practice in the activity in which they will eventually become experts. Instead, they undergo what researchers call a "sampling period." They play a variety of sports, usually in an unstructured or lightly structured environment; they gain a range of physical proficiencies from which they can draw; they learn about their own abilities and proclivities; and only later do they focus in and ramp up technical practice in one area. The title of one study of athletes in individual sports proclaimed "Late Specialization" as "the Key to Success"; another, "Making It to the Top in Team Sports: Start Later, Intensify, and Be Determined."

When I began to write about these studies, I was met with thoughtful criticism, but also denial. "Maybe in some other sport," fans often said, "but that's not true of *our* sport." The community of the world's most popular sport, soccer, was the loudest. And then, as if on cue, in late

2014 a team of German scientists published a study showing that members of their national team, which had just won the World Cup, were typically late specializers who didn't play more organized soccer than amateur-league players until age twenty-two or later. They spent more of their childhood and adolescence playing nonorganized soccer and other sports. Another soccer study published two years later matched players for skill at age eleven and tracked them for two years. Those who participated in more sports and nonorganized soccer, "but not more organized soccer practice/training," improved more by age thirteen. Findings like these have now been echoed in a huge array of sports, from hockey to volleyball.

The professed necessity of hyperspecialization forms the core of a vast, successful, and sometimes well-meaning marketing machine, in sports and beyond. In reality, the Roger path to sports stardom is far more prevalent than the Tiger path, but those athletes' stories are much more quietly told, if they are told at all. Some of their names you know, but their backgrounds you probably don't.

I started writing this introduction right after the 2018 Super Bowl, in which a quarterback who had been drafted into professional baseball before football (Tom Brady), faced off against one who participated in football, basketball, baseball, and karate and had chosen between college basketball and football (Nick Foles). Later that very same month, Czech athlete Ester Ledecká became the first woman ever to win gold in two different sports (skiing and snowboarding) at the same Winter Olympics. When she was younger, Ledecká participated in multiple sports (she still plays beach volleyball and windsurfs), focused on school, and never rushed to be number one in teenage competition categories. The *Washington Post* article the day after her second gold proclaimed, "In an era of sports specialization, Ledecká has been an evangelist for maintaining variety." Just after her feat, Ukrainian boxer Vasyl Lomachenko set a record for the fewest fights needed to win world titles in three different weight classes. Lomachenko, who took four years off boxing as a kid to learn traditional Ukrainian dance, reflected, "I was doing so many different sports as a young boy—gymnastics, basketball, football, tennis—and I think, ultimately, everything came together with all those different kinds of sports to enhance my footwork."

Prominent sports scientist Ross Tucker summed up research in the field simply: "We know that early sampling is key, as is diversity."

In 2014, I included some of the findings about late specialization in sports in the afterword of my first book, *The Sports Gene*. The following year, I got an invitation to talk about that research from an unlikely audience—not athletes or coaches, but military veterans. In preparation, I perused scientific journals for work on specialization and career-swerving outside of the sports world. I was struck by what I found. One study showed that early career specializers jumped out to an earnings lead after college, but that later specializers made up for the head start by finding work that better fit their skills and personalities. I found a raft of studies that showed how technological inventors increased their creative impact by accumulating experience in different domains, compared to peers who drilled more deeply into one; they actually benefited by proactively sacrificing a modicum of depth for breadth as their careers progressed. There was a nearly identical finding in a study of artistic creators.

I also began to realize that some of the people whose work I deeply admired from afar—from Duke Ellington (who shunned music lessons to focus on drawing and baseball as a kid) to Maryam Mirzakhani (who dreamed of becoming a novelist and instead became the first woman to win math's most famous prize, the Fields Medal)—seemed to have more Roger than Tiger in their development stories. I delved further and encountered remarkable individuals who succeeded not in spite of their range of experiences and interests, but because of it: a CEO who took her first job around the time her peers were getting ready to retire; an artist who cycled through five careers before he discovered his vocation and changed the world; an inventor who stuck to a self-made antispecialization philosophy and turned a small company founded in the nineteenth century into one of the most widely resonant names in the world today.

I had only dipped my toe into research on specialization in the wider world of work, so in my talk to the small group of military veterans I mostly stuck to sports. I touched on the other findings only briefly, but the audience seized on it. All were late specializers or career changers, and as they filed up one after another to introduce themselves after the talk, I could tell that all were at least moderately concerned, and some were borderline ashamed of it.

They had been brought together by the Pat Tillman Foundation, which, in the spirit of the late NFL player who left a professional football career to become an Army Ranger, provides scholarships to veterans, active-duty military, and military spouses who are undergoing career changes or going back to school. They were all scholarship recipients, former paratroopers and translators who were becoming teachers, scientists, engineers, and entrepreneurs. They brimmed with enthusiasm, but rippled with an undercurrent of fear. Their LinkedIn profiles didn't show the linear progression toward a particular career they had been told employers wanted. They were anxious starting grad school alongside younger (sometimes much younger) students, or changing lanes later than their peers, all because they had been busy accumulating inimitable life and leadership experiences. Somehow, a unique advantage had morphed in their heads into a liability.

A few days after I spoke to the Tillman Foundation group, a former Navy SEAL who came up after the talk emailed me: "We are all transitioning from one career to another. Several of us got together after you

had left and discussed how relieved we were to have heard you speak."
I was slightly bemused to find that a former Navy SEAL with an undergraduate degree in history and geophysics pursuing graduate degrees in
business and public administration from Dartmouth and Harvard
needed me to affirm his life choices. But like the others in the room, he
had been told, both implicitly and explicitly, that changing directions
was dangerous.

The talk was greeted with so much enthusiasm that the foundation
invited me to give a keynote speech at the annual conference in 2016,
and then to small group gatherings in different cities. Before each occasion, I read more studies and spoke with more researchers and found
more evidence that it takes time—and often forgoing a head start—to
develop personal and professional range, but it is worth it.

I dove into work showing that highly credentialed experts can become so narrow-minded that they actually get worse with experience,
even while becoming more confident—a dangerous combination. And I
was stunned when cognitive psychologists I spoke with led me to an
enormous and too often ignored body of work demonstrating that learning itself is best done slowly to accumulate lasting knowledge, even when
that means performing poorly on tests of immediate progress. That is,
the most effective learning looks inefficient; it looks like falling behind.

Starting something new in middle age might look that way too.
Mark Zuckerberg famously noted that "young people are just smarter."
And yet a tech founder who is fifty years old is nearly twice as likely to
start a blockbuster company as one who is thirty, and the thirty-year-
old has a better shot than a twenty-year-old. Researchers at Northwestern, MIT, and the U.S. Census Bureau studied new tech companies and
showed that among the fastest-growing start-ups, the average age of a
founder was forty-five when the company was launched.

Zuckerberg was twenty-two when he said that. It was in his interest
to broadcast that message, just as it is in the interest of people who run

youth sports leagues to claim that year-round devotion to one activity is necessary for success, never mind evidence to the contrary. But the drive to specialize goes beyond that. It infects not just individuals, but entire systems, as each specialized group sees a smaller and smaller part of a large puzzle.

One revelation in the aftermath of the 2008 global financial crisis was the degree of segregation within big banks. Legions of specialized groups optimizing risk for their own tiny pieces of the big picture created a catastrophic whole. To make matters worse, responses to the crisis betrayed a dizzying degree of specialization-induced perversity. A federal program launched in 2009 incentivized banks to lower monthly mortgage payments for homeowners who were struggling but still able to make partial payments. A nice idea, but here's how it worked out in practice: a bank arm that specialized in mortgage lending started the homeowner on lower payments; an arm of the same bank that specialized in foreclosures then noticed that the homeowner was suddenly paying less, declared them in default, and seized the home. "No one imagined silos like that inside banks," a government adviser said later. Overspecialization can lead to collective tragedy even when every individual separately takes the most reasonable course of action.

Highly specialized health care professionals have developed their own versions of the "if all you have is a hammer, everything looks like a nail" problem. Interventional cardiologists have gotten so used to treating chest pain with stents—metal tubes that pry open blood vessels—that they do so reflexively even in cases where voluminous research has proven that they are inappropriate or dangerous. A recent study found that cardiac patients were actually less likely to die if they were admitted during a national cardiology meeting, when thousands of cardiologists were away; the researchers suggested it could be because common treatments of dubious effect were less likely to be performed.

An internationally renowned scientist (whom you will meet toward the end of this book) told me that increasing specialization has created a "system of parallel trenches" in the quest for innovation. Everyone is digging deeper into their own trench and rarely standing up to look in the next trench over, even though the solution to their problem happens to reside there. The scientist is taking it upon himself to attempt to despecialize the training of future researchers; he hopes that eventually it will spread to training in every field. He profited immensely from cultivating range in his own life, even as he was pushed to specialize. And now he is broadening his purview again, designing a training program in an attempt to give others a chance to deviate from the Tiger path. "This may be the most important thing I will ever do in my life," he told me.

I hope this book helps you understand why.

When the Tillman Scholars spoke of feeling unmoored, and worried they were making a mistake, I understood better than I let on. I was working on a scientific research vessel in the Pacific Ocean after college when I decided for sure that I wanted to be a writer, not a scientist. I never expected that my path from science into writing would go through work as the overnight crime reporter at a New York City tabloid, nor that I would shortly thereafter be a senior writer at *Sports Illustrated,* a job that, to my own surprise, I would soon leave. I began worrying that I was a job-commitment-phobic drifter who must be doing this whole career thing wrong. Learning about the advantages of breadth and delayed specialization has changed the way I see myself and the world. The research pertains to every stage of life, from the development of children in math, music, and sports, to students fresh out of college trying to find their way, to midcareer professionals in need of a change and would-be retirees looking for a new vocation after moving on from their previous one.

The challenge we all face is how to maintain the benefits of breadth, diverse experience, interdisciplinary thinking, and delayed concentration in a world that increasingly incentivizes, even demands, hyperspecialization. While it is undoubtedly true that there are areas that require individuals with Tiger's precocity and clarity of purpose, as complexity increases—as technology spins the world into vaster webs of interconnected systems in which each individual only sees a small part—we also need more Rogers: people who start broad and embrace diverse experiences and perspectives while they progress. People with range.

CHAPTER 1

The Cult of the Head Start

ONE YEAR AND FOUR DAYS after World War II in Europe ended in unconditional surrender, Laszlo Polgar was born in a small town in Hungary—the seed of a new family. He had no grandmothers, no grandfathers, and no cousins; all had been wiped out in the Holocaust, along with his father's first wife and five children. Laszlo grew up determined to have a family, and a special one.

He prepped for fatherhood in college by poring over biographies of legendary thinkers, from Socrates to Einstein. He decided that traditional education was broken, and that he could make his own children into geniuses, if he just gave them the right head start. By doing so, he would prove something far greater: that any child can be molded for eminence in any discipline. He just needed a wife who would go along with the plan.

Laszlo's mother had a friend, and the friend had a daughter, Klara. In 1965, Klara traveled to Budapest, where she met Laszlo in person. Laszlo didn't play hard to get; he spent the first visit telling Klara that he planned to have six children and that he would nurture them to brilliance. Klara returned home to her parents with a lukewarm review: she had "met a very interesting person," but could not imagine marrying him.

They continued to exchange letters. They were both teachers and agreed that the school system was frustratingly one-size-fits-all, made for producing "the gray average mass," as Laszlo put it. A year and a half of letters later, Klara realized she had a very special pen pal. Laszlo finally wrote a love letter, and proposed at the end. They married, moved to Budapest, and got to work. Susan was born in early 1969, and the experiment was on.

For his first genius, Laszlo picked chess. In 1972, the year before Susan started training, American Bobby Fischer defeated Russian Boris Spassky in the "Match of the Century." It was considered a Cold War proxy in both hemispheres, and chess was suddenly pop culture. Plus, according to Klara, the game had a distinct benefit: "Chess is very objective and easy to measure." Win, lose, or draw, and a point system measures skill against the rest of the chess world. His daughter, Laszlo decided, would become a chess champion.

Laszlo was patient, and meticulous. He started Susan with "pawn wars." Pawns only, and the first person to advance to the back row wins. Soon, Susan was studying endgames and opening traps. She enjoyed the game and caught on quickly. After eight months of study, Laszlo took her to a smoky chess club in Budapest and challenged grown men to play his four-year-old daughter, whose legs dangled from her chair. Susan won her first game, and the man she beat stormed off. She entered the Budapest girls' championship and won the under-eleven title. At age four she had not lost a game.

By six, Susan could read and write and was years ahead of her grade peers in math. Laszlo and Klara decided they would educate her at home and keep the day open for chess. The Hungarian police threatened to throw Laszlo in jail if he did not send his daughter to the compulsory school system. It took him months of lobbying the Ministry of Education to gain permission. Susan's new little sister, Sofia, would be homeschooled too, as would Judit, who was coming soon, and whom

Laszlo and Klara almost named Zseni, Hungarian for "genius." All three became part of the grand experiment.

On a normal day, the girls were at the gym by 7 a.m. playing table tennis with trainers, and then back home at 10:00 for breakfast, before a long day of chess. When Laszlo reached the limit of his expertise, he hired coaches for his three geniuses in training. He spent his extra time cutting two hundred thousand records of game sequences from chess journals—many offering a preview of potential opponents—and filing them in a custom card catalog, the "cartotech." Before computer chess programs, it gave the Polgars the largest chess database in the world to study outside of—maybe—the Soviet Union's secret archives.

When she was seventeen, Susan became the first woman to qualify for the men's world championship, although the world chess federation did not allow her to participate. (A rule that would soon be changed, thanks to her accomplishments.) Two years later, in 1988, when Sofia was fourteen and Judit twelve, the girls comprised three of the four Hungarian team members for the women's Chess Olympiad. They won, and beat the Soviet Union, which had won eleven of the twelve Olympiads since the event began. The Polgar sisters became "national treasures," as Susan put it. The following year, communism fell, and the girls could compete all over the world. In January 1991, at the age of twenty-one, Susan became the first woman to achieve grandmaster status through tournament play against men. In December, Judit, at fifteen years and five months, became the youngest grandmaster ever, male or female. When Susan was asked on television if she wanted to win the world championship in the men's or women's category, she cleverly responded that she wanted to win the "absolute category."

None of the sisters ultimately reached Laszlo's highest goal of becoming the overall world champion, but all were outstanding. In 1996, Susan participated in the women's world championship, and won. Sofia peaked at the rank of international master, a level down from grand-master. Judit went furthest, climbing up to eighth in the overall world ranking in 2004.

Laszlo's experiment had worked. It worked so well that in the early 1990s he suggested that if his early specialization approach were applied to a thousand children, humanity could tackle problems like cancer and AIDS. After all, chess was just an arbitrary medium for his universal point. Like the Tiger Woods story, the Polgar story entered an endless pop culture loop in articles, books, TV shows, and talks as an example of the life-hacking power of an early start. An online course called "Bring Up Genius!" advertises lessons in the Polgar method to "build up your own Genius Life Plan." The bestseller *Talent Is Overrated* used the Polgar sisters and Tiger Woods as proof that a head start in deliberate practice is the key to success in "virtually any activity that matters to you."

The powerful lesson is that anything in the world can be conquered in the same way. It relies on one very important, and very unspoken, assumption: that chess and golf are representative examples of all the activities that matter to you.

Just how much of the world, and how many of the things humans want to learn and do, are really like chess and golf?

Psychologist Gary Klein is a pioneer of the "naturalistic decision making" (NDM) model of expertise; NDM researchers observe expert performers in their natural course of work to learn how they make high-stakes decisions under time pressure. Klein has shown that experts in an array of fields are remarkably similar to chess masters in that they instinctively recognize familiar patterns.

When I asked Garry Kasparov, perhaps the greatest chess player in history, to explain his decision process for a move, he told me, "I see a move, a combination, almost instantly," based on patterns he has seen before. Kasparov said he would bet that grandmasters usually make the move that springs to mind in the first few seconds of thought. Klein studied firefighting commanders and estimated that around 80 percent of their decisions are also made instinctively and in seconds. After years of firefighting, they recognize repeating patterns in the behavior of flames and of burning buildings on the verge of collapse. When he studied nonwartime naval commanders who were trying to avoid disasters, like mistaking a commercial flight for an enemy and shooting it down, he saw that they very quickly discerned potential threats. Ninety-five percent of the time, the commanders recognized a common pattern and chose a common course of action that was the first to come to mind.

One of Klein's colleagues, psychologist Daniel Kahneman, studied human decision making from the "heuristics and biases" model of human judgment. His findings could hardly have been more different from Klein's. When Kahneman probed the judgments of highly trained experts, he often found that experience had not helped at all. Even worse, it frequently bred confidence but not skill.

Kahneman included himself in that critique. He first began to doubt the link between experience and expertise in 1955, as a young lieutenant in the psychology unit of the Israel Defense Forces. One of his duties was to assess officer candidates through tests adapted from the British army. In one exercise, teams of eight had to get themselves and a length of telephone pole over a six-foot wall without letting the pole touch the ground, and without any of the soldiers or the pole touching the wall.* The difference in individuals' performances were so stark, with clear leaders, followers, braggarts, and wimps naturally emerging under the

---

* A common solution was for several team members to hold the pole at an angle as others took turns crawling up it and jumping over the wall. The pole could eventually be passed over the wall, held at an angle, and the remaining team members could jump and grab on to it and shimmy along it until they could jump over the wall.

stress of the task, that Kahneman and his fellow evaluators grew confident they could analyze the candidates' leadership qualities and identify how they would perform in officer training and in combat. They were completely mistaken. Every few months, they had a "statistics day" where they got feedback on how accurate their predictions had been. Every time, they learned they had done barely better than blind guessing. Every time, they gained experience and gave confident judgments. And every time, they did not improve. Kahneman marveled at the "complete lack of connection between the statistical information and the compelling experience of insight." Around that same time, an influential book on expert judgment was published that Kahneman told me impressed him "enormously." It was a wide-ranging review of research that rocked psychology because it showed experience simply did not create skill in a wide range of real-world scenarios, from college administrators assessing student potential to psychiatrists predicting patient performance to human resources professionals deciding who will succeed in job training. In those domains, which involved human behavior and where patterns did not clearly repeat, repetition did not cause learning. Chess, golf, and firefighting are exceptions, not the rule.

The difference between what Klein and Kahneman documented in experienced professionals comprised a profound conundrum: Do specialists get better with experience, or not?

In 2009, Kahneman and Klein took the unusual step of coauthoring a paper in which they laid out their views and sought common ground. And they found it. Whether or not experience inevitably led to expertise, they agreed, depended entirely on the domain in question. Narrow experience made for better chess and poker players and firefighters, but not for better predictors of financial or political trends, or of how employees or patients would perform. The domains Klein studied, in which instinctive pattern recognition worked powerfully, are what psychologist Robin Hogarth termed "kind" learning environments. Patterns repeat over and over, and feedback is extremely accurate and usually very rapid. In golf or chess, a ball or piece is moved according to rules and within defined boundaries, a consequence is quickly apparent, and similar challenges occur repeatedly. Drive a golf ball, and it either goes too far or not far enough; it slices, hooks, or flies straight. The player observes what happened, attempts to correct the error, tries again, and repeats for years. That is the very definition of deliberate practice, the type identified with both the ten-thousand-hours rule and the rush to early specialization in technical training. The learning environment is kind because a learner improves simply by engaging in the activity and trying to do better. Kahneman was focused on the flip side of kind learning environments; Hogarth called them "wicked."

In wicked domains, the rules of the game are often unclear or incomplete, there may or may not be repetitive patterns and they may not be obvious, and feedback is often delayed, inaccurate, or both.

In the most devilishly wicked learning environments, experience will reinforce the exact wrong lessons. Hogarth noted a famous New York City physician renowned for his skill as a diagnostician. The man's particular specialty was typhoid fever, and he examined patients for it by feeling around their tongues with his hands. Again and again, his testing yielded a positive diagnosis before the patient displayed a single symptom. And over and over, his diagnosis turned out to be correct. As another physician later pointed out, "He was a more productive carrier, using only his hands, than Typhoid Mary." Repetitive success, it turned out, taught him the worst possible lesson. Few learning environments are that wicked, but it doesn't take much to throw experienced pros off course. Expert firefighters, when faced with a new situation, like a fire in a skyscraper, can find themselves suddenly deprived of the intuition formed in years of house fires, and prone to poor decisions. With a change of the status quo, chess masters too can find that the skill they took years to build is suddenly obsolete.

———

In a 1997 showdown billed as the final battle for supremacy between natural and artificial intelligence, IBM supercomputer Deep Blue defeated Garry Kasparov. Deep Blue evaluated two hundred million positions per second. That is a tiny fraction of possible chess positions—the number of possible game sequences is more than atoms in the observable universe—but plenty enough to beat the best human. According to Kasparov, "Today the free chess app on your mobile phone is stronger than me." He is not being rhetorical.

"Anything we can do, and we know how to do it, machines will do it better," he said at a recent lecture. "If we can codify it, and pass it to computers, they will do it better." Still, losing to Deep Blue gave him an idea. In playing computers, he recognized what artificial intelligence scholars call Moravec's paradox: machines and humans frequently have opposite strengths and weaknesses.

There is a saying that "chess is 99 percent tactics." Tactics are short combinations of moves that players use to get an immediate advantage on the board. When players study all those patterns, they are mastering tactics. Bigger-picture planning in chess—how to manage the little battles to win the war—is called strategy. As Susan Polgar has written, "you can get a lot further by being very good in tactics"—that is, knowing a lot of patterns—"and have only a basic understanding of strategy."

Thanks to their calculation power, computers are tactically flawless compared to humans. Grandmasters predict the near future, but computers do it better. What if, Kasparov wondered, computer tactical prowess were combined with human big-picture, strategic thinking?

In 1998, he helped organize the first "advanced chess" tournament, in which each human player, including Kasparov himself, paired with a computer. Years of pattern study were obviated. The machine partner could handle tactics so the human could focus on strategy. It was like Tiger Woods facing off in a golf video game against the best gamers.

His years of repetition would be neutralized, and the contest would shift to one of strategy rather than tactical execution. In chess, it changed the pecking order instantly. "Human creativity was even more paramount under these conditions, not less," according to Kasparov. Kasparov settled for a 3–3 draw with a player he had trounced four games to zero just a month earlier in a traditional match. "My advantage in calculating tactics had been nullified by the machine." The primary benefit of years of experience with specialized training was outsourced, and in a contest where humans focused on strategy, he suddenly had peers.

A few years later, the first "freestyle chess" tournament was held. Teams could be made up of multiple humans and computers. The lifetime-of-specialized-practice advantage that had been diluted in advanced chess was obliterated in freestyle. A duo of amateur players with three normal computers not only destroyed Hydra, the best chess supercomputer, they also crushed teams of grandmasters using computers. Kasparov concluded that the humans on the winning team were the best at "coaching" multiple computers on what to examine, and then synthesizing that information for an overall strategy. Human/Computer combo teams—known as "centaurs"—were playing the highest level of chess ever seen. If Deep Blue's victory over Kasparov signaled the transfer of chess power from humans to computers, the victory of centaurs over Hydra symbolized something more interesting still: humans empowered to do what they do best without the prerequisite of years of specialized pattern recognition.

In 2014, an Abu Dhabi–based chess site put up $20,000 in prize money for freestyle players to compete in a tournament that also included games in which chess programs played without human intervention. The winning team comprised four people and several computers. The captain and primary decision maker was Anson Williams, a British engineer with no official chess rating. His teammate, Nelson Hernandez, told me, "What people don't understand is that freestyle involves an integrated set of skills that in some cases have nothing to do with playing chess." In traditional chess, Williams was probably at the level of a decent amateur. But he was well versed in computers and adept at integrating streaming information for strategy decisions. As a teenager, he had been outstanding at the video game *Command & Conquer,* known as a "real time strategy" game because players move simultaneously. In freestyle chess, he had to consider advice from teammates and various chess programs and then very quickly direct the computers to examine particular possibilities in more depth. He was like an executive with a team of mega-grandmaster tactical advisers, deciding whose advice to probe more deeply and ultimately whose to heed. He played each game cautiously, expecting a draw, but trying to set up situations that could lull an opponent into a mistake.

In the end, Kasparov did figure out a way to beat the computer: by outsourcing tactics, the part of human expertise that is most easily replaced, the part that he and the Polgar prodigies spent years honing.

In 2007, National Geographic TV gave Susan Polgar a test. They sat her at a sidewalk table in the middle of a leafy block of Manhattan's Greenwich Village, in front of a cleared chessboard. New Yorkers in jeans and fall jackets went about their jaywalking business as a white truck bearing a large diagram of a chessboard with twenty-eight pieces in midgame play took a left turn onto Thompson Street, past the deli, and past Susan Polgar. She glanced at the diagram as the truck drove by, and then perfectly re-created it on the board in front of her. The show was reprising a series of famous chess experiments that pulled back the curtain on kind-learning-environment skills.

The first took place in the 1940s, when Dutch chess master and psychologist Adriaan de Groot flashed midgame chessboards in front of players of different ability levels, and then asked them to re-create the boards as well as they could. A grandmaster repeatedly re-created the entire board after seeing it for only three seconds. A master-level player managed that half as often as the grandmaster. A lesser, city champion player and an average club player were never able to re-create the board accurately. Just like Susan Polgar, grandmasters seemed to have photographic memories.

After Susan succeeded in her first test, National Geographic TV turned the truck around to show the other side, which had a diagram with pieces placed at random. When Susan saw that side, even though there were fewer pieces, she could barely re-create anything at all.

That test reenacted an experiment from 1973, in which two Carnegie Mellon University psychologists, William G. Chase and soon-to-be Nobel laureate Herbert A. Simon, repeated the De Groot exercise, but added a wrinkle. This time, the chess players were also given boards with the pieces in an arrangement that would never actually occur in a game. Suddenly, the experts performed just like the lesser players. The grandmasters never had photographic memories after all. Through repetitive study of game patterns, they had learned to do what Chase and Simon called "chunking." Rather than struggling to remember the location of every individual pawn, bishop, and rook, the brains of elite players grouped pieces into a smaller number of meaningful chunks based on familiar patterns. Those patterns allow expert players to immediately assess the situation based on experience, which is why Garry Kasparov told me that grandmasters usually know their move within seconds. For Susan Polgar, when the van drove by the first time, the diagram was not twenty-eight items, but five different meaningful chunks that indicated how the game was progressing.

Chunking helps explain instances of apparently miraculous, domain-specific memory, from musicians playing long pieces by heart to quarterbacks recognizing patterns of players in a split second and making a decision to throw. The reason that elite athletes seem to have superhuman reflexes is that they recognize patterns of ball or body movements that tell them what's coming before it happens. When tested outside of their sport context, their superhuman reactions disappear.

We all rely on chunking every day in skills in which we are expert. Take ten seconds and try to memorize as many of these twenty words as you can:

Because groups twenty patterns
meaningful are words easier into chunk remember
really sentence familiar can to you much in a.

Okay, now try again:

Twenty words are really much easier to
remember in a meaningful sentence because
you can chunk familiar patterns into groups.

Those are the same twenty pieces of information, but over the course of your life, you've learned patterns of words that allow you to instantly make sense of the second arrangement, and to remember it much more easily. Your restaurant server doesn't just happen to have a miraculous memory; like musicians and quarterbacks, they've learned to group recurring information into chunks.

Studying an enormous number of repetitive patterns is so important in chess that early specialization in technical practice is critical. Psychologists Fernand Gobet (an international master) and Guillermo Campitelli (coach to future grandmasters) found that the chances of a competitive chess player reaching international master status (a level down from grandmaster) dropped from one in four to one in fifty-five if rigorous training had not begun by age twelve. Chunking can seem like magic, but it comes from extensive, repetitive practice. Laszlo Polgar was right to believe in it. His daughters don't even constitute the most extreme evidence.

For more than fifty years, psychiatrist Darold Treffert studied savants, individuals with an insatiable drive to practice in one domain, and ability in that area that far outstrips their abilities in other areas. "Islands of genius," Treffert calls it.* Treffert documented the almost unbelievable feats of savants like pianist Leslie Lemke, who can play thousands of songs from memory. Because Lemke and other savants have seemingly limitless retrieval capacity, Treffert initially attributed their abilities to perfect memories; they are human tape recorders. Except, when they are tested after hearing a piece of music for the first time, musical savants reproduce "tonal" music—the genre of nearly all pop and most classical music—more easily than "atonal" music, in which successive notes do not follow familiar harmonic structures. If savants were human tape recorders playing notes back, it would make no difference whether they were asked to re-create music that follows popular rules of composition or not. But in practice, it makes an enormous difference. In one study of a savant pianist, the researcher, who had heard the man play hundreds of songs flawlessly, was dumbstruck when the savant could not re-create an atonal piece even after a practice session with it. "What I heard seemed so unlikely that I felt obliged to check that the keyboard had not somehow slipped into transposing mode," the researcher recorded. "But he really had made a mistake, and the errors continued." Patterns and familiar structures were critical to the savant's extraordinary recall ability. Similarly, when artistic savants are briefly shown pictures and asked to reproduce them, they do much better with images of real-life objects than with more abstract depictions.

It took Treffert decades to realize he had been wrong, and that

---

* About half of savants are autistic, and many others have a disability, but not all do.

savants have more in common with prodigies like the Polgar sisters than he thought. They do not merely regurgitate. Their brilliance, just like the Polgar brilliance, relies on repetitive structures, which is precisely what made the Polgars' skill so easy to automate.

With the advances made by the AlphaZero chess program (owned by an AI arm of Google's parent company), perhaps even the top centaurs would be vanquished in a freestyle tournament. Unlike previous chess programs, which used brute processing force to calculate an enormous number of possible moves and rate them according to criteria set by programmers, AlphaZero actually taught itself to play. It needed only the rules, and then to play itself a gargantuan number of times, keeping track of what tends to work and what doesn't, and using that to improve. In short order, it beat the best chess programs. It did the same with the game of Go, which has many more possible positions. But the centaur lesson remains: the more a task shifts to an open world of big-picture strategy, the more humans have to add.

AlphaZero programmers touted their impressive feat by declaring that their creation had gone from "tabula rasa" (blank slate) to master on its own. But starting with a game is anything but a blank slate. The program is still operating in a constrained, rule-bound world. Even in video games that are less bound by tactical patterns, computers have faced a greater challenge.

The latest video game challenge for artificial intelligence is *StarCraft*, a franchise of real-time strategy games in which fictional species go to war for supremacy in some distant reach of the Milky Way. It requires much more complex decision making than chess. There are battles to manage, infrastructure to plan, spying to do, geography to explore, and resources to collect, all of which inform one another. Computers struggled to win at *StarCraft*, Julian Togelius, an NYU professor who studies gaming AI, told me in 2017. Even when they did beat humans in individual games, human players adjusted with "long-term adaptive strategy" and started winning. "There are so many layers of thinking," he said. "We humans sort of suck at all of them individually, but we have some kind of very approximate idea about each of them and can combine them and be somewhat adaptive. That seems to be what the trick is."

In 2019, in a limited version of *StarCraft*, AI beat a pro for the first time. (The pro adapted and earned a win after a string of losses.) But the game's strategic complexity provides a lesson: the bigger the picture, the more unique the potential human contribution. Our greatest strength is the exact opposite of narrow specialization. It is the ability to integrate broadly. According to Gary Marcus, a psychology and neural science professor who sold his machine learning company to Uber, "In narrow enough worlds, humans may not have much to contribute much longer. In more open-ended games, I think they certainly will. Not just games, in open ended real-world problems we're still crushing the machines."

The progress of AI in the closed and orderly world of chess, with instant feedback and bottomless data, has been exponential. In the rule-bound but messier world of driving, AI has made tremendous progress, but challenges remain. In a truly open-world problem devoid of rigid rules and reams of perfect historical data, AI has been disastrous. IBM's Watson destroyed at *Jeopardy!* and was subsequently pitched as a revolution in cancer care, where it flopped so spectacularly that several AI experts told me they worried its reputation would taint AI research in health-related fields. As one oncologist put it, "The difference between winning at *Jeopardy!* and curing all cancer is that we know the answer to *Jeopardy!* questions." With cancer, we're still working on posing the right questions in the first place.

In 2009, a report in the esteemed journal *Nature* announced that Google Flu Trends could use search query patterns to predict the winter spread of flu more rapidly than and just as accurately as the Centers for Disease Control and Prevention. But Google Flu Trends soon got shakier, and in the winter of 2013 it predicted more than double the prevalence of flu that actually occurred in the United States. Today, Google Flu Trends is no longer publishing estimates, and just has a holding page saying that "it is still early days" for this kind of forecasting. Tellingly, Marcus gave me this analogy for the current limits of expert machines: "AI systems are like savants." They need stable structures and narrow worlds.

When we know the rules and answers, and they don't change over time—chess, golf, playing classical music—an argument can be made for savant-like hyperspecialized practice from day one. But those are poor models of most things humans want to learn.

When narrow specialization is combined with an unkind domain, the human tendency to rely on experience of familiar patterns can backfire horribly—like the expert firefighters who suddenly make poor choices when faced with a fire in an unfamiliar structure. Chris Argyris, who helped create the Yale School of Management, noted the danger of treating the wicked world as if it is kind. He studied high-powered consultants from top business schools for fifteen years, and saw that they did really well on business school problems that were well defined and quickly assessed. But they employed what Argyris called single-loop learning, the kind that favors the first familiar solution that comes to mind. Whenever those solutions went wrong, the consultant usually got defensive. Argyris found their "brittle personalities" particularly surprising given that "the essence of their job is to teach others how to do things differently."

Psychologist Barry Schwartz demonstrated a similar, learned inflexibility among experienced practitioners when he gave college students a logic puzzle that involved hitting switches to turn light bulbs on and off in sequence, and that they could play over and over. It could be solved in seventy different ways, with a tiny money reward for each success.

The students were not given any rules, and so had to proceed by trial and error.* If a student found a solution, they repeated it over and over to get more money, even if they had no idea why it worked. Later on, new students were added, and all were now asked to discover the general rule of all solutions. Incredibly, every student who was brand-new to the puzzle discovered the rule for all seventy solutions, while only one of the students who had been getting rewarded for a single solution did. The subtitle of Schwartz's paper: "How Not to Teach People to Discover Rules"—that is, by providing rewards for repetitive short-term success with a narrow range of solutions.

All this is bad news for some of the business world's favorite successful-learning analogies—the Polgars, Tiger, and to some degree analogies based in any sport or game. Compared to golf, a sport like tennis is much more dynamic, with players adjusting to opponents every second, to surfaces, and sometimes to their own teammates. (Federer was a 2008 Olympic gold medalist in doubles.) But tennis is still very much on the kind end of the spectrum compared to, say, a hospital emergency room, where doctors and nurses do not automatically find out what happens to a patient after their encounter. They have to find ways to learn beyond practice, and to assimilate lessons that might even contradict their direct experience.

The world is not golf, and most of it isn't even tennis. As Robin Hogarth put it, much of the world is "Martian tennis." You can see the players on a court with balls and rackets, but nobody has shared the rules. It is up to you to derive them, and they are subject to change without notice.

---

* Twenty-five bulbs were mounted behind a translucent board, and the puzzle started with the upper left bulb lit and a scoreboard at zero. Subjects were told that accumulating points would earn them money, but they were not told how to score. By experimenting, they could figure out that pressing buttons in a sequence that resulted in the bottom right bulb being lit was the way to score points and earn money. Essentially, they had to move the light from upper left to bottom right.

_____

We have been using the wrong stories. Tiger's story and the Polgar story give the false impression that human skill is always developed in an extremely kind learning environment. If that were the case, specialization that is both narrow and technical and that begins as soon as possible would usually work. But it doesn't even work in most sports.

If the amount of early, specialized practice in a narrow area were the key to innovative performance, savants would dominate every domain they touched, and child prodigies would always go on to adult eminence. As psychologist Ellen Winner, one of the foremost authorities on gifted children, noted, no savant has ever been known to become a "Big-C creator," who changed their field.

There are domains beyond chess in which massive amounts of narrow practice make for grandmaster-like intuition. Like golfers, surgeons improve with repetition of the same procedure. Accountants and bridge and poker players develop accurate intuition through repetitive experience. Kahneman pointed to those domains' "robust statistical regularities." But when the rules are altered just slightly, it makes experts appear to have traded flexibility for narrow skill. In research in the game of bridge where the order of play was altered, experts had a more difficult time adapting to new rules than did nonexperts. When experienced accountants were asked in a study to use a new tax law for deductions that replaced a previous one, they did worse than novices. Erik Dane, a Rice University professor who studies organizational behavior, calls this phenomenon "cognitive entrenchment." His suggestions for avoiding it are about the polar opposite of the strict version of the ten-thousand-hours school of thought: vary challenges within a domain drastically, and, as a fellow researcher put it, insist on "having one foot outside your world."

Scientists and members of the general public are about equally likely to have artistic hobbies, but scientists inducted into the highest national academies are much more likely to have avocations outside of their vocation. And those who have won the Nobel Prize are more likely still. Compared to other scientists, Nobel laureates are at least twenty-two times more likely to partake as an amateur actor, dancer, magician, or other type of performer. Nationally recognized scientists are much more likely than other scientists to be musicians, sculptors, painters, printmakers, woodworkers, mechanics, electronics tinkerers, glass-blowers, poets, or writers, of both fiction and nonfiction. And, again, Nobel laureates are far more likely still. The most successful experts also belong to the wider world. "To him who observes them from afar," said Spanish Nobel laureate Santiago Ramón y Cajal, the father of modern neuroscience, "it appears as though they are scattering and dissipating their energies, while in reality they are channeling and strengthening them." The main conclusion of work that took years of studying scientists and engineers, all of whom were regarded by peers as true technical experts, was that those who did not make a creative contribution to their field lacked aesthetic interests outside their narrow area. As psychologist and prominent creativity researcher Dean Keith Simonton observed, "rather than obsessively focus[ing] on a narrow topic," creative achievers tend to have broad interests. "This breadth often supports insights that cannot be attributed to domain-specific expertise alone."

Those findings are reminiscent of a speech Steve Jobs gave, in which he famously recounted the importance of a calligraphy class to his design aesthetics. "When we were designing the first Macintosh computer, it all came back to me," he said. "If I had never dropped in on that single course in college, the Mac would have never had multiple typefaces or proportionally spaced fonts." Or electrical engineer Claude Shannon, who launched the Information Age thanks to a philosophy course he took to fulfill a requirement at the University of Michigan. In it, he was exposed to the work of self-taught nineteenth-century English logician George Boole, who assigned a value of 1 to true statements and 0 to false statements and showed that logic problems could be solved like math equations. It resulted in absolutely nothing of practical impor-tance until seventy years after Boole passed away, when Shannon did a summer internship at AT&T's Bell Labs research facility. There he rec-ognized that he could combine telephone call-routing technology with Boole's logic system to encode and transmit any type of information electronically. It was the fundamental insight on which computers rely. "It just happened that no one else was familiar with both those fields at the same time," Shannon said.

In 1979, Christopher Connolly cofounded a psychology consultancy in the United Kingdom to help high achievers (initially athletes, but then others) perform at their best. Over the years, Connolly became curious about why some professionals floundered outside a narrow ex-pertise, while others were remarkably adept at expanding their careers—moving from playing in a world-class orchestra, for example, to running one. Thirty years after he started, Connolly returned to school to do a PhD investigating that very question, under Fernand Gobet, the psy-chologist and chess international master. Connolly's primary finding was that early in their careers, those who later made successful transi-tions had broader training and kept multiple "career streams" open even as they pursued a primary specialty. They "traveled on an eight-lane highway," he wrote, rather than down a single-lane one-way street. They had range. The successful adapters were excellent at taking knowl-edge from one pursuit and applying it creatively to another, and at avoiding cognitive entrenchment. They employed what Hogarth called a "circuit breaker." They drew on outside experiences and analogies to interrupt their inclination toward a previous solution that may no lon-ger work. Their skill was in *avoiding* the same old patterns. In the wicked world, with ill-defined challenges and few rigid rules, range can be a life hack.

Pretending the world is like golf and chess is comforting. It makes for a tidy kind-world message, and some very compelling books. The rest of this one will begin where those end—in a place where the popular sport is Martian tennis, with a view into how the modern world became so wicked in the first place.

CHAPTER 2

How the Wicked World Was Made

THE TOWN OF DUNEDIN sits at the base of a hilly peninsula that juts off of New Zealand's South Island into the South Pacific. The peninsula is famous for yellow-eyed penguins, and Dunedin boasts, demurely, the world's steepest residential street. It also features the University of Otago, the oldest university in New Zealand, and home to James Flynn, a professor of political studies who changed how psychologists think about thinking.

He started in 1981, intrigued by a thirty-year-old paper that reported IQ test scores of American soldiers in World Wars I and II. The World War II soldiers had performed better, by a lot. A World War I soldier who scored smack in the middle of his peers—the 50th percentile—would have made only the 22nd percentile compared to soldiers in World War II. Flynn wondered if perhaps civilians had experienced a similar improvement. "I thought, if IQ gains had occurred anywhere," he told me, "maybe they had occurred everywhere." If he was right, psychologists had been missing something big right before their eyes.

Flynn wrote to researchers in other countries asking for data, and on a dull November Saturday in 1984, he found a letter in his university mailbox. It was from a Dutch researcher, and it contained years of raw data from IQ tests given to young men in the Netherlands. The data were from a test known as Raven's Progressive Matrices, designed to gauge the test taker's ability to make sense of complexity. Each question of the test shows a set of abstract designs with one design missing. The test taker must try to fill in the missing design to complete a pattern. Raven's was conceived to be the epitome of a "culturally reduced" test; performance should be unaffected by material learned in life, inside or outside of school. Should Martians alight on Earth, Raven's should be the test capable of determining how bright they are. And yet Flynn could immediately see that young Dutchmen had made enormous gains from one generation to the next.

Flynn found more clues in test reference manuals. IQ tests are all standardized so that the average score is always 100 points. (They are graded based on a curve, with 100 in the middle.) Flynn noticed that the tests had to be restandardized from time to time to keep the average at 100, because test takers were giving more correct answers than they had in the past. In the twelve months after he received the Dutch letter, Flynn collected data from fourteen countries. Every single one showed huge gains for both children and adults. "Our advantage over our ancestors," as he put it, is "from the cradle to the grave."

Flynn had asked the right question. Score gains *had* occurred everywhere. Other academics had stumbled upon pieces of the same data earlier, but none had investigated whether it was part of a global pattern, even those who were having to tweak the test scoring system to keep the average at 100. "As an outsider," Flynn told me, "things strike me as surprising that I think people trained in psychometrics just accepted."

The Flynn effect—the increase in correct IQ test answers with each new generation in the twentieth century—has now been documented in more than thirty countries. The gains are startling: three points every ten years. To put that in perspective, if an adult who scored average today were compared to adults a century ago, she would be in the 98th percentile.

When Flynn published his revelation in 1987, it hit the community of researchers who study cognitive ability like a firebomb. The American Psychological Association convened an entire meeting on the issue, and psychologists invested in the immutable nature of IQ test scores offered an array of explanations to usher the effect away, from more education and better nutrition—which presumably contributed—to test-taking experience, but none fit the unusual pattern of score improvements. On tests that gauged material picked up in school or with independent reading or study—general knowledge, arithmetic, vocabulary—scores hardly budged. Meanwhile, performance on more abstract tasks that are never formally taught, like the Raven's matrices, or "similarities" tests, which require a description of how two things are alike, skyrocketed.

A young person today asked to give similarities between "dusk" and "dawn" might immediately realize that both connote times of day. But they would be far more likely than their grandmothers to produce a higher-level similarity: both separate day from night. A child today who scores average on similarities would be in the 94th percentile of her grandparents' generation. When a group of Estonian researchers used national test scores to compare word understandings of schoolkids in the 1930s to those in 2006, they saw that improvement came very specifically on the most abstract words. The more abstract the word, the bigger the improvement. The kids barely bested their grandparents on words for directly observable objects or phenomena ("hen," "eating," "illness"), but they improved massively on imperceptible concepts ("law," "pledge," "citizen").

The gains around the world on Raven's Progressive Matrices—where change was least expected—were the biggest of all. "The huge Raven's gains show that today's children are far better at solving problems on the spot without a previously learned method for doing so," Flynn concluded. They are more able to extract rules and patterns where none are given. Even in countries that have recently had a *decrease* in verbal and math IQ test scores, Raven's scores went up. The cause, it seemed, was some ineffable thing in modern air. Not only that, but the mystery air additive somehow supercharged modern brains specifically for the most abstract tests. What manner of change, Flynn wondered, could be at once so large and yet so particular?

Through the late 1920s and early 1930s, remote reaches of the Soviet Union were forced through social and economic changes that would normally take generations. Individual farmers in isolated areas of what is now Uzbekistan had long survived by cultivating small gardens for food, and cotton for everything else. Nearby in the mountain pasture-lands of present-day Kyrgyzstan, herders kept animals. The population was entirely illiterate, and a hierarchical social structure was enforced by strict religious rules. The socialist revolution dismantled that way of life almost overnight.

The Soviet government forced all that agricultural land to become large collective farms and began industrial development. The economy quickly became interconnected and complex. Farmers had to form collective work strategies, plan ahead for production, divvy up functions, and assess work along the way. Remote villages began communicating with distant cities. A network of schools opened in regions with 100 percent illiteracy, and adults began learning a system of matching symbols to sounds. Villagers had used numbers before, but only in practical transactions. Now they were taught the concept of a number as an abstraction that existed even without reference to counting animals or apportioning food. Some village women remained fully illiterate but took short courses on how to teach kindergartners. Other women were admitted for longer study at a teachers' school. Classes in preschool education and the science and technology of agriculture were offered to students who had no formal education of any kind. Secondary schools and technical institutes soon followed. In 1931, amid that incredible transformation, a brilliant young Russian psychologist named Alexander Luria recognized a fleeting "natural experiment," unique in the history of the world. He wondered if changing citizens' work might also change their minds.

When Luria arrived, the most remote villages had not yet been touched by the warp-speed restructuring of traditional society. Those villages gave him a control group. He learned the local language and brought fellow psychologists to engage villagers in relaxed social situations—teahouses or pastures—and discuss questions or tasks designed to discern their habits of mind.

Some were very simple: present skeins of wool or silk in an array of hues and ask participants to describe them. The collective farmers and farm leaders, as well as the female students, easily picked out blue, red, and yellow, sometimes with variations, like dark blue or light yellow. The most remote villagers, who were still "premodern," gave more diversified descriptions: cotton in bloom, decayed teeth, a lot of water, sky, pistachio. Then they were asked to sort the skeins into groups. The collective farmers, and young people with even a little formal education, did so easily, naturally forming color groups. Even when they did not know the name of a particular color, they had little trouble putting together darker and lighter shades of the same one. The remote villagers, on the other hand, refused, even those whose work was embroidery. "It can't be done," they said, or, "None of them are the same, you can't put them together." When prodded vigorously, and only if they were allowed to make many small groups, some relented and created sets that were apparently random. A few others appeared to sort the skeins according to color saturation, without regard to the color.

Geometric shapes followed suit. The greater the dose of modernity, the more likely an individual grasped the abstract concept of "shapes" and made groups of triangles, rectangles, and circles, even if they had no formal education and did not know the shapes' names. The remote villagers, meanwhile, saw nothing alike in a square drawn with solid lines and the same exact square drawn with dotted lines. To Alieva, a twenty-six-year-old remote villager, the solid-line square was obviously a map, and the dotted-line square was a watch. "How can a map and a watch be put together?" she asked, incredulous. Khamid, a twenty-four-year-old remote villager, insisted that filled and unfilled circles could not go together because one was a coin and the other a moon.

The pattern continued for every genre of question. Pressed to make conceptual groupings—akin to the similarities questions on IQ tests—remote villagers reverted to practical narratives based on their direct experience. When psychologists attempted to explain a "which one does not belong" grouping exercise to thirty-nine-year-old Rakmat, they gave him the example of three adults and one child, with the child obviously different from the others. Except Rakmat could not see it that way. "The boy must stay with the others!" he argued. The adults are working, "and if they have to keep running out to fetch things, they'll never get the job done, but the boy can do the running for them." Okay, then, how about a hammer, a saw, a hatchet, and a log—three of them are tools. They are not a group, Rakmat replied, because they are useless without the log, so why would they be together?

Other villagers removed either the hammer or the hatchet, which they saw as less versatile for use with the log, unless they considered pounding the hatchet into the log with the hammer, in which case it could stay. Perhaps, then, bird/rifle/dagger/bullet? You can't possibly remove one and have a group, a remote villager insisted. The bullet must be loaded in the rifle to kill the bird, and "then you have to cut the bird up with the dagger, since there's no other way to do it." These were just the introductions explaining the grouping task, not the actual questions. No amount of cajoling, explanation, or examples could get remote villagers to use reasoning based on any concept that was not a concrete part of their daily lives.

The farmers and students who had begun to join the modern world were able to practice a kind of thinking called "eduction," to work out guiding principles when given facts or materials, even in the absence of instructions, and even when they had never seen the material before. This, it turns out, is precisely what Raven's Progressive Matrices tests. Imagine presenting the villagers living in premodern circumstances with abstract designs from the Raven's test.

Some of the changes wrought by modernity and collective culture seem almost magical. Luria found that most remote villagers were not subject to the same optical illusions as citizens of the industrialized world, like the Ebbinghaus illusion. Which middle circle below looks bigger?

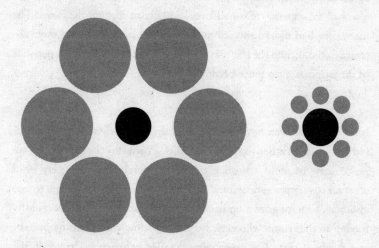

If you said the one on the right, you're probably a citizen of the industrialized world. The remote villagers saw, correctly, that they are the same, while the collective farmers and women in teachers' school picked the one on the right. Those findings have been repeated in other traditional societies, and scientists have suggested it may reflect the fact that premodern people are not as drawn to the holistic context—the relationship of the various circles to one another—so their perception is not changed by the presence of extra circles. To use a common metaphor, premodern people miss the forest for the trees; modern people miss the trees for the forest.

Since Luria's voyage to the interior, scientists have replicated his work in other cultures. The Kpelle people in Liberia were subsistence rice farmers, but in the 1970s roads began snaking toward them, connecting the Kpelle to cities. Given similarities tests, teenagers who were engaged with modern institutions grouped items by abstract categories ("All of these things can keep us warm"), while the traditional teens generated groups that were comparatively arbitrary, and changed frequently even when they were asked to repeat the exact same task. Because the touched-by-modernity teens had constructed meaningful thematic groups, they also had far superior recall when asked later to recount the items. The more they had moved toward modernity, the more powerful their abstract thinking, and the less they had to rely on their concrete experience of the world as a reference point.

In Flynn's terms, we now see the world through "scientific spectacles." He means that rather than relying on our own direct experiences, we make sense of reality through classification schemes, using layers of abstract concepts to understand how pieces of information relate to one another. We have grown up in a world of classification schemes totally foreign to the remote villagers; we classify some animals as mammals, and inside of that class make more detailed connections based on the similarity of their physiology and DNA.

Words that represent concepts that were previously the domain of scholars became widely understood in a few generations. The word "percent" was almost absent from books in 1900. By 2000 it appeared about once every five thousand words. (This chapter is 5,500 words long.) Computer programmers pile layers of abstraction. (They do very well on

Raven's.) In the progress bar on your computer screen that fills up to indicate a download, abstractions are legion, from the fundamental—the programming language that created it is a representation of binary code, the raw 1s and 0s the computer uses—to the psychological: the bar is a visual projection of time that provides peace of mind by estimating the progress of an immense number of underlying activities.

Lawyers might consider how results of one court case brought by an individual in Oklahoma could be relevant to a different one brought by a company in California. In order to prep, they might try out different hypothetical arguments while putting themselves in the shoes of an opposing attorney to predict how they will argue. Conceptual schemes are flexible, able to arrange information and ideas for a wide variety of uses, and to transfer knowledge between domains. Modern work demands knowledge transfer: the ability to apply knowledge to new situations and different domains. Our most fundamental thought processes have changed to accommodate increasing complexity and the need to derive new patterns rather than rely only on familiar ones. Our conceptual classification schemes provide a scaffolding for connecting knowledge, making it accessible and flexible.

Research on thousands of adults in six industrializing nations found that exposure to modern work with self-directed problem solving and nonrepetitive challenges was correlated with being "cognitively flexible." As Flynn makes sure to point out, this does not mean that brains now have more inherent potential than a generation ago, but rather that utilitarian spectacles have been swapped for spectacles through which the world is classified by concepts.* Even recently, within some very traditional or orthodox religious communities that have modernized but that still block women from engaging in modern work, the Flynn

---

* Psychologists still hotly debate the contributions to and implications of the Flynn effect. Harvard psychologist Steven Pinker characterized the gains as more than just a shift of thinking: "No historian who takes in the sweep of human history on the scale of centuries could miss the fact that we are now living in a period of extraordinary brainpower."

effect has proceeded more slowly for women than for men in the same community. Exposure to the modern world has made us better adapted for complexity, and that has manifested as flexibility, with profound implications for the breadth of our intellectual world.

In every cognitive direction, the minds of premodern citizens were severely constrained by the concrete world before them. With cajoling, some solved the following logic sequence: "Cotton grows well where it is hot and dry. England is cold and damp. Can cotton grow there or not?" They had direct experience growing cotton, so some of them could answer (tentatively and when pushed) for a country they had never visited. The same exact puzzle with different details stumped them: "In the Far North, where there is snow, all bears are white. Novaya Zemlya is in the Far North and there is always snow there. What colors are the bears there?" That time, no amount of pushing could get the remote villagers to answer. They would respond only with principles. "Your words can be answered only by someone who was there," one man said, even though he had never been to England but had just answered the cotton question. But even a faint taste of modern work began to change that. Given the white bear puzzle, Abdull, forty-five and barely literate but chairman of a collective farm, would not give an answer confidently, but he did exercise formal logic. "To go by your words," he said, "they should all be white."

The transition completely transformed the villagers' inner worlds. When the scientists from Moscow asked the villagers what they would like to know about them or the place they came from, the isolated farmers and herders generally could not come up with a single question. "I haven't seen what people do in other cities," one said, "so how can I ask?" Whereas those engaged in collective farming were readily curious. "Well, you just spoke about white bears," said thirty-one-year-old Akhmetzhan, a collective farmer. "I don't understand where they come from." He stopped for a moment to ponder. "And then you mentioned America. Is it governed by us or by some other power?" Nineteen-year-old Siddakh, who worked on a collective farm and had studied in a school for two years, was brimming with imaginative questions that probed self-improvement, from the personal to the local and global: "Well, what could I do to make our kolkhozniks [collective farmers] better people? How can we obtain bigger plants, or plant ones which will grow to be like big trees? And then I'm interested in how the world exists, where things come from, how the rich became rich and why the poor are poor."

Where the very thoughts of premodern villagers were circumscribed by their direct experiences, modern minds are comparatively free. This is not to say that one way of life is uniformly better than another. As Arab historiographer Ibn Khaldun, considered a founder of sociology, pointed out centuries ago, a city dweller traveling through the desert will be completely dependent on a nomad to keep him alive. So long as they remain in the desert, the nomad is a genius.

But it is certainly true that modern life requires range, making connections across far-flung domains and ideas. Luria addressed this kind of "categorical" thinking, which Flynn would later style as scientific spectacles. "[It] is usually quite flexible," Luria wrote. "Subjects readily shift from one attribute to another and construct suitable categories. They classify objects by substance (animals, flowers, tools), materials (wood, metal, glass), size (large, small), and color (light, dark), or other property. The ability to move freely, to shift from one category to another, is one of the chief characteristics of 'abstract thinking.'"

Flynn's great disappointment is the degree to which society, and particularly higher education, has responded to the broadening of the mind by pushing specialization, rather than focusing early training on conceptual, transferable knowledge.

Flynn conducted a study in which he compared the grade point averages of seniors at one of America's top state universities, from neuroscience to English majors, to their performance on a test of critical thinking.

The test gauged students' ability to apply fundamental abstract concepts from economics, social and physical sciences, and logic to common, real-world scenarios. Flynn was bemused to find that the correlation between the test of broad conceptual thinking and GPA was about zero. In Flynn's words, "the traits that earn good grades at [the university] do not include critical ability of any broad significance."*

Each of twenty test questions gauged a form of conceptual thinking that can be put to widespread use in the modern world. For test items that required the kind of conceptual reasoning that can be gleaned with no formal training—detecting circular logic, for example—the students did well. But in terms of frameworks that can best put their conceptual reasoning skills to use, they were horrible. Biology and English majors did poorly on everything that was not directly related to their field. None of the majors, including psychology, understood social science methods. Science students learned the facts of their specific field without understanding how science should work in order to draw true conclusions. Neuroscience majors did not do particularly well on anything. Business majors performed very poorly across the board, including in economics. Econ majors did the best overall. Economics is a broad field by nature, and econ professors have been shown to apply the reasoning principles they've learned to problems outside their area.† Chemists, on the other hand, are extraordinarily bright, but in several studies struggled to apply scientific reasoning to nonchemistry problems.

Students Flynn tested often mistook subtle value judgments for scientific conclusions, and in a question that presented a tricky scenario and required students *not* to mistake a correlation for evidence of

---

* Flynn also told me that he gave the test to pupils at a British secondary school that sends a lot of students to the London School of Economics, as well as to juniors and seniors at LSE. His conclusion: "They were no better at thinking critically when they came out of university than when they went in."

† As psychologist Robin Hogarth noted of economists, "What strikes me about their discourse . . . is how the terminology and reasoning processes of economics work their way into almost all topics. Whether the topic is sports, economic phenomena, politics, or even academic curricula."

causation, they performed worse than random. Almost none of the students in any major showed a consistent understanding of how to apply methods of evaluating truth they had learned in their own discipline to other areas. In that way, the students had something in common with Luria's remote villagers—even the science majors were typically unable to generalize research methods from their own field to other fields. Flynn's conclusion: "There is no sign that any department attempts to develop [anything] other than narrow critical competence."

Flynn is now in his eighties. He has a full white beard, the wind-buffeted cheeks of a lifelong runner, and piles of white curls that tuft and billow like cumulus clouds around his head. His house on a hill in Dunedin looks out over a gently rolling green farmscape.

When he recounts his own education at the University of Chicago, where he was captain of the cross-country team, he raises his voice. "Even the best universities aren't developing critical intelligence," he told me. "They aren't giving students the tools to analyze the modern world, except in their area of specialization. Their education is too narrow." He does not mean this in the simple sense that every computer science major needs an art history class, but rather that *everyone* needs habits of mind that allow them to dance across disciplines.

Chicago has long prided itself on a core curriculum dedicated to interdisciplinary critical thinking. The two-year core, according to the university, "is intended as an introduction to the tools of inquiry used in every discipline—science, mathematics, humanities, and social sciences. The goal is not just to transfer knowledge, but to raise fundamental questions and to become familiar with the powerful ideas that shape our society." But even at Chicago, Flynn argues, his education did not maximize the modern potential for applying conceptual thinking across domains.

Professors, he told me, are just too eager to share their favorite facts gleaned from years of acceleratingly narrow study. He has taught for fifty years, from Cornell to Canterbury, and is quick to include himself in that criticism. When he taught intro to moral and political philosophy, he couldn't resist the urge to impart his favorite minutiae from Plato, Aristotle, Hobbes, Marx, and Nietzsche.

Flynn introduced broad concepts in class, but he is sure that he often buried them in a mountain of other information specific to that class alone—a bad habit he worked to overcome. The study he conducted at the state university convinced him that college departments rush to develop students in a narrow specialty area, while failing to sharpen the tools of thinking that can serve them in every area. This must change, he argues, if students are to capitalize on their unprecedented capacity for abstract thought. They must be taught to think before being taught what to think about. Students come prepared with scientific spectacles, but do not leave carrying a scientific-reasoning Swiss Army knife.

Here and there, professors have begun to pick up the challenge. A class at the University of Washington titled "Calling Bullshit" (in staid coursebook language: INFO 198/BIOL 106B), focused on broad principles fundamental to understanding the interdisciplinary world and critically evaluating the daily firehose of information. When the class was first posted in 2017, registration filled up in the first minute.

Jeannette Wing, a computer science professor at Columbia University and former corporate vice president of Microsoft Research, has pushed broad "computational thinking" as the mental Swiss Army knife. She advocated that it become as fundamental as reading, even for those who will have nothing to do with computer science or programming. "Computational thinking is using abstraction and decomposition when attacking a large complex task," she wrote. "It is choosing an appropriate representation for a problem."

Mostly, though, students get what economist Bryan Caplan called narrow vocational training for jobs few of them will ever have. Three-quarters of American college graduates go on to a career unrelated to their major—a trend that includes math and science majors—after having become competent only with the tools of a single discipline.

One good tool is rarely enough in a complex, interconnected, rapidly changing world. As the historian and philosopher Arnold Toynbee said when he described analyzing the world in an age of technological and social change, "No tool is omnicompetent."

Flynn's passion resonated deeply with me. Before turning to journalism, I was in grad school, living in a tent in the Arctic, studying how changes in plant life might impact the subterranean permafrost. Classes consisted of stuffing my brain with the details of Arctic plant physiology. Only years later—as an investigative journalist writing about poor scientific research—did I realize that I had committed statistical malpractice in one section of the thesis that earned me a master's degree from Columbia University. Like many a grad student, I had a big database and hit a computer button to run a common statistical analysis, never having been taught to think deeply (or at all) about how that statistical analysis even worked. The stat program spit out a number summarily deemed "statistically significant." Unfortunately, it was almost certainly a false positive, because I did not understand the limitations of the statistical test in the context in which I applied it. Nor did the scientists who reviewed the work. As statistician Doug Altman put it, "Everyone is so busy doing research they don't have time to stop and think about the *way* they're doing it." I rushed into extremely specialized scientific research without having learned scientific reasoning. (And then I was rewarded for it, with a master's degree, which made for a very wicked learning environment.) As backward as it sounds, I only began to think broadly about how science should work years after I left it.

Fortunately, as an undergrad, I did have a chemistry professor who embodied Flynn's ideal. On every exam, amid typical chemistry questions, was something like this: "How many piano tuners are there in New York City?" Students had to estimate, just by reasoning, and try to get the right order of magnitude. The professor later explained that these were "Fermi problems," because Enrico Fermi—who created the first nuclear reactor beneath the University of Chicago football field—constantly made back-of-the-envelope estimates to help him approach problems.* The ultimate lesson of the question was that detailed prior knowledge was less important than a way of thinking.

On the first exam, I went with gut instinct ("I have no clue, maybe ten thousand?")—*way too high*. By the end of the class, I had a new tool in my conceptual Swiss Army knife, a way of using what little I did know to make a guess at what I didn't. I knew the population of New York City; most single people in studio apartments probably don't have pianos that get tuned, and most of my friends' parents had one to three children, so how many households are in New York? What portion might have pianos? How often are pianos tuned? How long might it take to tune a piano? How many homes can one tuner reach in a day? How many days a year does a tuner work? None of the individual estimates has to be particularly accurate in order to get a reasonable overall answer. Remote Uzbek villagers would not perform well on Fermi problems, but neither did I before taking that class. It was easy to learn, though. Having grown up in the twentieth century, I was already wearing the spectacles, I just needed help capitalizing on them. I remember nothing about stoichiometry, but I use Fermi thinking regularly, breaking down a problem so I can leverage what little I know to start investigating what I don't, a "similarities" problem of sorts.

Fortunately, several studies have found that a little training in broad thinking strategies, like Fermi-izing, can go a long way, and can be applied across domains. Unsurprisingly, Fermi problems were a topic in the

---

* Fermi was present at the first atomic bomb test and dropped pieces of paper "before, during, and after the passage of the blast wave," he wrote in documents that were classified at the time. He used the distance the paper traveled to estimate the explosion strength.

"Calling Bullshit" course. It used a deceptive cable news report as a case study to demonstrate "how Fermi estimation can cut through bullshit like a hot knife through butter." It gives anyone consuming numbers, from news articles to advertisements, the ability quickly to sniff out deceptive stats. That's a pretty handy hot butter knife. I would have been a much better researcher in any domain, including Arctic plant physiology, had I learned broadly applicable reasoning tools rather than the finer details of Arctic plant physiology.

Like chess masters and firefighters, premodern villagers relied on things being the same tomorrow as they were yesterday. They were extremely well prepared for what they had experienced before, and extremely poorly equipped for everything else. Their very thinking was highly specialized in a manner that the modern world has been telling us is increasingly obsolete. They were perfectly capable of learning from experience, but failed at learning *without* experience. And that is what a rapidly changing, wicked world demands—conceptual reasoning skills that can connect new ideas and work across contexts. Faced with any problem they had not directly experienced before, the remote villagers were completely lost. That is not an option for us. The more constrained and repetitive a challenge, the more likely it will be automated, while great rewards will accrue to those who can take conceptual knowledge from one problem or domain and apply it in an entirely new one.

The ability to apply knowledge broadly comes from broad training. A particular skilled group of performers in another place and time turned broad training into an art form. Their story is older, and yet a much better parable than chess prodigies for the modern age.

CHAPTER 3

When Less of the Same Is More

ANYWHERE A TRAVELER to seventeenth-century Venice turned an ear, they could hear music exploding from its traditional bounds. Even the name of the musical era, "Baroque," is taken from a jewelers' term to describe a pearl that was extravagantly large and unusually shaped.

Instrumental music—music that did not depend on words—underwent a complete revolution. Some of the instruments were brand-new, like the piano; others were enhanced—violins made by Antonio Stradivari would sell centuries later for millions of dollars. The modern system of major and minor keys was created. Virtuosos, the original musical celebrities, were anointed. Composers seized on their skill and wrote elaborate solos to push the boundaries of the best players' abilities. The concerto was born—in which a virtuoso soloist plays back and forth against an orchestra—and Venetian composer Antonio Vivaldi (known as *il Prete Rosso,* the Red Priest, for his flame-red hair) became the form's undisputed champion. *The Four Seasons* is as close to a pop hit as three-hundred-year-old music gets. (A mashup with a song from Disney's *Frozen* has ninety million YouTube plays.)

Vivaldi's creativity was facilitated by a particular group of musicians who could learn new music quickly on a staggering array of instruments.

They drew emperors, kings, princes, cardinals, and countesses from across Europe to be regaled by the most innovative music of the time. They were the all-female cast known as the *figlie del coro,* literally, "daughters of the choir." Leisure activities like horseback riding and field sports were scarce in the floating city, so music bore the full weight of entertainment for its citizens. The sounds of violins, flutes, horns, and voices spilled into the night from every bobbing barge and gondola. And in a time and place seething with music, the *figlie* dominated for a century.

"Only in Venice," a prominent visitor wrote, "can one see these musical prodigies." They were both ground zero of a musical revolution and an oddity. Elsewhere, their instruments were reserved for men. "They sing like angels, play the violin, the flute, the organ, the oboe, the cello, and the bassoon," an astonished French politician remarked. "In short, no instrument is large enough to frighten them." Others were less diplomatic. Aristocratic British writer Hester Thrale complained, "The sight of girls handling the double bass, and blowing into the bassoon did not much please me." After all, "suitable feminine instruments" were more along the lines of the harpsichord or musical glasses.

The *figlie* left the king of Sweden in awe. Literary rogue Casanova marveled at the standing-room-only crowds. A dour French concert reviewer singled out a particular violinist: "She is the first of her sex to challenge the success of our great artists." Even listeners not obviously disposed to support the arts were moved. Francesco Coli described "angelic Sirens," who exceeded "even the most ethereal of birds" and "threw open for listeners the doors of Paradise." Especially surprising praise, perhaps, considering that Coli was the official book censor for the Venetian Inquisition.

The best *figlie* became Europe-wide celebrities, like Anna Maria della Pietà. A German baron flatly declared her "the premier violinist in Europe." The president of the parliament of Burgundy said she was "unsurpassed" even in Paris. An expense report that Vivaldi recorded in

1712 shows that he spent twenty ducats on a violin for sixteen-year-old Anna Maria, an engagement-ring-like sum for Vivaldi, who made that much in four months. Among the hundreds of concertos Vivaldi wrote for the *figlie del coro* are twenty-eight that survived in the "Anna Maria notebook." Bound in leather and dyed Venetian scarlet, it bears Anna Maria's name in gold leaf calligraphy. The concertos, written specifically to showcase her prowess, are filled with high-speed passages that require different notes to be played on multiple strings at the same time. In 1716, Anna Maria and the *figlie* were ordered by the Senate to intensify their musical work in an effort to bring God's favor to the Venetian armies as they battled the Ottoman Empire on the island of Corfu. (In that siege, the Venetian violin, and a well-timed storm, proved mightier than the Turkish cannon.)

Anna Maria was middle-aged in the 1740s, when Jean-Jacques Rousseau came to visit. The rebel philosopher who would fuel the French Revolution was also a composer. "I had brought with me from Paris the national prejudice against Italian music," Rousseau wrote. And yet he declared that the music played by the *figlie del coro* "has not its like, either in Italy, or the rest of the world." Rousseau had one problem, though, that "drove me to despair." He could not *see* the women. They performed behind a thin crepe hung in front of wrought-iron latticework grilles in elevated church balconies. They could be heard, but only their silhouettes seen, tilting and swaying with the tides of the music, like shadow pictures in a vaudeville stage set. The grilles "concealed from me the angels of beauty," Rousseau wrote. "I could talk of nothing else."

He talked about it so much that he happened to talk about it with one of the *figlie*'s important patrons. "If you are so desirous to see those little girls," the man told Rousseau, "it will be an easy matter to satisfy your wishes."

Rousseau *was* so desirous. He pestered the man incessantly until he took him to meet the musicians. And there, Rousseau, whose fearless writing would be banned and burned before it fertilized the soil of democracy, grew anxious. "When we entered the salon which confined these longed-for beauties," he wrote, "I felt an amorous trembling, which I had never before experienced."

The patron introduced the women, the siren prodigies whose fame had spread like a grassfire through Europe—and Rousseau was stunned.

There was Sophia—"horrid," Rousseau wrote. Cattina—"she had but one eye." Bettina—"the smallpox had entirely disfigured her." "Scarcely one of them," according to Rousseau, "was without some striking defect."

A poem had recently been written about one of the best singers: "Missing are the fingers of her left hand / Also absent is her left foot." An accomplished instrumentalist was the "poor limping lady." Other guests left even less considerate records.

Like Rousseau, English visitor Lady Anna Miller was entranced by the music and pleaded to see the women perform with no barrier hiding them. "My request was granted," Miller wrote, "but when I entered I was seized with so violent a fit of laughter, that I am surprised they had not driven me out again. . . . My eyes were struck with the sight of a dozen or fourteen beldams ugly and old . . . these with several young girls." Miller changed her mind about watching them play, "so much had the sight of the performers disgusted me."

The girls and women who delighted delicate ears had not lived delicate lives. Many of their mothers worked in Venice's vibrant sex industry and contracted syphilis before they had babies and dropped them off at the Ospedale della Pietà. The name literally means "Hospital of Pity," but figuratively it was the House of Mercy, where the girls grew up and learned music. It was the largest of four *ospedali,* charitable institutions in Venice founded to ameliorate particular social ills. In the Pietà's case, the ill was that fatherless babies (mostly girls) frequently ended up in the canals.

Most of them would never know their mothers. They were dropped off in the *scaffetta,* a drawer built into the outer wall of the Pietà. Like the size tester for carry-on luggage at the airport, if a baby was small enough to fit, the Pietà would raise her.

The great Anna Maria was a representative example. Someone, probably her mother, who was probably a prostitute, took baby Anna Maria to the doorstep of the Pietà on the waterfront of Venice's St. Mark's Basin, along a bustling promenade. A bell attached to the *scaffetta* alerted staff of each new arrival. Babies were frequently delivered with a piece of fabric, a coin, ring, or some trinket left in the *scaffetta* as a form of identification should anyone ever return to claim them. One mother left half of a brilliantly illustrated weather chart, hoping one day to return with the other half. As with many of the objects, and many of the girls, it remained forever in the Pietà. Like Anna Maria, most of the foundlings would never know a blood relative, and so they were named for their home: Anna Maria della Pietà—Anna Maria of the Pieta. An eighteenth-century roster lists Anna Maria's de facto sisters: Adelaide della Pietà, Agata della Pietà, Ambrosina della Pietà, and on and on, all the way through Violeta, Virginia, and Vittoria della Pietà.

The *ospedali* were public-private partnerships, each overseen by a volunteer board of upper-class Venetians. The institutions were officially secular, but they were adjoined to churches, and life inside ran according to quasi-monastic rules. Residents were separated according to age and gender. Daily Mass was required before breakfast, and regular confession was expected. Everyone, even children, worked constantly to keep the institution running. One day a year, girls were allowed a trip to the countryside, chaperoned, of course. It was a rigid existence, but there were benefits.

The children were taught to read, write, and do arithmetic, as well as vocational skills. Some became pharmacists for the residents, others laundered silk or sewed ship sails that could be sold. The *ospedali* were fully functioning, self-contained communities. Everyone was compensated for their work, and the Pietà had its own interest-paying bank meant to help wards learn to manage their own money. Boys learned a trade or joined the navy and left as teenagers. For girls, marriage was the primary route to emancipation. Dowries were kept ready, but many wards stayed forever.

As the *ospedali* accrued instruments, music was added to the education of dozens of girls so that they could play during religious ceremonies in the adjacent churches. After a plague in 1630 wiped out one-third of the population, Venetians found themselves in an especially "penitential mood," as one historian put it. The musicians suddenly became more important.

The *ospedali* governors noticed that a lot more people were attending church, and that the institutional endowments swelled with donations proportional to the quality of the girls' music. By the eighteenth century, the governors were openly promoting the musicians for fundraising. Each Saturday and Sunday, concerts began before sunset. The church was so packed that the Eucharist had to be moved. Visitors were still welcome for free, of course, but if a guest wanted to sit, *ospedali* staff were happy to rent out chairs. Once the indoor space was full, listeners crowded outside windows, or paused their gondolas in the basin outside. Foundlings became an economic engine not just sustaining the social welfare system in Venice, but drawing tourists from abroad. Entertainment and penitence mixed in amusing ways. Audience members were not allowed to applaud in church, so after the final note they coughed and hemmed and scraped their feet and blew their noses in admiration.

The *ospedali* commissioned composers for original works. Over one six-year period, Vivaldi wrote 140 concertos exclusively for the Pietà musicians. A teaching system evolved, where the older *figlie* taught the younger, and the younger the beginners. They held multiple jobs—Anna Maria was a teacher and copyist—and yet they produced star after virtuoso star. After Anna Maria, her soloist successor, Chiara della Pietà, was hailed as the greatest violinist in all of Europe.

It all raises the question: Just what magical training mechanism was deployed to transform the orphan foundlings of the Venetian sex industry, who but for the grace of charity would have died in the city's canals, into the world's original international rock stars?

The Pietà's music program was not unique for its rigor. According to a list of Pietà directives, formal lessons were Tuesdays, Thursdays, and Saturdays, and *figlie* were free to practice on their own. Early in the rise of the *figlie del coro,* work and chores took most of their time, so they were only allowed an hour a day of music study.

The most surprising feature was how many instruments they learned. Shortly after he received his music doctorate from Oxford, eighteenth-century English composer and historian Charles Burney set out to write a definitive history of modern music, which involved several *ospedali* visits. Burney, who became famous as both a travel writer and the foremost music scholar of the day, was astounded by what he saw in Venice. On one *ospedali* trip, he was given a two-hour private performance, with no curtain between him and the performers. "It was really curious to *see,* as well as to *hear,* every part of this excellent concert, performed by female violins, hautbòis [oboes], tenors, bases, harpsichords, french-horns, and even double bases," Burney wrote. More curious still, "these young persons frequently change instruments."

Figlie took singing lessons, and learned to play every instrument their institution owned. It helped that they were paid for learning new skills. A musician named Maddalena married and left institutional life, and toured from London to St. Petersburg, performing as a violinist, harpsichordist, cellist, and soprano. She wrote of "acquiring skills not expected of my sex," and became so famous that her personal life was covered by one of the day's gossip writers.

For those who stayed a lifetime in the institution, their multi-instrument background had practical importance. Pelegrina della Pietà, who arrived at the *scaffetta* swaddled in rags, started on the bass, moved to violin, and then to oboe, all while working as a nurse. Vivaldi wrote oboe parts specifically for Pelegrina, but in her sixties her teeth fell out, abruptly ending her oboe career. So she switched back to violin, and continued performing into her seventies.

The Pieta's musicians loved to show off their versatility. According to a French writer, they were trained "in all styles of music, sacred or profane," and gave concerts that "lent themselves to the most varied vocal and instrumental combinations." Audience members commonly remarked on the wide range of instruments the *figlie* could play, or on their surprise at seeing a virtuosa singer come out during intermission to improvise an instrumental solo.

Beyond instruments the *figlie* played in concert, they learned instruments that were probably used primarily for teaching or experimentation: a harpsichord-like spinet; a chamber organ; a giant string instrument known as a tromba marina; a wooden, flutelike instrument covered with leather called a zink; and a viola da gamba, a string instrument played upright and with a bow like a cello, but with more strings, a subtly different shape, and frets befitting a guitar. The *figlie* weren't merely playing well, they were participants in an extraordinary period for instrument invention and reinvention. According to musicologist Marc Pincherle, in the multiskilled *figlie* and their menagerie of instruments, "Vivaldi had at his disposal a musical laboratory of unlimited resources."

Some of the instruments the *figlie* learned are so obscure that nobody knows what exactly they were. A young Pietà musician named Prudenza apparently sang beautifully, and performed fluently with the violin and the "violoncello all'inglese." Music scholars have argued about what that even is, but, as with anything else the Pietà could get its musical mitts on—like the chalumeau (wind) and the psaltery (string)—the *figlie* learned to play it.

They lifted composers to unexplored heights. They were part of the bridge that carried music from Baroque composers to the classical masters: Bach (who transcribed Vivaldi's concertos); Haydn (who composed specifically for one of the *figlie*, Bianchetta, a singer, harpist, and organist); and perhaps Mozart, who visited an *ospedale* with his father as a boy, and returned as a teen. The *figlie*'s skills on a vast array of instruments enabled musical experimentation so profound that it laid a foundation for the modern orchestra. According to musicologist Denis Arnold, the modernization of church music that occurred through the *figlie* was so influential that one of Mozart's iconic sacred pieces, without the girls of the Venetian orphanages, "might never have been composed at all."

But their stories were largely forgotten, or thrown away, literally. When Napoleon's troops arrived in 1797, they tossed manuscripts and records out the *ospedali* windows. When, two hundred years later, a famous eighteenth-century painting of women giving a concert was displayed at the National Gallery of Art in Washington, D.C., the mysterious figures dressed in black, in an upper balcony above the audience, went entirely unidentified.

Maybe the memories of the *figlie* faded because they were women— playing music in public religious ceremonies defied papal authority. Or because so many of them neither came with families nor left any behind. They lacked family names, but the abandoned girls were so synonymous with their instruments that those became their names. The baby who came through a notch in the wall and began her way in the world as Anna Maria della Pietà left the world having been, by various stages, Anna Maria del violino, Anna Maria del theorbo, Anna Maria del cembalo, Anna Maria del violoncello, Anna Maria del luta, Anna Maria della viola d'amore, and Anna Maria del mandolin.

Imagine it today: click a tourism site and the entertainment recommendation is the world-famous orchestra comprised of orphans left at the doorstep of the music venue. You will be treated to virtuoso solos on instruments you know and love, as well as those you've never heard of. Occasionally the musicians will switch instruments during the show. And please follow us on Twitter, @FamousFoundlings. Never mind 200-ducat dowries, the *figlie* would have speaking agents and feature film deals.

Just like Tiger Woods's television appearance when he was two, it would foment a frenzy of parents and media seeking to excavate the mysterious secret to success. Parents actually did flock in the eighteenth century. Noblemen vied (and paid) to get their daughters a chance to play with those "able indigents," as one historian put it.

But the strategies of their musical development would be a hard sell. Today, the massively multi-instrument approach seems to go against everything we know about how to get good at a skill like playing music. It certainly goes against the deliberate practice framework, which only counts highly focused attempts at exactly the skill to be performed. Multiple instruments, in that view, should be a waste of time.

In the genre of modern self-help narratives, music training has stood beside golf atop the podium, exemplars of the power of a narrowly focused head start in highly technical training. Whether it is the story of Tiger Woods or the Yale law professor known as the Tiger Mother, the message is the same: choose early, focus narrowly, never waver.

The Tiger Mother's real name is Amy Chua, and she coined the term in her 2011 book *Battle Hymn of the Tiger Mother*. Like Tiger, the Tiger Mother permeated popular culture. Chua advertised the secrets to "how Chinese parents raise such stereotypically successful kids." On the very first page of the very first chapter is the litany of things Sophia and Lulu must never do, including: "play any instrument other than the piano or the violin." (Sophia gets piano, Lulu is assigned violin.) Chua supervised three, four, and sometimes five hours of music practice a day.

Parents in online forums agonize over what instrument to pick for their child, because the child is too young to pick for herself and will fall irredeemably behind if she waits. "I am slowly trying to convince him how nice playing music is," a parent of a two-and-a-half-year-old posted. "I am just not too sure which instrument would be best." Another post advised nixing violin if a child has not started by seven, as she will be too far behind. In response to such concerns, the director of a private music school wrote a "how to choose" advice column with tips for picking an instrument for a child who can't yet stick with the same favorite color from one week to the next.

There are, of course, many routes to expertise. Some outstanding musicians have focused very young. The supreme cellist Yo-Yo Ma is a well-known example. Less well known, though, is that Ma started on violin, moved to piano, and then to the cello because he didn't really like the first two instruments. He just went through the sampling period a lot faster than the typical student.

Tiger parents are trying to skip that phase entirely. It reminds me of a conversation I had with Ian Yates, a British sports scientist and coach who helped develop future professional athletes in a range of sports. Parents, Yates told me, increasingly come to him and "want their kids doing what the Olympians are doing right now, not what the Olympians were doing when they were twelve or thirteen," which included a wider variety of activities that developed their general athleticism and allowed them to probe their talents and interests before they focused narrowly on technical skills. The sampling period is not incidental to the development of great performers—something to be excised in the interest of a head start—it is integral.

John Sloboda is undoubtedly one of the most influential researchers in the psychology of music. His 1985 book *The Musical Mind* ranged from the origins of music to the acquisition of playing skill, and set a research agenda that the field is still carrying out today. Through the

1990s, Sloboda and his colleagues studied strategies for musical growth. Practice, unsurprisingly, was crucial in the development of musicians. But the details were less intuitive.

A study of music students aged eight to eighteen and ranging in skill from rank novices to students in a highly selective music school found that when they began training there was no difference in the amount of practice undertaken between any of the groups of players, from the least to the most accomplished. The students who would go on to be most successful only started practicing much more once they identified an instrument they wanted to focus on, whether because they were better at it or just liked it more. The instrument, it appeared, was driving the practitioner, rather than the reverse.

In a separate study of twelve hundred young musicians, those who quit reported "a mismatch between the instruments [they] wanted to learn to play and the instruments they actually played." Amy Chua described her daughter Lulu as a "natural musician." Chua's singer friend called Lulu "extraordinary," with a gift "no one can teach." Lulu made rapid progress on the violin, but pretty soon told her mother ominously, "You picked it, not me." At thirteen, she quit most of her violin activities. Chua, candid and introspective, wondered in the coda of her book if Lulu would still be playing if she had been allowed to choose her own instrument.

When Sloboda and a colleague conducted a study with students at a British boarding school that recruited from around the country—admission rested entirely on an audition—they were surprised to find that the students classified as exceptional by the school came from less musically active families compared to less accomplished students, did not start playing at a younger age, were less likely to have had an instrument in the home at a very young age, had taken fewer lessons prior to entering the school, and had simply practiced less overall before arriving—a lot less. "It seems very clear," the psychologists wrote, "that sheer amount of lesson or practice time is not a good indicator of exceptionality." As to structured lessons, every single one of the students who had received a large amount of structured lesson time early in development fell into the "average" skill category, and not one was in the exceptional group. "The strong implication," the researchers wrote, is "that that too many lessons at a young age may not be helpful."

"However," they added, "the distribution of effort across different instruments seems important. Those children identified as exceptional by [the school] turn out to be those children who distributed their effort more evenly across three instruments." The less skilled students tended to spend their time on the first instrument they picked up, as if they could not give up a perceived head start. The exceptional students developed more like the *figlie del coro*. "The modest investment in a third instrument paid off handsomely for the exceptional children," the scientists concluded.

The psychologists highlighted the variety of paths to excellence, but the most common was a sampling period, often lightly structured with some lessons and a breadth of instruments and activities, followed only later by a narrowing of focus, increased structure, and an explosion of practice volume. Sound familiar? A study that followed up on Sloboda's work two decades later compared young musicians admitted to a competitive conservatory to similarly committed but less skilled music students. Nearly all of the more accomplished students had played at least three instruments, proportionally much more than the lower-level students, and more than half played four or five. Learning to play classical music is a narrative linchpin for the cult of the head start; as music goes, it is a relatively golflike endeavor. It comes with a blueprint; errors are immediately apparent; it requires repetitive practice of the exact same task until execution becomes automatic and deviation is minimal. How could picking an instrument as early as possible and starting in technical training not be the standard path to success? And yet even classical music defies a simple Tiger story.

The Cambridge Handbook of Expertise and Expert Performance, published in 2006, is a sort of bible for popular writers, speakers, and researchers in the ten-thousand-hours school. It is a compilation of essayistic chapters, each written by different researchers who delve into dance, math, sports, surgery, writing, and chess. The music section focuses very conspicuously on classical playing. At nine hundred oversized pages, it is a handbook for large hands. In the chapter on developing music expertise, there is just one single substantive mention of the beginnings of expert players in all the genres of music in the world that are not classical. The *Handbook* simply notes that, in contrast to classical players, jazz and folk and modern popular musicians and singers do not follow a simple, narrow trajectory of technical training, and they "start much later."

Jack Cecchini can thank two stumbles, one metaphorical and one literal, for making him one of the rare musicians who is world class in both jazz and classical.

The first was in 1950 in Chicago, when he was thirteen and stumbled across a guitar resting on his landlord's couch. He ran his fingers over the strings as he walked by. The landlord picked it up, demonstrated two chords, and immediately asked Cecchini to play accompaniment with them. Of course, he couldn't. "He'd shake his head when it was time for me to change the chord, and if I didn't he'd start swearing," Cecchini recalled with a chuckle. Cecchini's interest was ignited, and he started trying to imitate songs he heard on the radio. By sixteen, he was playing jazz in the background of Chicago clubs he was too young to patronize. "It was like a factory," he told me. "If you had to go to the bathroom, you had to get one of the other guys to pick it up. But you're experimenting every night." He took the only free music lessons he could find, in clarinet, and tried to transfer what he learned to the guitar. "There are eight million places on the guitar to play the same notes," he said. "I was just trying to find solutions to problems, and you start to learn the fingerboard." Pretty soon he was performing with Frank Sinatra at the Villa Venice, Miriam Makeba at the Apollo, and touring with Harry Belafonte from Carnegie Hall to packed baseball stadiums. That's where the second stumble came in.

During a show when Cecchini was twenty-three, one of Belafonte's stage dancers stepped on the cable that connected his guitar to an amplifier. His instrument was reduced to a whisper. "Harry freaked out," Cecchini recalled. "He said, 'Get rid of that thing and get yourself a classical guitar!'" Getting one was easy, but he had been using a pick, and for acoustic he had to learn fingering, so the trouble was learning to play it on tour.

He fell in love with the instrument, and by thirty-one was so adept that he was chosen as the soloist to play a concerto by none other than Vivaldi accompanied by an orchestra for a crowd in Chicago's Grant Park. The next day, the *Chicago Tribune*'s music critic began his review: "Despite the ever-increasing number of enthusiasts who untiringly promote the resurrection of the guitar as a classical instrument, there are but few men who possess the talent and patience to master what remains one of the most beautiful but obstinately difficult of all instruments." Cecchini, he continued, "proved to be one of those few."

Despite his late and haphazard start, Cecchini also became a renowned teacher of both jazz and classical guitar. Students traveled from out of state to pick his brain, and by the early 1980s lines formed down the stairs of his Chicago school in the evenings. His own formal training, of course, had been those free clarinet lessons. "I'd say I'm 98 percent self-taught," he told me. He switched between instruments and found his way through trial and error. It might sound unusual, but when Cecchini reeled off legends he played with or admired, there was not a Tiger among them.

Duke Ellington was one of the few who ever actually took formal lessons, when he was seven, from the exuberantly named teacher Marietta Clinkscales. He lost interest immediately, before he learned to read notes, and quit music entirely to focus on baseball. In school, his interests were drawing and painting. (He later turned down a college art scholarship.) When he was fourteen, Ellington heard ragtime, and for the first time in seven years sat down at a piano and tried to copy what he had heard. "There was no connection between me and music, until I started fiddling with it myself," he remembered. "As far as anyone teaching me, there was too many rules and regulations. . . . As long as I could sit down and figure it out for myself, then that was all right." Even once he became arguably America's preeminent composer, he relied on copyists to decode his personal musical shorthand into traditional musical notation.

Johnny Smith was Cecchini's absolute favorite. Smith grew up in a shotgun house in Alabama. Neighbors gathered to play music, and young Johnny goofed around with whatever they left in a corner overnight. "John played anything," his brother Ben recalled. It allowed him to enter local competitions for any instrument, and the prizes were groceries. He once fiddled his way to a five-pound bag of sugar. He didn't particularly like violin, though. Smith said he would have walked fifty miles for a guitar lesson, but there were no teachers around, so he just had to experiment.

When the United States entered World War II, Smith enlisted in the Army hoping to be a pilot, but a left-eye problem disqualified him. He was sent to the marching band, which had absolutely no use for a guitar player. He could not yet read music, but was assigned to teach himself a variety of instruments so he could play at recruiting events. Wide-ranging experience set him up for his postwar work as NBC's musical arranger. He had learned to learn, and his multi-instrument and poly-genre skill became so renowned that it got him into a tricky spot.

He was leaving NBC one Friday evening when he was stopped at the elevator and asked to learn a new guitar part. The classical player hired for the job couldn't hack it. It was for a live celebration of composer Arnold Schoenberg's seventy-fifth birthday, and would feature one of Schoenberg's atonal compositions, which had not been performed in twenty-five years. Smith had four days. He continued with his Friday night, got home at 5 a.m., and then joined an emergency rehearsal at 7 a.m. On Wednesday, he performed so beautifully that the audience demanded an encore of all seven movements. In 1998, alongside Sir Edmund Hillary, who with Tenzing Norgay was the first to summit Mount Everest, Smith was awarded Smithsonian's Bicentennial Medal for outstanding cultural contributions.

Pianist Dave Brubeck earned the medal as well. His song "Take Five" was chosen by NPR listeners as the quintessential jazz tune of all time. Brubeck's mother tried to teach him piano, but he refused to follow instructions. He was born cross-eyed, and his childhood reluctance was related to his inability to see the musical notation. His mother gave up, but he listened when she taught others and tried to imitate. Brubeck still could not read music when he dropped out of veterinary premed at the College of the Pacific and walked across the lawn to the music department, but he was a masterful faker. He put off studying piano for instruments that would more easily allow him to improvise his way through exercises. Senior year, he could hide no longer. "I got a wonderful piano teacher," he recalled, "who figured out I couldn't read in about five minutes." The dean informed Brubeck that he could not graduate and furthermore was a disgrace to the conservatory. Another teacher who had noticed his creativity stuck up for him, and the dean cut a deal. Brubeck was allowed to graduate on the condition that he promise never to embarrass the institution by teaching. Twenty years later, the college apparently felt it had sufficiently escaped embarrassment, and awarded him an honorary doctorate.

Perhaps the greatest improv master of all could not read, period— words or music. Django Reinhardt was born in Belgium in 1910, in a Romani caravan. His early childhood talents were chicken stealing and trout tickling—feeling along a riverbank for fish and rubbing their bellies until they relaxed and could be tossed ashore. Django grew up outside Paris in an area called la Zone, where the city's cesspool cleaners

unloaded waste each night. His mother, Négros, was too busy supporting the family making bracelets out of spent artillery shell casings she
gathered from a World War I battlefield to lord over anyone's music
practice. Django went to school if he felt like it, but he mostly didn't. He
crashed movie theaters and shot billiards, and was surrounded by music.
Wherever Romani gathered, there were banjos, harps, pianos, and especially violins.

The violin's portability made it the classic Romani instrument, and
Django started there, but he didn't love it. He learned in the call-and-
response style. An adult would play a section of music and he would try
to copy it. When he was twelve, an acquaintance gave him a hybrid
banjo-guitar. He had found his thing, and became obsessed. He experimented with different objects as picks when his fingers needed a break:
spoons, sewing thimbles, coins, a piece of whalebone. He teamed up
with a banjo-playing hunchback named Lagardère, and they wandered
the Paris streets, busking and improvising duets.

In his mid teens, Django was at a restaurant in Paris where the city's
accordionists had gathered. He and his banjo-guitar were asked to the
stage to play for the other musicians. Django launched into a polka that
was known as a skill-proving piece for accordionists because it was so
hard to play. When he finished the traditional form, rather than stopping he careened into a series of lightning improvisations, bending and
twisting the song into creations none of the veteran musicians had ever
heard. Django was playing "with a drawn knife," as the lingo went. He
was looking for a fight by warping a sacred dancehall tune, but he was
so original that he got away with it. His creativity was unbound. "I
wonder if, in his younger days," one of his music partners said, "he even
knew that printed music existed." Django would soon need all the versatility he had learned.

He was eighteen when a candle in his wagon ignited a batch of cel-
luloid flowers that his wife, Bella, had fashioned for a funeral. The

wagon exploded into an inferno. Django was burned over half his body and ended up bedridden for a year and a half. For the rest of his life the pinkie and ring finger of his left hand, his fret hand, were dangling flesh, useless on the strings. Django was used to improvising. Like Pelegrina of the *figlie del coro* when she lost her teeth, he pivoted. He taught himself how to play chords with a thumb and two fingers. His left hand had to sprint up and down the neck of his guitar, the index and middle finger flitting waterbug-like over the strings. He re-emerged with a new way of handling the instrument, and his creativity erupted.

With a French violinist, Django fused dancehall musette with jazz and invented a new form of improvisational music that defied easy characterization, so it was just called "Gypsy jazz." Some of his spontaneous compositions became "standards," pieces that enter the canon from which other musicians improvise. He revolutionized the now-familiar virtuosic guitar solo that pervaded the next generation's music, from Jimi Hendrix, who kept an album of Django's recordings and named one of his groups Band of Gypsys, to Prince (self-taught, played more than a half-dozen different genres of instruments on his debut album). Long before Hendrix melted "The Star-Spangled Banner" into his own wondrous creation, Django did it with the French national anthem, "La Marseillaise."

Even though he never learned to read music (or words—a fellow musician had to teach him to sign his autograph for fans), Django composed a symphony, playing on his guitar what he wanted each instrument in the ensemble to do while another musician struggled to transcribe it.

He died of a brain hemorrhage at forty-three, but music he made nearly a century ago continues to show up in pop culture, including Hollywood blockbusters like *The Matrix* and *The Aviator,* and in the hit *BioShock* video games. The author of *The Making of Jazz* anointed the man who could neither read music nor study it with the traditional fingerings "without question, the single most important guitarist in the history of jazz."

Cecchini has bushy eyebrows and a beard that parts and closes quickly like ruffled shrubbery when he talks excitedly. Like now: he's talking Django, and he's a huge fan. He used to have a black poodle named Django. He opens a sepia-toned YouTube clip and whispers conspiratorially, "Watch this."

There is Django, bow tie, pencil mustache, and slicked-back hair. The two useless fingers on his left hand are tucked into a claw. Suddenly, the hand shoots all the way up the guitar neck, and then all the way back down, firing a rapid succession of notes. "That's amazing!" Cecchini says. "The synchronization between the left and right hand is phenomenal."

The strict deliberate practice school describes useful training as focused consciously on error correction. But the most comprehensive examination of development in improvisational forms, by Duke University professor Paul Berliner, described the childhoods of professionals as "one of osmosis," not formal instruction. "Most explored the band room's diverse options as a prelude to selecting an instrument of specialization," he wrote. "It was not uncommon for youngsters to develop skills on a variety of instruments." Berliner added that aspiring improvisational musicians "whose educational background has fostered a fundamental dependence on [formal] teachers must adopt new approaches to learning." A number of musicians recounted Brubeck-like scenarios to Berliner, the time a teacher found out that they could not read music but had become adept enough at imitation and improvisation that "they had simply pretended to follow the notation." Berliner relayed the advice of professional musicians to a young improvisational learner as "not to think about playing—just play."

While I was sitting with Cecchini, he reeled off an impressive improvisation. I asked him to repeat it so I could record it. "I couldn't play that again if you put a gun to my head," he said. Charles Limb, a musician, hearing specialist, and auditory surgeon at the University of California, San Francisco, designed an iron-free keyboard so that jazz musicians could improvise while inside an MRI scanner. Limb saw that brain areas associated with focused attention, inhibition, and self-censoring turned down when the musicians were creating. "It's almost as if the brain turned off its own ability to criticize itself," he told *National Geographic*. While improvising, musicians do pretty much the opposite of consciously identifying errors and stopping to correct them.

Improv masters learn like babies: dive in and imitate and improvise first, learn the formal rules later. "At the beginning, your mom didn't give you a book and say, 'This is a noun, this is a pronoun, this is a dangling participle,'" Cecchini told me. "You acquired the sound first. And then you acquire the grammar later."

Django Reinhardt was once in a taxi with Les Paul, inventor of the solid-body electric guitar. Paul was a self-taught musician, and the only person in both the Rock and Roll and National Inventors halls of fame. Reinhardt tapped Paul on the shoulder and asked if he could read music. "I said no, I didn't," Paul recounted, "and he laughed till he was crying and said, 'Well, I can't read either. I don't even know what a C is; I just play them.'"

Cecchini told me that he was regularly stunned when he would ask an exceptional jazz performer onstage to play a certain note, and find the musician could not understand him. "It's an old joke among jazz musicians," Cecchini said. "You ask, 'Can you read music?' And the guy says, 'Not enough to hurt my playing.'" There is truth in the joke. Cecchini has taught musicians who played professionally for the Chicago Symphony, which in 2015 was rated as the top orchestra in the country and fifth in the world by a panel of critics. "It's easier for a jazz musician to learn to play classical literature than for a classical player to learn how to play jazz," he said. "The jazz musician is a creative artist, the classical musician is a re-creative artist."

After Django Reinhardt lit the nightclub music scene on fire, classically trained musicians began trying to transition to jazz. According to Michael Dregni, who wrote multiple books on that period, improvisation was "a concept that went against conservatory training. . . . After years of rigorous conservatory training, it was an impossible transition for some." Leon Fleisher, regarded as one of the great classical pianists of the twentieth century, told the coauthor of his 2010 memoir that his "greatest wish" was to be able to improvise. But despite a lifetime of masterful interpretation of notes on the page, he said, "I can't improvise at all."

Cecchini's analogy to language learning is hardly unique. Even the Suzuki Method of music instruction, synonymous in the public consciousness with early drilling, was designed by Shinichi Suzuki to mimic natural language acquisition. Suzuki grew up around his father's violin factory, but considered the instrument nothing more than a toy. When he fought with his siblings, they beat one another with violins. He did not attempt to play the instrument until he was seventeen, moved by a recording of *Ave Maria*. He brought a violin home from the factory and tried to imitate a classical recording by ear. "My complete self-taught technique was more a scraping than anything else," he said of that initial foray, "but somehow I finally got so I could play the piece." Only later did he seek out technical lessons and become a performer and then an educator. According to the Suzuki Association of the Americas, "Children do not practice exercises to learn to talk. . . . Children learn to read after their ability to talk has been well established."

In totality, the picture is in line with a classic research finding that is not specific to music: breadth of training predicts breadth of transfer.

That is, the more contexts in which something is learned, the more the learner creates abstract models, and the less they rely on any particular example. Learners become better at applying their knowledge to a situation they've never seen before, which is the essence of creativity.

Compared to the Tiger Mother's tome, a parenting manual oriented toward creative achievement would have to open with a much shorter list of rules. In offering advice to parents, psychologist Adam Grant noted that creativity may be difficult to nurture, but it is easy to thwart. He pointed to a study that found an average of six household rules for typical children, compared to one in households with extremely creative children. The parents with creative children made their opinions known after their kids did something they didn't like, they just did not proscribe it beforehand. Their households were low on prior restraint.

"It's strange," Cecchini told me at the end of one of our hours-long discussions, "that some of the greatest musicians were self-taught or never learned to read music. I'm not saying one way is the best, but now I get a lot of students from schools that are teaching jazz, and they all sound the same. They don't seem to find their own voice. I think when you're self-taught you experiment more, trying to find the same sound in different places, you learn how to solve problems."

Cecchini stopped speaking for a moment, reclined in his chair, and stared at the ceiling. A few moments passed. "I could show somebody in two minutes what would take them years of screwing around on the fingerboard like I did to find it. You don't know what's right or what's wrong. You don't have that in your head. You're just trying to find a solution to problems, and after fifty lifetimes, it starts to come together for you. It's slow," he told me, "but at the same time, there's something to learning that way."

CHAPTER 4

Learning, Fast and Slow

"**OKAY? YOU'RE GOING** to an Eagles game," the charismatic math teacher tells her eighth-grade class. She takes care to frame problems using situations that motivate students. "They're selling hot dogs," she continues. "They're very good, by the way, in Philadelphia." Students giggle. One interjects, "So are the cheesesteaks."

The teacher brings them back to today's lesson, simple algebraic expressions: "The hot dogs at [the] stadium where the Eagles play sell for three dollars. I want you to give me a variable expression for [the cost of] N hot dogs." The students need to learn what it means for a letter to represent an undetermined number. It is an abstraction they must grasp in order to progress in math, but not a particularly easy one to explain.

Marcus volunteers: "N over three dollars."

"Not *over*," the teacher responds, "because that means divided." She gives the correct expression: "Three N. Three N means however many I buy I have to pay three dollars for [each], right?" Another student is confused. "Where do you get the N from?" he asks.

"That's the N number of hot dogs," the teacher explains. "That's what I'm using as my variable." A student named Jen asks if that means you should multiply. "That's right. So if I got two hot dogs, how much money am I spending?"

Six dollars, Jen answers correctly.

"Three times two. Good, Jen." Another hand shoots up. "Yes?"

"Can it be any letter?" Michelle wants to know. Yes, it can.

"But isn't it confusing?" Brandon asks.

It can be any letter at all, the teacher explains. On to part two of today's lesson: evaluating expressions.

"What I just did with the three dollars for a hot dog was 'evaluating an expression,'" the teacher explains. She points to "7H" on the board and asks, if you make seven dollars an hour and work two hours this week, how much would you earn? Fourteen, Ryan answers correctly. What about if you worked ten hours? Seventy, Josh says. The teacher can see they're getting it. Soon, though, it will become clear that they never actually understood the expression, they just figured out to multiply whatever two numbers the teacher said aloud.

"What we just did was we took the number of hours and did what? Michelle?" Multiplied it by seven, Michelle answers. Right, but really what we did, the teacher explains, was put it into the expression where H is. "That's what evaluating means," she adds, "substituting a number for a variable."

But now another girl is confused. "So for the hot-dog thing, would the N be two?" she asks. "Yes. We substituted two for the N," the teacher replies. "We evaluated that example." Why, then, the girl wants to know, can't you just write however many dollars a hot dog costs times two? If N is just two, what sense does it make to write "N" instead of "2"?

The students ask more questions that slowly make clear they have failed to connect the abstraction of a variable to more than a single particular number for any given example. When she tries to move back to a realistic context—"social studies class is three times as long as math"—they are totally lost. "I thought fifth period was the longest?"

one chimes in. When the students are asked to turn phrases into variable expressions, they have to start guessing.

"What if I say 'six less than a number'? Michelle?" the teacher asks.

"Six minus N," Michelle answers. Incorrect.

Aubrey guesses the only other possibility: "N minus six." Great.

The kids repeat this form of platoon multiple choice. Watched in real time, it can give the impression that they understand.

"What if I gave you 15 minus B?" the teacher asks the class, telling them to transform that back into words. Multiple-choice time. "Fifteen less than B?" Patrick offers. The teacher does not respond immediately, so he tries something else. "B less than 15." This time the response is immediate; he nailed it. The pattern repeats. *Kim is six inches shorter than her mother.* "N minus negative six," Steve offers. No. "N minus six." Good. *Mike is three years older than Jill.* Ryan? "Three X," he says. No, that would be multiply, wouldn't it? "Three plus X." Great.

Marcus has now figured out the surefire way to get to the right answer. His hand shoots up for the next question. *Three divided by W.* Marcus? "W over three, or three over W," he answers, covering his bases. Good, three over W, got it.

Despite the teacher's clever vignettes, it is clear that students do not understand how these numbers and letters might be useful anywhere but on a school worksheet. When she asks where variable expressions might be used in the world, Patrick answers: when you're trying to figure out math problems. Still, the students have figured out how to get the right answers on their worksheets: shrewdly interrogating their teacher.

She mistakes the multiple-choice game they are mastering for productive exploration. Sometimes, the students team up. In staccato succession: "K over eight," one offers, "K into eight," another says, "K of eight," a third tries. The teacher is kind and encouraging even if they don't manage to toss out the right answer. "It's okay," she says, "you're thinking." The problem, though, is the way in which they are thinking.

———

That was one American class period out of hundreds in the United States, Asia, and Europe that were filmed and analyzed in an effort to understand effective math teaching. Needless to say, classrooms were very different. In the Netherlands, students regularly trickled into class late, and spent a lot of class time working on their own. In Hong Kong, class looked pretty similar to the United States: lectures rather than individual work filled most of the time. Some countries used a lot of problems in real-world contexts, others relied more on symbolic math. Some classes kept kids in their seats, others had them approach the blackboard. Some teachers were very energetic, others staid. The litany of differences was long, but not one of those features was associated with differences in student achievement across countries. There were similarities too. In every classroom in every country, teachers relied on two main types of questions.

The more common were "using procedures" questions: basically, practice at something that was just learned. For instance, take the formula for the sum of the interior angles of a polygon (180 × (number of polygon sides − 2)), and apply it to polygons on a worksheet. The other common variety was "making connections" questions, which connected students to a broader concept, rather than just a procedure. That was more like when the teacher asked students *why* the formula works, or made them try to figure out if it works for absolutely any polygon from a triangle to an octagon. Both types of questions are useful and both were posed by teachers in every classroom in every country studied. But an important difference emerged in what teachers did *after* they asked a making-connections problem.

Rather than letting students grapple with some confusion, teachers often responded to their solicitations with hint-giving that morphed a making-connections problem into a using-procedures one. That is exactly what the charismatic teacher in the American classroom was doing.

Lindsey Richland, a University of Chicago professor who studies learning, watched that video with me, and told me that when the students were playing multiple choice with the teacher, "what they're actually doing is seeking rules." They were trying to turn a conceptual problem they didn't understand into a procedural one they could just execute. "We're very good, humans are, at trying to do the least amount of work that we have to in order to accomplish a task," Richland told me. Soliciting hints toward a solution is both clever and expedient. The problem is that when it comes to learning concepts that can be broadly wielded, expedience can backfire.

In the United States, about one-fifth of questions posed to students began as making-connections problems. But by the time the students were done soliciting hints from the teacher and solving the problems, a grand total of zero percent remained making-connections problems. Making-connections problems did not survive the teacher-student interactions.

Teachers in every country fell into the same trap at times, but in the higher-performing countries plenty of making-connections problems remained that way as the class struggled to figure them out. In Japan, a little more than half of all problems were making-connections problems, and half of those stayed that way through the solving. An entire class period could be just one problem with many parts. When a student offered an idea for how to approach a problem, rather than engaging in multiple choice, the teacher had them come to the board and put a magnet with their name on it next to the idea. By the end of class, one problem on a blackboard the size of an entire wall served as a captain's log of the class's collective intellectual voyage, dead ends and all. Richland originally tried to label the videotaped lessons with a single topic of the day, "but we couldn't do it with Japan," she said, "because you could engage with these problems using so much different content." (There is a specific Japanese word to describe chalkboard writing that tracks conceptual connections over the course of collective problem solving: *bansho*.)

Just as it is in golf, procedure practice is important in math. But when it comprises the entire math training strategy, it's a problem. "Students do not view mathematics as a *system*," Richland and her colleagues wrote. They view it as just a set of procedures. Like when Patrick was asked how variable expressions connected to the world, and answered that they were good for answering questions in math class.

In their research, Richland and her collaborators highlighted the stunning degree of reliance community college students—41 percent of all undergraduate students in the United States—have on memorized algorithms. Asked whether $a/5$ or $a/8$ is greater, 53 percent of students answered correctly, barely better than guessing. Asked to explain their answers, students frequently pointed to some algorithm. Students remembered that they should focus on the bottom number, but a lot of them recalled that a larger denominator meant $a/8$ was bigger than $a/5$. Others remembered that they should try to get a common denominator, but weren't sure why. There were students who reflexively cross-multiplied, because they knew that's what you do when you see fractions, even though it had no relevance to the problem at hand. Only 15 percent of the students began with broad, conceptual reasoning that if you divide something into five parts, each piece will be larger than if you divide the same thing into eight parts. Every single one of those students got the correct answer.

Some of the college students seemed to have unlearned number sense that most children have, like that adding two numbers gives you a third comprised of the first two. A student who was asked to verify that $462 + 253 = 715$, subtracted 253 from 715, and got 462. When he was asked for another strategy, he could not come up with subtracting 462 from 715 to see that it equals 253, because the rule he learned was to subtract the number to the right of the plus sign to check the answer.

When younger students bring home problems that force them to make connections, Richland told me, "parents are like, 'Lemme show you, there's a faster, easier way.'" If the teacher didn't already turn the work into using-procedures practice, well-meaning parents will. They aren't comfortable with bewildered kids, and they want understanding to come quickly and easily. But for learning that is both durable (it sticks) and flexible (it can be applied broadly), *fast and easy* is precisely the problem.

"Some people argue that part of the reason U.S. students don't do as well on international measures of high school knowledge is that they're doing too well in class," Nate Kornell, a cognitive psychologist at Williams College, told me. "What you want is to make it easy to make it hard."

Kornell was explaining the concept of "desirable difficulties," obstacles that make learning more challenging, slower, and more frustrating in the short term, but better in the long term. Excessive hint-giving, like in the eighth-grade math classroom, does the opposite; it bolsters immediate performance, but undermines progress in the long run. Several desirable difficulties that can be used in the classroom are among the most rigorously supported methods of enhancing learning, and the engaging eighth-grade math teacher accidentally subverted all of them in the well-intended interest of before-your-eyes progress.

One of those desirable difficulties is known as the "generation effect." Struggling to generate an answer on your own, even a wrong one, enhances subsequent learning. Socrates was apparently on to something when he forced pupils to generate answers rather than bestowing them. It requires the learner to intentionally sacrifice current performance for future benefit.

Kornell and psychologist Janet Metcalfe tested sixth graders in the South Bronx on vocabulary learning, and varied how they studied in order to explore the generation effect. Students were given some of the words and definitions together. For example, *To discuss something in order to come to an agreement: Negotiate.* For others, they were shown only the definition and given a little time to think of the right word, even if they had no clue, before it was revealed. When they were tested later, students did way better on the definition-first words. The experiment was repeated on students at Columbia University, with more obscure words (*Characterized by haughty scorn: Supercilious*). The results were the same. Being forced to generate answers improves subsequent learning even if the generated answer is wrong. It can even help to be wildly wrong. Metcalfe and colleagues have repeatedly demonstrated a "hypercorrection effect." The more confident a learner is of their wrong answer, the better the information sticks when they subsequently learn the right answer. Tolerating big mistakes can create the best learning opportunities.*

Kornell helped show that the long-run benefits of facilitated screwups extend to primates only slightly less studious than Columbia students. Specifically, to Oberon and Macduff, two rhesus macaques trained to learn lists by trial and error. In a fascinating experiment, Kornell worked with an animal cognition expert to give Oberon and Macduff lists of random pictures to memorize, in a particular order. (Example: a tulip, a school of fish, a cardinal, Halle Berry, and a raven.) The pictures were all displayed simultaneously on a screen. By pressing them in trial-and-error fashion, the monkeys had to learn the desired order and then practice it repeatedly. But all practice was not designed equal.

In some practice sessions, Oberon (who was generally brighter) and Macduff were automatically given hints on every trial, showing them the next picture in the list. For other lists, they could voluntarily touch

---

* This is another instance where extrapolating from sports to the rest of the world can mislead. With motor-skill learning, some bad habits once formed can be laborious to undo. Elite coaches expend a lot of energy undoing motor habits that athletes who were overcoached as children formed years earlier. In the nonsports world, repeated wrong answers can set up learning, so long as the right answer is provided eventually.

a hint box on the screen whenever they were stuck and wanted to be shown the next item. For still other lists, they could ask for a hint on half of their practice attempts. And for a final group of lists, no hints at all.

In the practice sessions with hints upon request, the monkeys behaved a lot like humans. They almost always requested hints when they were available, and thus got a lot of the lists right. Overall, they had about 250 trials to learn each list.

After three days of practice, the scientists took off the training wheels. Starting on day four, the memorizing monkeys had to repeat all the lists from every training condition without any hints whatsoever. It was a performance disaster. Oberon only got about one-third of the lists right. Macduff got less than one in five. There was, though, an exception: the lists on which they never had hints at all.

For those lists, on day one of practice the duo had performed terribly. They were literally monkeys hitting buttons. But they improved steadily each training day. On test day, Oberon nailed almost three-quarters of the lists that he had learned with no hints. Macduff got about half of them.

The overall experiment results went like this: the more hints that were available during training, the better the monkeys performed during early practice, and the worse they performed on test day. For the lists that Macduff spent three days practicing with automatic hints, he got *zero* correct. It was as if the pair had suddenly unlearned every list that they practiced with hints. The study conclusion was simple: "training with hints did not produce any lasting learning."

Training without hints is slow and error-ridden. It is, essentially, what we normally think of as testing, except for the purpose of learning rather than evaluation—when "test" becomes a dreaded four-letter word. The eighth-grade math teacher was essentially testing her students in class, but she was facilitating or outright giving them the answers.

Used for learning, testing, including self-testing, is a very desirable difficulty. Even testing prior to studying works, at the point when wrong answers are assured. In one of Kornell's experiments, participants were made to learn pairs of words and later tested on recall. At test time, they did the best with pairs that they learned via practice quizzes, even if they had gotten the answers on those quizzes wrong. Struggling to retrieve information primes the brain for subsequent learning, even when the retrieval itself is unsuccessful. The struggle is real, and really useful. "Like life," Kornell and team wrote, "retrieval is all about the journey."

If that eighth-grade classroom followed a typical academic plan over the course of the year, it is precisely the opposite of what science recommends for durable learning—one topic was probably confined to one week and another to the next. Like a lot of professional development efforts, each particular concept or skill gets a short period of intense focus, and then on to the next thing, never to return. That structure makes intuitive sense, but it forgoes another important desirable difficulty: "spacing," or distributed practice.

It is what it sounds like—leaving time between practice sessions for the same material. You might call it deliberate not-practicing between bouts of deliberate practice. "There's a limit to how long you should wait," Kornell told me, "but it's longer than people think. It could be anything, studying foreign language vocabulary or learning how to fly a plane, the harder it is, the more you learn." Space between practice sessions creates the hardness that enhances learning. One study separated Spanish vocabulary learners into two groups—a group that learned the vocab and then was tested on it the same day, and a second that learned the vocab but was tested on it a month later. Eight years later, with no studying in the interim, the latter group retained 250 percent more. For a given amount of Spanish study, spacing made learning more productive by making it easy to make it hard.

It does not take nearly that long to see the spacing effect. Iowa State researchers read people lists of words, and then asked for each list to be recited back either right away, after fifteen seconds of rehearsal, or after fifteen seconds of doing very simple math problems that prevented rehearsal. The subjects who were allowed to reproduce the lists right after hearing them did the best. Those who had fifteen seconds to rehearse before reciting came in second. The group distracted with math problems finished last. Later, when everyone thought they were finished, they were all surprised with a pop quiz: write down every word you can recall from the lists. Suddenly, the worst group became the best. Short-term rehearsal gave purely short-term benefits. Struggling to hold on to information and then recall it had helped the group distracted by math problems transfer the information from short-term to long-term memory. The group with more and immediate rehearsal opportunity recalled nearly nothing on the pop quiz. Repetition, it turned out, was less important than struggle.

It isn't bad to get an answer right while studying. Progress just should not happen too quickly, unless the learner wants to end up like Oberon (or, worse, Macduff), with a knowledge mirage that evaporates when it matters most. As with excessive hint-giving, it will, as a group of psychologists put it, "produce misleadingly high levels of immediate mastery that will not survive the passage of substantial periods of time." For a given amount of material, learning is most efficient in the long run when it is really inefficient in the short run. If you are doing too well when you test yourself, the simple antidote is to wait longer before practicing the same material again, so that the test will be more difficult when you do. Frustration is not a sign you are not learning, but ease is.

Platforms like Medium and LinkedIn are absolutely rife with posts about shiny new, unsupported learning hacks that lead to mind-blowingly rapid progress—from special dietary supplements and "brain-training" apps to audio cues meant to alter brain waves. In 2007, the U.S. Department of Education published a report by six scientists and an accomplished teacher who were asked to identify learning strategies that truly have scientific backing. Spacing, testing, and using making-connections questions were on the extremely short list. All three impair performance in the short term.

As with the making-connections questions Richland studied, it is difficult to accept that the best learning road is slow, and that doing poorly now is essential for better performance later. It is so deeply counterintuitive that it fools the learners themselves, both about their own progress and their teachers' skill. Demonstrating that required an extraordinarily unique study. One that only a setting like the U.S. Air Force Academy could provide.

In return for full scholarships, cadets at the Air Force Academy commit to serve as military officers for a minimum of eight years after graduation.* They submit to a highly structured and rigorous academic program heavy on science and engineering. It includes a minimum of three math courses for every student.

Every year, an algorithm randomly assigns incoming cadets to sections of Calculus I, each with about twenty students. To examine the impact of professors, two economists compiled data on more than ten thousand cadets who had been randomly assigned to calculus sections taught by nearly a hundred professors over a decade. Every section used the exact same syllabus, the exact same exam, and the exact same post-course professor evaluation form for cadets to fill out.

After Calculus I, students were randomized again to Calculus II sections, again with the same syllabus and exam, and then again to more advanced math, science, and engineering courses. The economists confirmed that standardized test scores and high school grades were spread evenly across sections, so the instructors were facing similar challenges. The Academy even standardized test-grading procedures, so every student was evaluated in the same manner. "Potential 'bleeding heart'

---

* Five years must be active duty.

professors," the economists wrote, "had no discretion to boost grades." That was important, because they wanted to see what differences individual teachers made.

Unsurprisingly, there was a group of Calculus I professors whose instruction most strongly boosted student performance on the Calculus I exam, and who got sterling student evaluation ratings. Another group of professors consistently added less to student performance on the exam, and students judged them more harshly in evaluations. But when the economists looked at another, longer-term measure of teacher value added—how those students did on subsequent math and engineering courses that required Calculus I as a prerequisite—the results were stunning. The Calculus I teachers who were the best at promoting student overachievement in their own class were somehow not great for their students in the long run. "Professors who excel at promoting contemporaneous student achievement," the economists wrote, "on average, harm the subsequent performance of their students in more advanced classes." What looked like a head start evaporated.

The economists suggested that the professors who caused short-term struggle but long-term gains were facilitating "deep learning" by making connections. They "broaden the curriculum and produce students with a deeper understanding of the material." It also made their courses more difficult and frustrating, as evidenced by both the students' lower Calculus I exam scores and their harsher evaluations of their instructors. And vice versa. The calculus professor who ranked dead last in deep learning out of the hundred studied—that is, his students underperformed in subsequent classes—was sixth in student evaluations, and seventh in student performance during his own class. Students evaluated their instructors based on how they performed on tests *right now*— a poor measure of how well the teachers set them up for later development—so they gave the best marks to professors who provided them with the least long-term benefit. The economists concluded that students were actually selectively *punishing* the teachers who provided them the most long-term benefit. Tellingly, Calculus I students whose teachers had fewer qualifications and less experience did better in that class, while the students of more experienced and qualified teachers struggled in Calculus I but did better in subsequent courses.

A similar study was conducted at Italy's Bocconi University, on twelve hundred first-year students who were randomized into introductory course sections in management, economics, or law, and then the courses that followed them in a prescribed sequence over four years. It showed precisely the same pattern. Teachers who guided students to overachievement in their own course were rated highly, and undermined student performance in the long run.

Psychologist Robert Bjork first used the phrase "desirable difficulties" in 1994. Twenty years later, he and a coauthor concluded a book chapter on applying the science of learning like this: "Above all, the most basic message is that teachers and students must avoid interpreting current performance as learning. Good performance on a test during the learning process can indicate mastery, but learners and teachers need to be aware that such performance will often index, instead, fast but fleeting progress."

Here is the bright side: over the past forty years, Americans have increasingly said in national surveys that current students are getting a worse education than they themselves did, and they have been wrong. Scores from the National Assessment of Educational Progress, "the nation's report card," have risen steadily since the 1970s. Unquestionably, students today have mastery of basic skills that is superior to students of the past. School has not gotten worse. The goals of education have just become loftier.

Education economist Greg Duncan, one of the most influential education professors in the world, has documented this trend. Focusing on "using procedures" problems worked well forty years ago when the world was flush with jobs that paid middle-class salaries for procedural tasks, like typing, filing, and working on an assembly line. "Increasingly," according to Duncan, "jobs that pay well require employees to be able to solve unexpected problems, often while working in groups. . . . These shifts in labor force demands have in turn put new and increasingly stringent demands on schools."

Here is a math question from the early 1980s basic skills test of all public school sixth graders in Massachusetts:

Carol can ride her bike 10 miles per hour. If Carol rides her bike to the store, how long will it take?

To solve this problem, you would need to know:

A) How far it is to the store.
B) What kind of bike Carol has.
C) What time Carol will leave.
D) How much Carol has to spend.

And here is a question Massachusetts sixth graders got in 2011:

Paige, Rosie, and Cheryl each spent exactly $9.00 at the same snack bar.

• Paige bought 3 bags of peanuts.
• Rosie bought 2 bags of peanuts and 2 pretzels.
• Cheryl bought 1 bag of peanuts, 1 pretzel, and 1 milk shake.

   A. What is the cost, in dollars, of 1 bag of peanuts? Show or explain how you got your answer.
   B. What is the cost, in dollars, of 1 pretzel? Show or explain how you got your answer.

C. What is the total number of pretzels that can be bought for the cost of 1 milk shake? Show or explain how you got your answer.

For every problem like the first one, the simple formula "distance = rate × time" could be memorized and applied. The second problem requires the connection of multiple concepts that are then applied to a new situation. The teaching strategies that current teachers experienced when they were students are no longer good enough. Knowledge increasingly needs not merely to be durable, but also flexible—both sticky and capable of broad application.

Toward the end of the eighth-grade math class that I watched with Lindsey Richland, the students settled into a worksheet for what psychologists call "blocked" practice. That is, practicing the same thing repeatedly, each problem employing the same procedure. It leads to excellent immediate performance, but for knowledge to be flexible, it should be learned under varied conditions, an approach called varied or mixed practice, or, to researchers, "interleaving."

Interleaving has been shown to improve inductive reasoning. When presented with different examples mixed together, students learn to create abstract generalizations that allow them to apply what they learned to material they have never encountered before. For example, say you plan to visit a museum and want to be able to identify the artist (Cézanne, Picasso, or Renoir) of paintings there that you have never seen. Before you go, instead of studying a stack of Cézanne flash cards, and then a stack of Picasso flash cards, and then a stack of Renoir, you should put the cards together and shuffle, so they will be interleaved. You will struggle more (and probably feel less confident) during practice, but be better equipped on museum day to discern each painter's style, even for paintings that weren't in the flash cards.

In a study using college math problems, students who learned in blocks—all examples of a particular type of problem at once—performed a lot worse come test time than students who studied the exact same problems but all mixed up. The blocked-practice students learned procedures for each type of problem through repetition. The mixed-practice students learned how to differentiate types of problems.

The same effect has appeared among learners studying everything from butterfly species identification to psychological-disorder diagnosis. In research on naval air defense simulations, individuals who engaged in highly mixed practice performed worse than blocked practicers during training, when they had to respond to potential threat scenarios that became familiar over the course of the training. At test time, everyone faced completely new scenarios, and the mixed-practice group destroyed the blocked-practice group.

And yet interleaving tends to fool learners about their own progress. In one of Kornell and Bjork's interleaving studies, 80 percent of students were sure they had learned better with blocked than mixed practice, whereas 80 percent performed in a manner that proved the opposite. The feeling of learning, it turns out, is based on before-your-eyes progress, while deep learning is not. "When your intuition says block," Kornell told me, "you should probably interleave."

Interleaving is a desirable difficulty that frequently holds for both physical and mental skills. A simple motor-skill example is an experiment in which piano students were asked to learn to execute, in one-fifth of a second, a particular left-hand jump across fifteen keys. They were allowed 190 practice attempts. Some used all of those practicing the fifteen-key jump, while others switched between eight-, twelve-, fifteen-, and twenty-two-key jumps. When the piano students were invited back for a test, those who underwent the mixed practice were faster and more accurate at the fifteen-key jump than the students who had only practiced that exact jump. The "desirable difficulty" coiner himself, Robert Bjork, once commented on Shaquille O'Neal's perpetual free-throw woes to say that instead of continuing to practice from the free-throw line, O'Neal should practice from a foot in front of and behind it to learn the motor modulation he needed.

Whether the task is mental or physical, interleaving improves the ability to match the right strategy to a problem. That happens to be a hallmark of expert problem solving. Whether chemists, physicists, or political scientists, the most successful problem solvers spend mental energy figuring out what type of problem they are facing before matching a strategy to it, rather than jumping in with memorized procedures. In that way, they are just about the precise opposite of experts who develop in kind learning environments, like chess masters, who rely heavily on intuition. Kind learning environment experts choose a strategy and then evaluate; experts in less repetitive environments evaluate and then choose.

Desirable difficulties like testing and spacing make knowledge stick. It becomes durable. Desirable difficulties like making connections and interleaving make knowledge flexible, useful for problems that never appeared in training. All slow down learning and make performance suffer, in the short term. That can be a problem, because like the Air Force cadets, we all reflexively assess our progress by how we are doing *right now*. And like the Air Force cadets, we are often wrong.

In 2017, Greg Duncan, the education economist, along with psychologist Drew Bailey and colleagues, reviewed sixty-seven early childhood education programs meant to boost academic achievement. Programs like Head Start did give a head start, but academically that was about it. The researchers found a pervasive "fadeout" effect, where a temporary academic advantage quickly diminished and often completely vanished. On a graph, it looks eerily like the kind that show future elite athletes catching up to their peers who got a head start in deliberate practice.

A reason for this, the researchers concluded, is that early childhood education programs teach "closed" skills that can be acquired quickly with repetition of procedures, but that everyone will pick up at some point anyway. The fadeout was not a disappearance of skill so much as the rest of the world catching up. The motor-skill equivalent would be teaching a kid to walk a little early. Everyone is going to learn it anyway, and while it might be temporarily impressive, there is no evidence that rushing it matters.

The research team recommended that if programs want to impart lasting academic benefits they should focus instead on "open" skills that scaffold later knowledge. Teaching kids to read a little early is not a lasting advantage. Teaching them how to hunt for and connect contextual clues to understand what they read can be. As with all desirable difficulties, the trouble is that a head start comes fast, but deep learning is slow. "The slowest growth," the researchers wrote, occurs "for the most complex skills."

Duncan landed on the *Today* show discussing his team's findings. The counteropinion was supplied by parents and an early childhood teacher who were confident that they could *see* a child's progress. That is not in dispute. The question is how well they can judge the impact on future learning, and the evidence says that, like the Air Force cadets, the answer is not very well.*

Before-our-eyes progress reinforces our instinct to do more of the same, but just like the case of the typhoid doctor, the feedback teaches the wrong lesson. Learning deeply means learning slowly. The cult of the head start fails the learners it seeks to serve.

---

* Two of the most famously intensive early childhood education programs showed the fadeout pattern on several cognitive measures they targeted for improvement, but also demonstrated some important long-term social benefits, like decreased rates of incarceration. Even when the intended academic effects disappear, it seems that an extended program of positive interactions between adults and children can leave a lasting mark. In my opinion, youth sports programs should take note: coach/athlete interactions may have a longer life than the fleeting advantage of a head start in closed skills.

Knowledge with enduring utility must be very flexible, composed of mental schemes that can be matched to new problems. The virtual naval officers in the air defense simulation and the math students who engaged in interleaved practice were learning to recognize deep structural commonalities in types of problems. They could not rely on the same type of problem repeating, so they had to identify underlying conceptual connections in simulated battle threats, or math problems, that they had never actually seen before. They then matched a strategy to each new problem. When a knowledge structure is so flexible that it can be applied effectively even in new domains or extremely novel situations, it is called "far transfer."

There is a particular type of thinking that facilitates far transfer—a type that Alexander Luria's Uzbek villagers could not employ—and that can seem far-fetched precisely because of how far it transfers. And it's a mode of broad thinking that none of us employ enough.

CHAPTER 5

Thinking Outside Experience

THE SEVENTEENTH CENTURY was approaching. The universe was one in which celestial bodies moved around the stationary Earth powered by individual spirits, ineffable planetary souls. The Polish astronomer Nicolaus Copernicus had proposed that planets moved around the sun, but the idea was still so unorthodox that Italian philosopher Giordano Bruno was censured for teaching it, and later burned at the stake as a heretic for insisting there were other suns surrounded by other planets.

Their spirits may have been driving, but the planets also needed a vehicle for motion, so they were assumed to be riding on pure crystalline spheres. The spheres were invisible from Earth and interlocked, like the gears of a clock, to produce collective motion at a constant speed for all eternity. Plato and Aristotle had laid the foundation for the accepted model, and it dominated for two thousand years. That clockwork universe was the one German astronomer Johannes Kepler inherited. He accepted it, at first.

When the constellation Cassiopeia suddenly gained a new star (it was actually a supernova, the bright explosion at the end of a star's life), Kepler recognized that the idea of the unchanging heavens could not be correct. A few years later, a comet tracked across the European sky.

Shouldn't it have cracked the crystalline spheres as it traveled, Kepler wondered? He began to doubt two millennia worth of accepted wisdom.

By 1596, when he turned twenty-five, Kepler had accepted the Copernican model of planets orbiting the sun, and now he posed another profound question: Why do planets that are farther away from the sun move more slowly? Perhaps the more distant planets had weaker "moving souls." But why would that be? Just coincidence? Maybe, he thought, rather than many spirits, there was just one, inside the sun, which for some reason acted more powerfully on nearby planets. Kepler was so far outside the bounds of previous thought that there was no evidence in existence for him to work from. He had to use analogies.

Smells and heat dissipate predictably farther from their source, which meant that a mysterious planet-moving power from the sun might as well. But smells and heat are also detectable everywhere along their path, whereas the sun's moving soul, Kepler wrote, is "poured out throughout the whole world, and yet does not exist anywhere but where there is something movable." Was there any proof that such a thing could exist?

Light "makes its nest in the sun," Kepler wrote, and yet appears not to exist between its source and an object it lights up. If light can do it, so could some other physical entity. He began using the words "power" or "force" instead of "soul" and "spirit." Kepler's "moving power" was a precursor to gravity, an astounding mental leap because it came before science embraced the notion of physical forces that act throughout the universe.

Given how the moving power seemed to emanate from the sun and disperse in space, Kepler wondered if light itself or some light-like force caused planetary motion. Well, then, could the moving power be blocked like light? Planetary motion did not stop during an eclipse, Kepler reasoned, so the moving power could not be just like light, or depend on light. He needed a new analogy.

Kepler read a newly published description of magnetism, and thought maybe the planets were like magnets, with poles at either end. He realized that each planet moved more slowly when it was farther in its orbit from the sun, so perhaps the planets and the sun were attracting and repelling one another depending on which poles were nearby. That might explain why the planets moved toward and away from the sun, but why did they keep moving forward in their orbits? The sun's power seemed somehow to also push them forward. On to the next analogy.

The sun rotates on its axis and creates a whirlpool of moving power that sweeps the planets around like boats in a current. Kepler liked that, but it raised a new problem. He had realized that orbits were not perfectly circular, so what kind of strange current was the sun creating? The whirlpool analogy was incomplete without boatmen.

Boatmen in a whirling river can steer their boats perpendicular to the current, so maybe planets could steer in the sun's current, Kepler surmised. A circular current could explain why all the planets move in the same direction, and then each planet steered through the current to keep from getting sucked into the center, which made the orbits not quite circular. But then who was captaining each ship? That brought Kepler all the way back to spirits, and he was not happy about it. "Kepler," he wrote to himself, "does't thou wish then to equip each planet with two eyes?"

Each time he got stuck, Kepler unleashed a fusillade of analogies. Not just light, heat, odor, currents and boatmen, but optics of lenses, balance scales, a broom, magnets, a magnetic broom, orators gazing at a crowd, and more. He interrogated each one ruthlessly, every time alighting on new questions.

He eventually decided that celestial bodies pulled one another, and larger bodies had more pull. That led him to claim (correctly) that the moon influenced tides on Earth. Galileo, the embodiment of bold truths, mocked him for the ridiculous idea of "the moon's dominion over the waters."

Kepler's intellectual wanderings traced a staggering journey, from planets imbued with souls and riding on interlocking crystalline spheres in perfect circles around the stationary Earth, to his illumination of the laws of planetary motion, which showed that the planets move in ellipses that are predictable based on their relation to the sun.

More important, Kepler invented astrophysics. He did not inherit an idea of universal physical forces. There was no concept of gravity as a force, and he had no notion of momentum that keeps the planets in motion. Analogies were all he had. He became the first discoverer of causal physical laws for phenomena in the heavens, and he realized it. "Ye physicists," he wrote when he published his laws of planetary motion, "prick your ears, for now we are going to invade your territory." The title of his magnum opus: *A New Astronomy Based upon Causes*.

In an age when alchemy was still a common approach to natural phenomena, Kepler filled the universe with invisible forces acting all around us, and helped usher in the Scientific Revolution. His fastidious documentation of every meandering path his brain blazed is one of the great records of a mind undergoing creative transformation. It is a truism to say that Kepler thought outside the box. But what he really did, whenever he was stuck, was to think entirely outside the domain. He left a brightly lit trail of his favorite tools for doing that, the ones that allowed him to cast outside eyes upon wisdom his peers simply accepted. "I especially love analogies," he wrote, "my most faithful masters, acquainted with all the secrets of nature. . . . One should make great use of them."

Mention Kepler if you want to get Northwestern University psychologist Dedre Gentner excited. She gesticulates. Her tortoiseshell glasses bob up and down. She is probably the world's foremost authority on analogical thinking. Deep analogical thinking is the practice of recognizing conceptual similarities in multiple domains or scenarios that may seem to have little in common on the surface. It is a powerful tool for solving wicked problems, and Kepler was an analogy addict, so Gentner is naturally very fond of him. When she mentions a trivial historical detail about him that might be misunderstood by modern readers, she suggests that maybe it's best not to publish it as it might make him look bad, though he has been dead for nearly four hundred years.

"In my opinion," Gentner told me, "our ability to think relationally is one of the reasons we're running the planet. Relations are really hard for other species." Analogical thinking takes the new and makes it familiar, or takes the familiar and puts it in a new light, and allows humans to reason through problems they have never seen in unfamiliar contexts. It also allows us to understand that which we cannot *see* at all. Students might learn about the motion of molecules by analogy to billiard-ball collisions; principles of electricity can be understood with analogies to water flow through plumbing. Concepts from biology serve as analogies to inform the cutting edge of artificial intelligence: "neural networks" that learn how to identify images from examples (when you search cat pictures, for instance) were conceived as akin to the neurons of the brain, and "genetic algorithms" are conceptually based on evolution by natural selection—solutions are tried, evaluated, and the more successful solutions pass on properties to the next round of solutions, ad infinitum. It is the furthest extension of the type of thinking that was foreign to Luria's premodern villagers, whose problem solving depended on direct experience.

Kepler was facing a problem not just new to himself, but to all humanity. There was no experience database to draw on. To investigate whether he should be the first ever to propose "action at a distance" in the heavens (a mysterious power invisibly traversing space and then appearing at its target), he turned to analogy (odor, heat, light) to consider whether it was conceptually possible. He followed that up with a litany of distant analogies (magnets, boats) to think through the problem.

Most problems, of course, are not new, so we can rely on what

Gentner calls "surface" analogies from our own experience. "Most of the time, if you're reminded of things that are similar on the surface, they're going to be relationally similar as well," she explained. Remember how you fixed the clogged bathtub drain in the old apartment? That will probably come to mind when the kitchen sink is clogged in the new one.

But the idea that surface analogies that pop to mind work for novel problems is a "kind world" hypothesis, Gentner told me. Like kind learning environments, a kind world is based on repeating patterns. "It's perfectly fine," she said, "if you stay in the same village or the same savannah all your life." The current world is not so kind; it requires thinking that cannot fall back on previous experience. Like math students, we need to be able to pick a strategy for problems we have never seen before. "In the life we lead today," Gentner told me, "we need to be reminded of things that are only abstractly or relationally similar. And the more creative you want to be, the more important that is."

In the course of studying problem solving in the 1930s, Karl Duncker posed one of the most famous hypothetical problems in all of cognitive psychology. It goes like this:

Suppose you are a doctor faced with a patient who has a malignant stomach tumor. It is impossible to operate on this patient, but unless the tumor is destroyed the patient will die. There is a kind of ray that can be used to destroy the tumor. If the rays reach the tumor all at once at a sufficiently high intensity, the tumor will be destroyed. Unfortunately, at this intensity the healthy tissue that the rays pass through on the way to the tumor will also be destroyed. At lower intensities the rays are harmless to healthy tissue, but they will not affect the tumor either. What type of procedure might be used to destroy the tumor with the rays, and at the same time avoid destroying the healthy tissue?

It's on you to excise the tumor and save the patient, but the rays are either too powerful or too weak. How can you solve this? While you're thinking, a little story to pass the time: There once was a general who needed to capture a fortress in the middle of a country from a brutal dictator. If the general could get all of his troops to the fortress at the same time, they would have no problem taking it. Plenty of roads that the troops could travel radiated out from the fort like wheel spokes, but they were strewn with mines, so only small groups of soldiers could safely traverse any one road. The general came up with a plan. He divided the army into small groups, and each group traveled a different road leading to the fortress. They synchronized their watches, and made sure to converge on the fortress at the same time via their separate roads. The plan worked. The general captured the fortress and overthrew the dictator.

Have you saved the patient yet? Just one last story while you're still thinking: Years ago, a small-town fire chief arrived at a woodshed fire, concerned that it would spread to a nearby house if it was not extinguished quickly. There was no hydrant nearby, but the shed was next to a lake, so there was plenty of water. Dozens of neighbors were already taking turns with buckets throwing water on the shed, but they weren't making any progress. The neighbors were surprised when the fire chief yelled at them to stop, and to all go fill their buckets in the lake. When they returned, the chief arranged them in a circle around the shed, and on the count of three had them all throw their water at once. The fire was immediately dampened, and soon thereafter extinguished. The town gave the fire chief a pay raise as a reward for quick thinking.

Are you done saving your patient? Don't feel bad, almost no one solves it. At least not at first, and then nearly everyone solves it. Only about 10 percent of people solve "Duncker's radiation problem" initially. Presented with both the radiation problem and the fortress story, about 30 percent solve it and save the patient. Given both of those plus the fire chief story, half solve it. Given the fortress and the fire chief stories and then told to use them to help solve the radiation problem, 80 percent save the patient.

The answer is that you (the doctor) could direct multiple low-intensity rays at the tumor from different directions, leaving healthy tissue intact, but converging at the tumor site with enough collective intensity to destroy it. Just like how the general divided up troops and directed them to converge at the fortress, and how the fire chief arranged neighbors with their buckets around the burning shed so that their water would converge on the fire simultaneously.

Those results are from a series of 1980s analogical thinking studies. Really, don't feel bad if you didn't get it. In a real experiment you would have taken more time, and whether you got it or not is unimportant. The important part is what it shows about problem solving. A gift of a single analogy from a different domain tripled the proportion of solvers who got the radiation problem. Two analogies from disparate domains gave an even bigger boost. The impact of the fortress story alone was as large as if solvers were just straight out told this guiding principle: "If you need a large force to accomplish some purpose, but are prevented from applying such a force directly, many smaller forces applied simultaneously from different directions may work just as well."

The scientists who did that work expected that analogies would be fuel for problem solving, but they were surprised that most solvers working on the radiation problem did not find clues in the fortress story until they were directed to do so. "One might well have supposed," the scientists wrote, that "being in a psychology experiment would have led virtually all subjects to consider how the first part [of the study] might be related to the second."

Human intuition, it appears, is not very well engineered to make use of the best tools when faced with what the researchers called "ill-defined" problems. Our experience-based instincts are set up well for Tiger domains, the kind world Gentner described, where problems and solutions repeat.

An experiment on Stanford international relations students during the Cold War provided a cautionary tale about relying on kind-world reasoning—that is, drawing only on the first analogy that feels familiar. The students were told that a small, fictional democratic country was under threat from a totalitarian neighbor, and they had to decide how the United States should respond. Some students were given descriptions that likened the situation to World War II (refugees in boxcars; a president "from New York, the same state as FDR"; a meeting in "Winston Churchill Hall"). For others, it was likened to Vietnam, (a president "from Texas, the same state as LBJ," and refugees in boats). The international relations students who were reminded of World War II were far more likely to choose to go to war; the students reminded of Vietnam opted for nonmilitary diplomacy. That phenomenon has been documented all over the place. College football coaches rated the same player's potential very differently depending on what former player he was likened to in an introductory description, even with all other information kept exactly the same.

With the difficult radiation problem, the most successful strategy employed multiple situations that were not at all alike on the surface, but held deep structural similarities. Most problem solvers are not like Kepler. They will stay inside of the problem at hand, focused on the internal details, and perhaps summon other medical knowledge, since it is on the surface a medical problem. They will not intuitively turn to distant analogies to probe solutions. They should, though, and they should make sure some of those analogies are, on the surface, far removed from the current problem. In a wicked world, relying upon experience from a single domain is not only limiting, it can be disastrous.

———

The trouble with using no more than a single analogy, particularly one from a very similar situation, is that it does not help battle the natural impulse to employ the "inside view," a term coined by psychologists Daniel Kahneman and Amos Tversky. We take the inside view when we make judgments based narrowly on the details of a particular project that are right in front of us.

Kahneman had a personal experience with the dangers of the inside view when he assembled a team to write a high school curriculum on the science of decision making. After a full year of weekly meetings, he surveyed the entire team to find out how long everyone thought the project would take. The lowest estimate was one and a half years, the highest two and a half years. Kahneman then asked a team member named Seymour, a distinguished curriculum expert who had seen the process with other teams, how this one compared.

Seymour thought for a while. Moments earlier, he had estimated it would take about two more years. Faced with Kahneman's question about other teams, he said he had never even thought to compare this instance to separate projects, but that about 40 percent of the teams he'd seen never finished at all, and not a single one he could think of took less than seven years.

Kahneman's group was not willing to spend six more years on a curriculum project that might fail. They spent a few minutes debating the new opinion, and decided to forge ahead trusting the about-two-years wisdom of the group. Eight years later, they finished, by which point Kahneman was not even on the team or living in the country, and the agency that asked for the curriculum was no longer interested.

Our natural inclination to take the inside view can be defeated by following analogies to the "outside view." The outside view probes for deep structural similarities to the current problem in different ones. The outside view is deeply counterintuitive because it requires a decision maker to ignore unique surface features of the current project, on which they are the expert, and instead look outside for structurally similar analogies. It requires a mindset switch from narrow to broad.

For a unique 2012 experiment, University of Sydney business strategy professor Dan Lovallo—who had conducted inside-view research with Kahneman—and a pair of economists theorized that starting out by making loads of diverse analogies, Kepler style, would naturally lead to the outside view and improve decisions. They recruited investors from large private equity firms who consider a huge number of potential projects in a variety of domains. The researchers thought the investors' work might naturally lend itself to the outside view.

The private equity investors were told to assess a real project they were currently working on with a detailed description of the steps to success, and to predict the project's return on investment. They were then asked to write down a batch of other investment projects they knew of with broad conceptual similarity to theirs—for instance, other examples of a business owner looking to sell, or a start-up with a technologically risky product. They were instructed to estimate the return for each of those examples too.

In the end, the investors estimated that the return on their own project would be about 50 percent higher than the outside projects they had identified as conceptually similar. When given the chance at the end to rethink and revise, they slashed their own initial estimate. "They were sort of shocked," Lovallo told me, "and the senior people were the most shocked." The investors initially judged their own projects, where they knew all the details, completely differently from similar projects to which they were outsiders.

This is a widespread phenomenon. If you're asked to predict whether a particular horse will win a race or a particular politician will win an election, the more internal details you learn about any particular scenario—physical qualities of the specific horse, the background and strategy of the particular politician—the more likely you are to say that the scenario you are investigating will occur.

Psychologists have shown repeatedly that the more internal details an individual can be made to consider, the more extreme their judgment becomes. For the venture capitalists, they knew more details about their own project, and judged that it would be an extreme success, until they were forced to consider other projects with broad conceptual similarities. In another example, students rated a university a lot better if they were told about a few specific science departments that were ranked in the top ten nationally than if they were simply told that *every* science department at the university was ranked among the top ten. In one famous study, participants judged an individual as more likely to die from "heart disease, cancer, or other natural causes" than from "natural causes." Focusing narrowly on many fine details specific to a problem at hand feels like the exact right thing to do, when it is often exactly wrong.

Bent Flyvbjerg, chair of Major Programme Management at Oxford University's business school, has shown that around 90 percent of major infrastructure projects worldwide go over budget (by an average of 28 percent) in part because managers focus on the details of their project and become overly optimistic. Project managers can become like Kahneman's curriculum-building team, which decided that thanks to its roster of experts it would certainly not encounter the same delays as did other groups. Flyvbjerg studied a project to build a tram system in Scotland, in which an outside consulting team actually went through an analogy process akin to what the private equity investors were instructed to do. They ignored specifics of the project at hand and focused on others with structural similarities. The consulting team saw that the project group had made a rigorous analysis using all of the details of the work to be done. And yet, using analogies to separate projects, the consulting team concluded that the cost projection of £320 million (more than

$400 million) was probably a massive underestimate. When the tram opened three years late, it was headed toward £1 billion. After that, other UK infrastructure projects began implementing outside-view approaches, essentially forcing managers to make analogies to many outside projects of the past.

Following their private-equity-investor experiment, the outside-view researchers turned to the movie business, a notoriously uncertain realm with high risk, high reward, and a huge store of data on actual outcomes. They wondered if forcing analogical thinking on moviegoers could lead to accurate forecasts of film success. They started by giving hundreds of movie fans basic film information—lead actor names, the promotional poster, and a synopsis—for an upcoming release. At the time, those included *Wedding Crashers, Fantastic Four, Deuce Bigalow: European Gigolo,* and others. The moviegoers were also given a list of forty older movies, and asked to score how well each one probably served as an analogy to each upcoming release. The researchers used those similarity scores (and a little basic film information, like whether it was a sequel) to predict the eventual revenue of the upcoming releases. They pitted those predictions against a mathematical model stuffed with information about seventeen hundred past movies and each upcoming film, including genre, budget, star actors, release year, and whether it was a holiday release. Even without all that detailed information, the revenue predictions that used moviegoer analogy scores were vastly better. The moviegoer-analogies forecast performed better on fifteen of nineteen upcoming releases. Using the moviegoers' analogies gave revenue projections that were less than 4 percent off for *War of the Worlds, Bewitched,* and *Red Eye,* and 1.7 percent off for *Deuce Bigalow: European Gigolo.*

Netflix came to a similar conclusion for improving its recommendation algorithm. Decoding movies' traits to figure out what you like was very complex and less accurate than simply analogizing you to many other customers with similar viewing histories. Instead of predicting *what* you might like, they examine *who* you are like, and the complexity is captured therein.

Interestingly, if the researchers used only the single film that the movie fans ranked as most analogous to the new release, predictive power collapsed. What seemed like the single best analogy did not do well on its own. Using a full "reference class" of analogies—the pillar of the outside view—was immensely more accurate.

Think back to chapter 1, to the types of intuitive experts that Gary Klein studied in kind learning environments, like chess masters and firefighters. Rather than beginning by generating options, they leap to a decision based on pattern recognition of surface features. They may then evaluate it, if they have time, but often stick with it. This time will probably be like the last time, so extensive narrow experience works. Generating new ideas or facing novel problems with high uncertainty is nothing like that. Evaluating an array of options *before* letting intuition reign is a trick for the wicked world.

In another experiment, Lovallo and his collaborator Ferdinand Dubin asked 150 business students to generate strategies to help the fictitious Mickey Company, which was struggling with its computer mouse business in Australia and China. After business students learned about the company's challenges, they were told to write down all the strategies they could think of to try to improve Mickey's position.

Lovallo and Dubin gave some students one or more analogies in their instructions. (For example: "The profile of Nike Inc. and McDonald's Corp. may be helpful to supplement your recommendations but should not limit them.") Other students got none. The students prompted with one analogy came up with more strategies than those given no analogies, and students given multiple analogies came up with more strategies than those reminded only of one. And the more distant the analogy, the better it was for idea generation. Students who were pointed to Nike and McDonald's generated more strategic options than their peers who were reminded of computer companies Apple and Dell. Just being reminded to analogize widely made the business students more creative. Unfortunately, students also said that if they were to use analogy companies at all, they believed the best way to generate strategic options would be to focus on a single example in the same field. Like the venture capitalists, their intuition was to use too few analogies, and to rely on those that were the most superficially similar. "That's usually exactly the wrong way to go about it regardless of what you're using analogy for," Lovallo told me.

The good news is that it is easy to ride analogies from the intuitive inside view to the outside view. In 2001, the Boston Consulting Group, one of the most successful in the world, created an intranet site to provide consultants with collections of material to facilitate wide-ranging analogical thinking. The interactive "exhibits" were sorted by discipline (anthropology, psychology, history, and others), concept (change, logistics, productivity, and so on), and strategic theme (competition, cooperation, unions and alliances, and more). A consultant generating strategies for a post-merger integration might have perused the exhibit on how William the Conqueror "merged" England with the Norman Kingdom in the eleventh century. An exhibit that described Sherlock Holmes's observational strategies could have provided ideas for learning from details that experienced professionals take for granted. And a consultant working with a rapidly expanding start-up might have gleaned ideas from the writing of a Prussian military strategist who studied the fragile equilibrium between maintaining momentum after a victory and overshooting a goal by so much that it turns into a defeat. If that all sounds incredibly remote from pressing business concerns, that is exactly the point.

Dedre Gentner wanted to find out if everyone can be a bit more like Kepler, capable of wielding distant analogies to understand problems. So she helped create the "Ambiguous Sorting Task."

It consists of twenty-five cards, each one describing a real-world phenomenon, like how internet routers or economic bubbles work. Each
card falls into two main categories, one for its domain (economics, biology, and so on) and one for its deep structure. Participants are asked to
sort the cards into like categories.

For a deep structure example, you might put economic bubbles and
melting polar ice caps together as positive-feedback loops. (In economic
bubbles, consumers buy stocks or property with the idea that the price
will increase; that buying causes the price to increase, which leads to
more buying. When ice caps melt, they reflect less sunlight back to
space, which warms the planet, causing more ice to melt.) Or perhaps
you would put the act of sweating and actions of the Federal Reserve
together as negative-feedback loops. (Sweating cools the body so that
more sweating is no longer required. The Fed lowers interest rates to
spur the economy; if the economy grows too quickly, the Fed raises rates
to slow down the activity it launched.) The way gas prices lead to an
increase in grocery prices and the steps needed for a message to traverse
neurons in your brain are both examples of causal chains, where one
event leads to another, which leads to another, in linear order.

Alternatively, you might group Federal Reserve rate changes, economic bubbles, and gas price changes together because they are all in
the same domain: economics. And you might put sweating and neuro-
transmission together under biology.

Gentner and colleagues gave the Ambiguous Sorting Task to Northwestern University students from an array of majors and found that all
of the students figured out how to group phenomena by domains. But
fewer could come up with groupings based on causal structure. There
was a group of students, however, who were particularly good at finding common deep structures: students who had taken classes in a range
of domains, like those in the Integrated Science Program.

Northwestern's website for the program features an alum's description: "Think of the Integrated Science Program as a biology minor,

chemistry minor, physics minor, and math minor combined into a single major. The primary intent of this program is to expose students to all fields of the natural and mathematical sciences so that they can see commonalities among different fields of the natural sciences. . . . The ISP major allows you to see connections across different disciplines."

A professor I asked about the Integrated Science Program told me that specific academic departments are generally not big fans. They want students to take more specialized classes in a single department. They are concerned about the students falling behind. They would rather rush them to specialization than equip them with ideas from what Gentner referred to as a "variety of base domains," which foster analogical thinking and conceptual connections that can help students categorize the type of problem they are facing. That is precisely a skill that sets the most adept problem solvers apart.

In one of the most cited studies of expert problem solving ever conducted, an interdisciplinary team of scientists came to a pretty simple conclusion: successful problem solvers are more able to determine the deep structure of a problem before they proceed to match a strategy to it. Less successful problem solvers are more like most students in the Ambiguous Sorting Task: they mentally classify problems only by superficial, overtly stated features, like the domain context. For the best performers, they wrote, problem solving "begins with the typing of the problem."

As education pioneer John Dewey put it in *Logic, The Theory of Inquiry,* "a problem well put is half-solved."

Before he began his tortuous march of analogies toward reimagining the universe, Kepler had to get very confused on his homework. Unlike Galileo and Isaac Newton, he documented his confusion. "What matters to me," Kepler wrote, "is not merely to impart to the reader what I have to say, but above all to convey to him the reasons, subterfuges, and lucky hazards which led me to my discoveries."

Kepler was a young man when he showed up to work at Tycho Brahe's observatory—so cutting edge at the time that it cost 1 percent of the national budget of Denmark. He was given the assignment nobody wanted: Mars and its perplexing orbit. The orbit had to be a circle, Kepler was told, so he had to figure out why Brahe's observations didn't match that. Every once in a while, Mars appears to reverse course in the sky, do a little loop, and then carry on in the original direction, a feat known as retrograde motion. Astronomers proposed elaborate contortions to explain how Mars could accomplish this while riding the interlocking spheres of the sky.

As usual, Kepler could not accept contortions. He asked peers for help, but his pleas fell on deaf ears. His predecessors had always managed to explain away the Mars deviations without scrapping the overall scheme. Kepler's short Mars assignment (he guessed it would take eight days) turned into five years of calculations trying to describe where Mars appeared in the sky at any given moment. No sooner had Kepler done it with great accuracy than he threw it away.

It was close, but not perfect. The imperfection was minuscule. Just two of Brahe's observations differed from Kepler's calculations of where Mars should be, and by just eight minutes of arc, a sliver of sky one-eighth the width of a pinkie finger held at arm's length. Kepler could have assumed his model was correct and those two observations were slightly off, or he could dispense with five years of work. He chose to trash his model. "If I had believed we could ignore these eight minutes," he wrote, "I would have patched my hypothesis accordingly." The assignment no one wanted became Kepler's keyhole view into a new understanding of the universe. He was in uncharted territory. The analogies began in earnest, and he reinvented astronomy. Light, heat, smells, boats, brooms, magnets—it began with those pesky observations that didn't quite fit, and ended in the complete undoing of Aristotle's clockwork universe.

Kepler did something that turns out to be characteristic of today's world-class research labs. Psychologist Kevin Dunbar began documenting how productive labs work in the 1990s, and stumbled upon a modern version of Keplerian thinking. Faced with an unexpected finding, rather than assuming the current theory is correct and that an observation must be off, the unexpected became an opportunity to venture somewhere new—and analogies served as the wilderness guide.

When Dunbar started, he simply set out to document the process of discovery in real time. He focused on molecular biology labs because they were blazing new trails, particularly in genetics and treatments for viruses, like HIV. He spent a year with four labs in the United States, playing a fly on the wall, visiting the labs every day for months, and later extended the work to more labs in the United States, Canada, and Italy. He became such a familiar presence that scientists called him to make sure he knew about impromptu meetings. The surface features of the labs were very different. One had dozens of members, others were small. A few were all men, one was all women. All had international reputations.

The weekly lab meetings made the most interesting viewing. Once a week, the entire team came together—lab director, grad students, post-doctoral fellows, technicians—to discuss some challenge a lab member was facing. The meetings were nothing like the heads-down, solitary work in stereotypical portrayals of scientists, huddled over their test tubes. Dunbar saw free-flowing and spontaneous exchange. Ideas were batted back and forth, new experiments proposed, obstacles discussed. "Those are some of the most creative moments in science," he told me. So he recorded them.

The first fifteen minutes could be housekeeping—whose turn it was to order supplies, or who had left a mess. Then the action started. Someone presented an unexpected or confusing finding, their version of Kepler's Mars orbit. Prudently, scientists' first instinct was to blame themselves, some error in calculation or poorly calibrated equipment. If it kept up, the lab accepted the result as real, and ideas about what to try and what might be going on started flying. Every hour of lab meeting Dunbar recorded required eight hours of transcribing and labeling problem-solving behaviors so that he could analyze the process of scientific creativity, and he found an analogy fest.

Dunbar witnessed important breakthroughs live, and saw that the labs most likely to turn unexpected findings into new knowledge for humanity made a lot of analogies, and made them from a variety of base domains. The labs in which scientists had more diverse professional backgrounds were the ones where more and more varied analogies were offered, and where breakthroughs were more reliably produced when the unexpected arose. Those labs were Keplers by committee. They included members with a wide variety of experiences and interests. When the moment came to either dismiss or embrace and grapple with information that puzzled them, they drew on their range to make analogies. Lots of them.

For relatively straightforward challenges, labs started with analogies to other, very similar experiments. The more unusual the challenge, the more distant the analogies, moving away from surface similarities and toward deep structural similarities. In some lab meetings a new analogy entered the conversation every four minutes on average, some of them from outside of biology entirely.

In one instance, Dunbar actually saw two labs encounter the same experimental problem at around the same time. Proteins they wanted to measure would get stuck to a filter, which made them hard to analyze. One of the labs was entirely *E. coli* experts, and the other had scientists with chemistry, physics, biology, and genetics backgrounds, plus medical students. "One lab made an analogy drawing on knowledge from the person with a medical degree, and they figured it out right there at the meeting," Dunbar told me. "The other lab used *E. coli* knowledge to deal with every problem. That didn't work here so they had to just start experimenting for weeks to get rid of the problem. It put me in an awkward position because I had seen the answer in another lab's meeting." (As part of the conditions of the study, he was not allowed to share information between labs.)

In the face of the unexpected, the range of available analogies helped determine who learned something new. In the lone lab that did not make any new findings during Dunbar's project, everyone had similar and highly specialized backgrounds, and analogies were almost never used. "When all the members of the laboratory have the same knowledge at their disposal, then when a problem arises, a group of similar minded individuals will not provide more information to make analogies than a single individual," Dunbar concluded.

"It's sort of like the stock market," he told me. "You need a mixture of strategies."

The trouble with courses of study like Northwestern's Integrated Science Program, which impart a broad mixture of strategies, is that they may require abandoning a head start toward a major or career. That is a tough sell, even if it better serves learners in the long run.

Whether it is the making-connections knowledge Lindsey Richland studied, or the broad concepts that Flynn tested, or the distant, deep structural analogical reasoning that Gentner assessed, there is often no entrenched interest fighting on the side of range, or of knowledge that must be slowly acquired. All forces align to incentivize a head start and early, narrow specialization, even if that is a poor long-term strategy. That is a problem, because another kind of knowledge, perhaps the most important of all, is necessarily slowly acquired—the kind that helps you match yourself to the right challenge in the first place.

CHAPTER 6

The Trouble with Too Much Grit

THE BOY'S MOTHER APPRECIATED music and art, but when the boy tried to freehand sketch the family cat, he proved such a deficient draftsman that he destroyed the picture and refused to try again. Instead, he spent his childhood in the Netherlands playing marbles or sledding with his little brother, but mostly just looking at things. A prominent parenting handbook advised against unsupervised wanderings that might "intoxicate" a child's imagination, but he wandered alone for hours. He walked in storms, and at night. He walked for miles just to sit for hours watching a bird's nest, or following water bugs on their commutes across a brook. He was especially obsessed with collecting beetles, labeling each one with its proper Latin species name.

When he was thirteen, the boy was admitted to a brand-new school housed in a hulking former royal palace. It was so far from his home that he had to board with a local family. His mind was elsewhere during class, but he was a good student, and spent his free time memorizing poetry.

The art teacher was the faculty celebrity, an education pioneer who argued for design to become a central part of the national economic engine. That crusade was so successful it led the federal government to mandate freehand drawing classes in every public school. Rather than holding forth from the front of the class, the teacher arranged students in the center and meandered through them like a sewing needle, giving personal attention. Most students adored him. But he made no impression on the boy. As an adult, the boy would complain that nobody had ever told him what perspective was in drawing, even though it was so central to the teacher's tenets that knowledge of perspective was written into the new law expanding art education.

The boy didn't like living with strangers, so he left the school just before he turned fifteen. For the next sixteen months, he did little other than take long nature walks. That could not go on forever, but he had no idea what else to do. Fortunately, his uncle owned a fantastically successful art dealership, and had just been knighted. He offered his nephew a job in the big city. Making art had not inspired the boy, but selling it did. He turned the observational intensity he had practiced in nature to lithographs and photographs, categorizing what he saw just as he had his beetles. By twenty, he was dealing with important clients and traveling abroad for sales trips. The young man confidently told his parents that he would never have to look for a job again. He was wrong.

He was a country boy in the city, without enough social grace to smooth over disagreements with his boss, and he disliked bargaining, which felt like trying to take advantage of customers. He was soon transferred to a London office that did not deal directly with customers, and then at twenty-two he was transferred again, this time to Paris. He arrived in France amid an artistic revolution. On walks to work, the young man passed the studios of artists who were in the process of becoming famous. And yet, as with the art teacher, as a pair of his future biographers would write, "None of it registered." He was too busy with a new obsession: religion. Years later, when he and his little brother discussed those revolutionary artists, he would say he had "seen absolutely *nothing* of them."

When he was finally dismissed from the dealership, he went to work as an assistant teacher at a boarding school in a seaside town in England.

Working fourteen-hour days, he taught classes from French to math, oversaw the dorm, took the kids to church, and acted as the handyman. The school was simply a business venture for the owner, and the young man was cheap labor. He found another job as a tutor, this time at a fancier boarding school, but after a few months he decided he would become a missionary in South America. His parents talked him out of that, insisting that he needed to "stop following [his] own desires" and return to a stable life course. His mother wished he would do something in nature that would make him "happier and calmer." He decided to follow in his father's footsteps; he would train to become a full-fledged pastor.

In the meantime, his father arranged a job as a bookstore clerk. The young man loved books and worked from 8 a.m. until midnight. When the store flooded, he astounded his colleagues with his sheer physical endurance as he carried pile after pile of books to safety. His new goal was to get accepted to a university so that he could later train as a pastor. Again, he unleashed his tireless passion. He worked with a tutor, and copied by hand the text of entire books. "I must sit up as long as I can keep my eyes open," he told his brother. He reminded himself that "practice makes perfect," but Latin and Greek did not come easily to him. He moved in with an uncle, a stern war hero who urged him simply, "push on." The young man resolved to begin work before his peers rose and finish after they slept. His uncle would find him reading in the wee morning hours.

And still, he floundered in his studies. Nearing his twenty-fifth birthday, the young man heard a sermon about how the economic revolution had made certain citizens, like his art-dealer uncle, fabulously wealthy, while others had been thrust into abject poverty. He decided to forsake university to spread the Word more quickly. He opted for a shorter educational course, but was not adept at giving the succinct, punchy sermons that the school mandated. He failed in that program as well. But nobody could stop him from preaching, so he headed for coal country, where inspiration was needed most.

When the young man arrived and saw the blackened sky, he likened it to the shading of a Rembrandt. There he would preach to workers so downtrodden that they referred to the world above the mineshaft as "up in Hell." He dove in to spiritual service with his usual verve, giving away his clothes and money, and doting night and day on the ill and injured. They were legion.

Shortly after he arrived, a series of explosions killed 121 miners and sent gas streaming out of the ground, fueling a pillar of fire like some monstrous Bunsen burner nestled below the earth. The suffering locals marveled at the young man's endurance as he tried to soothe families. But they also found him odd; the children he taught did not listen. Soon, his makeshift ministry was finished. He was twenty-seven, and despondent. A decade after an exuberant start as an art dealer, he had no possessions, accomplishments, or direction.

He poured his heart out in a missive to his little brother, now a respected art dealer himself. He likened himself to a caged bird in spring who feels deeply that it is time for him to do something important but cannot recall what it is, and so "bangs his head against the bars of his cage. And then the cage stays there and the bird is mad with suffering." A man, too, he exhorted, "doesn't always know himself what he could do, but he feels by instinct, I'm good for something, even so! . . . I know that I could be a quite different man! . . . There's something within me, so what is it!" He had been a student, an art dealer, a teacher, a bookseller, a prospective pastor, and an itinerant catechist. After promising starts, he had failed spectacularly in every path he tried.

His brothers suggested he try carpentry, or look for work as a barber. His sister thought he would make a fine baker. He was an insatiable reader, so perhaps a librarian. But in the depths of his despair, he turned his ferocious energy on the last thing he could think of that he could start right away. His next letter to his brother was very short: "I'm writing to you while drawing and I'm in a hurry to get back to it." Previously, the man had seen drawing as a distraction from his aim of reaching people with truth. Now he began to seek truth by documenting the lives around him in drawings. He had stopped drawing freehand as a child when he realized he was a clumsy draftsman, so he started at the very beginning, reading *Guide to the ABCs of Drawing*.

In the coming years, he would make a few very brief attempts at formal training. His cousin-in-law was a painter and tried to teach him watercolor. The cousin would later be listed on the man's Wikipedia page as the sole entry beside "Education." In truth, the man struggled with the fragile touch required for watercolor, and the mentor/mentee relationship ended after a month. His former art-dealer boss, now an esteemed tastemaker in the art world, pronounced his drawings unworthy of being displayed for sale. "Of one thing I am sure," the boss told him, "you are no artist." He added flatly, "You started too late."

When he was nearly thirty-three, he enrolled in art school alongside students a decade younger, but lasted only a few weeks. He entered the class drawing competition, and the judges harshly suggested he revert to a beginner's class with ten-year-olds.

As he had between careers, he pinballed from one artistic passion to another. On one day he felt true artists only painted realistic figures, and then when his figures came out poorly, the next day true artists only cared for landscapes. One day he strived for realism, another for pure expression. This week art was a medium for declaring religious devotion, next week such concerns encumbered pure creation. One year he decided all true art consisted only of shades of black and gray, and then later that vibrant color was the real pearl inside the artist's shell. Each time he fell fully in love, and then just as fully and quickly back out.

One day, he dragged an easel and oil paints—with which he had almost no experience—out to a sand dune in a storm. He ran in and out of cover, slapping and slathering paint on the canvas in staccato strokes between gusts of wind that peppered the painting with grains of sand. He squeezed color right from the tube onto the canvas when he had to. The viscous oil paint and the speed required to apply it in the storm freed his imagination and his hand from the crippling deficiencies that plagued him when he strove for perfect realism. More than a century later, his definitive biographers would write of that day, "[He] made an astonishing discovery: he could paint." And he felt it. "I enjoy it tremendously," he wrote his brother. "Painting has proved less difficult than I expected."

He continued to whipsaw from one artistic experiment to another, avowing and disavowing, roundly condemning the attempt to capture sunlight in paint only to reverse course and place his canvas outside in the sunlight to do just that. He obsessed over deeper and darker blacks in colorless works, and then dispensed with that in an instant and forever in favor of vibrant color, his about-face so thorough that he would not even use black to depict the night sky. He started piano lessons because he thought musical tones might teach him something about color tones.

His peregrinations continued for the few remaining years of his short life, both geographically and artistically. He finally forsook the goal of ever becoming a master draftsman, and then one by one left behind all of the styles that he had previously claimed to be critical, but at which he had failed. He emerged with a new art: impetuous, slathered with paint, erupting with color, laden with no formality other than to capture something infinite.* He wanted to make art that anyone could understand, not haughty works for those with privileged training. For years he had tried and failed to capture every proportion of a figure accurately. Now he let that go so entirely that he left figures walking among trees with faces left blank and hands like mittens.

Whereas he had once demanded live models to portray and images to copy, now he wielded his mind's eye. One evening, he looked out his bedroom window toward the rolling hills in the distance and, as he had with birds and beetles as a boy, watched the sky pass for hours. When he picked up the brush, his imagination transformed a nearby

---

* He put the phrase in French in a letter to his brother: "*ce qui ne passe pas dans ce qui passe*"—that which endures in that which fades.

town into a tiny village, its towering church to a humble chapel. The dark green cypress tree in the foreground became massive, winding up the canvas like seaweed in the swirling rhythm of the night sky.

It was just a few years from the recommended relegation to a drawing class for ten-year-olds. But that starry night, along with scores of other paintings in his new style, the one he devised amid a succession of failures, would launch a new era of art and inspire new conceptions of beauty and expression. Works that he dashed off in hours as experiments over the final two years of his life would become some of the most valuable objects—culturally and monetarily—that have ever existed in the world.

It is a myth that Vincent van Gogh died in anonymity. An ecstatic review cast him as a revolutionary months before he died, and made him the talk of Paris. Claude Monet, the dean of impressionism—the movement Van Gogh ignored, lamented, and then innovated upon—declared Van Gogh's work the cream of an annual exhibition.

Adjusted for inflation, four of Van Gogh's paintings have sold for more than $100 million, and they weren't even the most famous ones. His work now graces everything from socks to cell phone covers and an eponymous vodka brand. But he reached far beyond commerce.

"What artists do changed because of Vincent Van Gogh," artist and writer Steven Naifeh told me. (Naifeh, with Gregory White Smith, wrote "the definitive biography," according to a curator of the Van Gogh Museum.) Van Gogh's paintings served as a bridge to modern art and inspired a widespread devotion that no artist, perhaps no person, has equaled. Teenagers who have never visited a museum tape his art to their walls; Japanese travelers leave the ashes of their ancestors at his grave. In 2016, the Art Institute of Chicago displayed together all three iconic "Bedrooms"—pictures meant "to rest the brain, or rather the imagination," according to Van Gogh; the record number of visitors forced them to create impromptu crowd control strategies, with a TSA-precheck-style express lane.

And yet had Van Gogh died at thirty-four rather than thirty-seven (life expectancy in the Netherlands when he was born was forty), he might not even merit a historical footnote. The same goes for Paul Gauguin, a painter who briefly lived with Van Gogh and innovated a style known as synthetism, in which bold lines separated sections of brilliant color, without the subtle gradations of classical painting. He, too, became one of the few artists to crack the $100 million barrier. He spent the first six years of his professional life with the merchant marine before he found his calling: bourgeois stockbroker. Only after the market crash of 1882 did Gauguin become a full-time artist, at the age of thirty-five. His switch is reminiscent of J. K. Rowling's. She "failed on an epic scale" in her twenties, she once said, personally and professionally. A short marriage "imploded," and she was a single mother and unemployed former teacher on welfare. Like Van Gogh in the coal country and Gauguin after the crash, she was "set free" by failure to try work that better matched her talents and interests.

They all appear to have excelled in spite of their late starts. It would be easy enough to cherry-pick stories of exceptional late developers overcoming the odds. But they aren't exceptions by virtue of their late starts, and those late starts did not stack the odds against them. Their late starts were integral to their eventual success.

"Match quality" is a term economists use to describe the degree of fit between the work someone does and who they are—their abilities and proclivities.

Northwestern University economist Ofer Malamud's inspiration for studying match quality was personal experience. He was born in Israel, but his father worked for a shipping company, and when Malamud was nine the family moved to Hong Kong, where he attended an English school. The English system required that a student home in on an academic specialization in the last two years of high school. "When you applied to a college in England, you had to apply to a specific major," Malamud told me. His father was an engineer, so he figured he should do engineering. At the last moment, he chose not to pick a specialty. "I decided to apply to the U.S. because I didn't know what I wanted to do," he said.

He started with computer science, but quickly learned that wasn't his thing. So he sampled subjects before settling on economics and then philosophy. The experience left him with an abiding curiosity about how the timing of specialization impacts career choice. In the late 1960s, future Nobel laureate economist Theodore Schultz argued that his field had done well to show that higher education increased worker productivity, but that economists had neglected the role of education in allowing individuals to delay specialization while sampling and finding out who they are and where they fit.

Malamud could not randomly assign people to life in order to study specialization timing, but he found a natural experiment in the British school system. For the period he studied, English and Welsh students had to specialize before college so that they could apply to specific, narrow programs. In Scotland, on the other hand, students were actually required to study different fields for their first two years of college, and could keep sampling beyond that.

In each country, every college course that a student took provided skills that could be applied in a specific field, as well as information about their match quality with the field itself. If students focused earlier, they compiled more skills that prepared them for gainful employment. If they sampled and focused later, they entered the job market with fewer domain-specific skills, but a greater sense of the type of work that fit their abilities and inclinations. Malamud's question was: Who usually won the trade-off, early or late specializers?

If the benefit of higher education was simply that it provided skills for work, then early-specializing students would be less likely to career switch after college to a field unrelated to their studies: they have amassed more career-specific skills, so they have more to lose by switching. But if a critical benefit of college was that it provided information about match quality, then early specializers should end up switching to unrelated career fields more often, because they did not have time to sample different matches before choosing one that fit their skills and interests.

Malamud analyzed data for thousands of former students, and found that college graduates in England and Wales were consistently more likely to leap entirely out of their career fields than their later-specializing Scottish peers. And despite starting out behind in income because they had fewer specific skills, the Scots quickly caught up. Their counterparts in England and Wales were more often switching fields after college and after beginning a career even though they had more disincentive to switch, having focused on that field. With less sampling opportunity, more students headed down a narrow path before figuring out if it was a good one. The English and Welsh students were specializing so early that they were making more mistakes. Malamud's conclusion: "The benefits to increased match quality . . . outweigh the greater loss in skills." Learning stuff was less important than learning about oneself. Exploration is not just a whimsical luxury of education; it is a central benefit.

It should come as no surprise that more students in Scotland ultimately majored in subjects that did not exist in their high schools, like engineering. In England and Wales, students were expected to pick a path with knowledge only of the limited menu they had been exposed to early in high school. That is sort of like being forced to choose at sixteen whether you want to marry your high school sweetheart. At the time it might seem like a great idea, but the more you experience, the less great that idea looks in hindsight. In England and Wales, adults were more likely to get divorced from the careers they had invested in because they settled down too early. If we treated careers more like dating, nobody would settle down so quickly.

For professionals who did switch, whether they specialized early or late, switching was a good idea. "You lose a good fraction of your skills, so there's a hit," Malamud said, "but you do actually have higher growth rates after switching." Regardless of when specialization occurred, switchers capitalized on experience to identify better matches.

Steven Levitt, the economist who coauthored *Freakonomics,* cleverly leveraged his readership for a test of switching. On the "Freakonomics Experiments" home page, he invited readers who were considering life changes to flip a digital coin. Heads meant they should go ahead and make the change, tails that they should not. Twenty thousand volunteers responded, agonizing over everything from whether they should get a tattoo, try online dating, or have a child, to the 2,186 people who were pondering a job change.* But could they really trust a momentous decision to chance? The answer for the potential job changers who flipped heads was: only if they wanted to be happier. Six months later, those who flipped heads and switched jobs were substantially happier than the stayers.† According to Levitt, the study suggested that "admonitions such as 'winners never quit and quitters never win,' while well-meaning, may actually be extremely poor advice." Levitt identified one of his own most important skills as "the willingness to jettison" a project or an entire area of study for a better fit.

Winston Churchill's "never give in, never, never, never, never" is an

---

* This made job changing the single most popular question.
† In a detailed analysis, Levitt showed that the result of the coin flip actually influenced the decisions people made. Someone pondering a job change who flipped heads was more likely to change jobs than someone in the same situation who flipped tails, even though, of course, everyone could do whatever they wanted with their life no matter the result of the flip. Among people who chose to follow the coin's advice, flipping heads (and changing jobs) was causally related to their subsequent increased happiness.

oft-quoted trope. The end of the sentence is always left out: "except to convictions of honor and good sense."

Labor economist Kirabo Jackson has demonstrated that even the dreaded administrative headache known as "teacher turnover" captures the value of informed switching. He found that teachers are more effective at improving student performance after they switch to a new school, and that the effect is not explained by switching to higher-achieving schools or better students. "Teachers tend to leave schools at which they are poorly matched," he concluded. "Teacher turnover . . . may in fact move us closer to an optimal allocation of teachers to schools."

Switchers are winners. It seems to fly in the face of hoary adages about quitting, and of far newer concepts in modern psychology.

Psychologist Angela Duckworth conducted the most famous study of quitting. She sought to predict which incoming freshmen would drop out of the U.S. Military Academy's basic-training-cum-orientation, traditionally known as "Beast Barracks."

Six and a half weeks of physical and emotional rigors are designed to transition young men and women from teenagers on summer break to officers-in-training. Cadets are in formation by 5:30 a.m. to begin running or calisthenics. In the mess hall for breakfast, new cadets, or "plebes," must sit straight in their chairs and bring food to their mouths, not their faces toward their plates. An upperclassman can pepper them with questions. "How's the cow?" is shorthand for "How much milk is left?" A plebe will learn to respond, "Sir/Ma'am, she walks, she talks, she's full of chalk! The lacteal fluid extracted from the female of the bovine species is highly prolific to the [nth] degree!" N represents the number of milk cartons left at the table.

The rest of the day is a mix of classroom and physical activities, like the windowless tear gas chamber where plebes have to remove their gas masks and recite facts while their faces are burning. Puking isn't required, nor is it discouraged. Lights-out at 10 p.m., so it can start all over in the morning. It is a precarious time for the morale of new student-soldiers. To get into the academy, all had to be excellent students, many were outstanding athletes, and most completed an application process that included a nomination from a member of Congress. Slackers do not arrive at Beast. Still, some will be gone before the first month is out.

Duckworth learned that the Whole Candidate Score—an agglomeration of standardized test scores, high school rank, physical fitness tests, and demonstrated leadership—is the single most important factor for admission, but that it is useless for predicting who will drop out before completing Beast. She had been talking to high performers across domains, and decided to study passion and perseverance, a combination she cleverly formulated as "grit." She designed a self-assessment that captured the two components of grit. One is essentially work ethic and resilience, and the other is "consistency of interests"—direction, knowing exactly what one wants.

In 2004, at the beginning of Beast, Duckworth gave 1,218 plebes in the incoming class the grit survey. They were asked to pick from five ratings how much each of twelve statements applied to them. Some of the statements were plainly about work ethic ("I am a hard worker"; "I am diligent"). Others probed persistence or singular focus ("I often set a goal but later choose to pursue a different one"; "My interests change from year to year").

Where the Whole Candidate Score failed to predict Beast dropouts, the Grit Scale was better. Duckworth extended the study to other domains, like the finals of the Scripps National Spelling Bee. She found that both verbal IQ tests and grit predicted how far a speller would get in the competition, but that they did so separately. It was best to have a ton of both, but spellers with little grit could make up for it with high verbal IQ scores, and spellers with lower verbal IQ scores could compensate with grit.

Duckworth's intriguing work spawned a cottage industry, for a very large cottage. Sports teams, Fortune 500 companies, charter school networks, and the U.S. Department of Education began touting grit, attempting to develop grit, even testing for grit. Duckworth won a Mac-Arthur "genius" grant for her work, but nonetheless responded thoughtfully to the fervor with an op-ed in the *New York Times*. "I worry I've contributed, inadvertently, to an idea I vigorously oppose: high-stakes character assessment," she wrote. That is not the only way in which grit research has been extended or exaggerated beyond its evidence.

The fact that cadets are selected based on their Whole Candidate Score leads to what statisticians call a "restriction of range." That is, because cadets were selected precisely for their Whole Candidate Score, a group of people who are very alike on Whole Candidate Score measures were siphoned from the rest of humanity. When that happens, other variables that were not part of the selection process can suddenly look much more important in comparison. To use a sports analogy, it would be like conducting a study of success in basketball that included only NBA players as subjects; the study might show that height is not an important predictor of success, but determination is. Of course, the NBA had already selected tall men from the wider population, so the range of height in the study was restricted. Thus height appears not to matter as much as it truly does.* Similarly, the relative predictiveness of grit and other traits in West Point cadets and spelling bee competitors may not look quite the same in less restricted populations. If a truly random sample of high school graduates was assessed for Whole Candidate Scores, not just those who were accepted to West Point, physical fitness, grades, and leadership experiences may well predict their Beast persistence, and perhaps more so than grit. Duckworth and her coauthors, to their credit,

---

* In some years, a scientist who studied basketball would find an inverse relationship between player height and scoring if the scientist looked only at players in the NBA. If the scientist did not acknowledge that the rest of humanity outside the NBA had been filtered out, he or she might give parents the advice to have short kids for them to score more points in the NBA.

point out that by studying highly preselected groups, "we have necessarily limited the external validity of our investigation."

The vast majority of plebes complete Beast, no matter their grit scores. In the first year Duckworth studied them, 71 out of 1,218 dropped out. In 2016, 32 of 1,308 plebes dropped out. The deeper question is whether dropping out might actually be a good decision. Alums told me that cadets drop out for varied reasons, during Beast and beyond it. "I think for the kids that are more cerebral and less physical, the short length makes it easy to just fight through to get to the academic year. For the more physical kids, Beast will be one of the best experiences they have," Ashley Nicolas, an '09 alum who worked as an intelligence officer in Afghanistan, told me. Some of those cadets make it through Beast only to realize that the academy was not the right place for their abilities or interests. "I remember a lot more leaving during first semester when they realized they could not hang academically. The ones who left earlier were either very homesick or just realized they were not a good fit. Most of the latter seemed to be kids who were pressured into coming to West Point without any real desire themselves." In other words, of the small number of cadets who left during Beast, rather than a failing of persistence, some of them were simply responding to match quality information—they weren't a good fit.

Similarly, some people might start memorizing root words for the National Spelling Bee and then realize it is not how they want to spend their learning time. That could be a problem of grit, or it could be a decision made in response to match quality information that could not have been gleaned without giving it a try.

Carnegie Mellon economics and statistics professor Robert A. Miller modeled career matching—and a decision to attend a military academy is a major career choice—as a "multi-armed bandit process." "One-armed bandit" is slang for a slot machine. A multi-armed bandit process refers to a hypothetical scenario: a single gambler is sitting in front of an entire row of slot machines; each machine has its own unique probability of reward with each pull; the gambler's challenge is to test the different machines and try to figure out the best way to allocate their lever pulls to maximize rewards. Miller showed that the process for match quality is the same. An individual starts with no knowledge, tests various possible paths in a manner that provides information as quickly as possible, and increasingly refines decisions about where to allocate energy. The expression "young and foolish," he wrote, describes the tendency of young adults to gravitate to risky jobs, but it is not foolish at all. It is ideal. They have less experience than older workers, and so the first avenues they should try are those with high risk and reward, and that have high informational value. Attempting to be a professional athlete or actor or to found a lucrative start-up is unlikely to succeed, but the potential reward is extremely high. Thanks to constant feedback and an unforgiving weed-out process, those who try will learn quickly if they might be a match, at least compared to jobs with less constant feedback. If they aren't, they go test something else, and continue to gain information about their options and themselves.

Seth Godin, author of some of the most popular career writing in the world, wrote a book disparaging the idea that "quitters never win." Godin argued that "winners"—he generally meant individuals who reach the apex of their domain—quit fast and often when they detect that a plan is not the best fit, and do not feel bad about it. "We fail," he wrote, when we stick with "tasks we don't have the guts to quit." Godin clearly did not advocate quitting simply because a pursuit is difficult. Persevering through difficulty is a competitive advantage for any traveler of a long road, but he suggested that knowing when to quit is such a big strategic advantage that every single person, before undertaking an endeavor, should enumerate conditions under which they should quit. The important trick, he said, is staying attuned to whether switching is simply a failure of perseverance, or astute recognition that better matches are available.

Beast Barracks is perfect for a multi-armed bandit approach to quitting. A group of high achievers, not one of whom has an iota of military experience, pulls the West Point "lever," so to speak. That is, they begin a high-risk, high-reward program and from week one get a massive information signal about whether military discipline is for them. The overwhelming majority stick it out, but it would be unrealistic to expect every single member of a large group of young adults to have understood exactly what they were getting into. Should those few who left have finished instead? Perhaps, if they quit in a moment of simple panic, rather than as a reassessment of the future they wanted in light of this new information about military life. But perhaps more should drop out early too.

In return for a five-year active-duty service commitment, every West Point cadet gets a taxpayer-funded scholarship valued at around a half million dollars. That's why it is particularly vexing to the Army that since the mid-1990s, about half of West Point graduates leave active military service after five years, which is as soon as they are allowed. It takes about five years just to offset the development costs for a trained officer. Three-quarters are gone before the twenty-year mark, which would bring them to their early forties having earned a lifetime pension.

A 2010 monograph published by the Army's Strategic Studies Institute warned that prospects for the Army officer corps "have been darkened by an ever-diminishing return on this investment, as evidenced by plummeting company-grade officer retention rates."

West Point cadets have been making it through Beast and a challenging curriculum, and then leaving, at around the highest rates of all officer training programs—more than officers who came through ROTC (officer training while enrolled at a nonmilitary college), or Officer Candidate School (OCS), which trains college-graduate civilians or enlisted soldiers to become officers. Investment in officer training has recently played out exactly backward: OCS trainees stay the longest, followed by ROTC trainees who did not receive any college scholarship, followed by ROTC trainees who received two-year scholarships, followed by ROTC trainees with three-year scholarships, followed finally by West Point graduates and full-scholarship ROTC trainees. The more likely the Army is to identify someone as a successful future officer and spend money on them, the more likely they are to leave as soon as possible. The Army's goal is developing career senior officers, not simply Beast survivors. From the military's perspective, this is all a major backfire.

The pattern reached such proportions that a high-ranking officer decided that West Point was actually creating quitters and declared that the military should reduce investment in an "institution that taught its cadets to get out of the Army."

Obviously, neither the academy nor ROTC are teaching cadets to leave. Did cadets suddenly lose the grit that had gotten them through Beast? It's not that either. The authors of the monograph—a major, a retired lieutenant colonel, and a colonel, all current or former West Point professors—pinpointed the problem as a match quality conundrum. The more skilled the Army thought a prospective officer could become, the more likely it was to offer a scholarship. And as those hardworking and talented scholarship recipients blossomed into young professionals, they tended to realize that they had a lot of career options outside the military. Eventually, they decided to go try something else. In other words, they learned things about themselves in their twenties and responded by making match quality decisions.

The academy's leaky officer pipeline began springing holes en masse in the 1980s, during the national transition to a knowledge economy. By the millennium, the leaks formed a torrent. The Army began offering retention bonuses—just cash payments to junior officers if they agreed to serve a few more years. It cost taxpayers $500 million, and was a massive waste. Officers who had planned to stay anyway took it, and those who already planned to leave did not. The Army learned a hard lesson: the problem was not a financial one; it was a matching one.

In the industrial era, or the "company man" era, as the monograph authors called it, "firms were highly specialized," with employees generally tackling the same suite of challenges repeatedly. Both the culture of the time—pensions were pervasive and job switching might be viewed as disloyal—and specialization were barriers to worker mobility outside of the company. Plus, there was little incentive for companies to recruit from outside when employees regularly faced kind learning environments, the type where repetitive experience alone leads to improvement. By the 1980s, corporate culture was changing. The knowledge economy created "overwhelming demand for . . . employees with talents for conceptualization and knowledge creation." Broad conceptual skills now helped in an array of jobs, and suddenly control over career trajectory shifted from the employer, who looked inward at a ladder of opportunity, to the employee, who peered out at a vast web of possibility. In the private sector, an efficient talent market rapidly emerged as workers shuffled around in pursuit of match quality. While the world changed, the Army stuck with the industrial-era ladder.

The West Point professors explained that the Army, like many bureaucratic organizations, missed out on match quality markets. "There is no talent matching market mechanism," they wrote. When a junior officer changed direction and left the Army, it did not signal a loss of drive. It signaled that a strong drive for personal development had changed the officer's goals entirely. "I've yet to meet a classmate who left the Army and regretted it," said Ashley Nicolas, the former intelligence officer. She went on to become a math teacher and then a lawyer. She added that all were grateful for the experience, even though it didn't become a lifelong career.

While the private sector adjusted to the burgeoning need for high match quality, the Army just threw money at people. It has, though,

begun to subtly change. That most hierarchical of entities has found success embracing match flexibility. The Officer Career Satisfaction Program was designed so that scholarship-ROTC and West Point graduates
can take more control of their own career progression. In return for
three additional years of active service, the program increased the number of officers who can choose a branch (infantry, intelligence, engineering, dental, finance, veterinary, communication technology, and many
more), or a geographic post. Where dangling money for junior officers
failed miserably, facilitating match quality succeeded. In the first four
years of the program, four thousand cadets agreed to extend their service commitments in exchange for choice.*

It is just a small step. When Defense Secretary Ash Carter visited
West Point in 2016 for student meetings, he was flooded with concerns
from very gritty cadets about rigid career paths that did not allow them
to adjust to their own development. Carter had pledged to drastically
reshape the Army's "industrial era" personnel management from the
strict "up-or-out" model to one that allows officers a shot to improve
their own match quality as they grow.

When they were high school graduates, with few skills and little
exposure to a world of career options, West Point cadets might easily
have answered "Not like me at all" to the Grit Scale statement "I often
set a goal but later choose to pursue a different one." A few years later,
with more knowledge of their skills and preferences, choosing to pursue
a different goal was no longer the gritless route; it was the smart one.

---

* The Army also started a process called "talent-based branching" in which it works with
cadets and young officers to help them assess their own talents and interests as they progress in training. The idea is to improve their occupational match quality. As Colonel
Joanne Moore noted in a presentation in 2017, the jobs that cadets enter the military
dreaming of often prove not to be a great fit. They only realize that after trying, so the ability to switch is critical for optimizing match quality.

———

Intuitively, grit research appeals to me. In the nonscientific, colloquial use of the word, I tend to think I have a lot of it. After running track and playing football, basketball, and baseball at a large public high school— and I'm only five foot six—I walked on to a Division I track team in college as an 800-meter runner.

I was not close to the worst 800 runner on my college team freshman year; I was *the* worst, by a landslide. I was allowed to keep practicing with the team because as long as you are not chosen for travel, it doesn't cost anybody anything, not even the pair of shoes the recruits got. When the traveling team went to South Carolina to train over spring break, I stayed on the eerily quiet campus rather than going home, to train without distraction. I stuck with it for two miserable years of vomit-inducing workouts and ego-bruising races, while blue-chip recruits quit and were replaced by others. There were plenty of days (and weeks, and an entire month or three) when I felt like I should probably quit. But I was learning about the kind of training that worked for me, and I was improving. In my senior season, I cracked the university's all-time top ten list indoors, was twice All-East, and part of a relay that set the university record. The only other guy in my class who held a university record was my gritty roommate, the other walk-on. Nearly the entire recruited class from our year quit. Hilariously, I was awarded the Gustave A. Jaeger Memorial Prize for the athlete who "achieved significant athletic success in the face of unusual challenge and difficulty"—my "unusual challenge and difficulty" just being that I epically stunk at first. After the presentation, the head coach, with whom I'd had little direct conversation as a walk-on, shared that he had felt sorry for me watching workouts my freshman year.

There's nothing particularly special about that story—it exists on every team. But I think it is indicative of my approach to work. Nonetheless, I scored at the 50th percentile on the Grit Scale compared to

American adults at large. I racked up points for assessing myself as a very hard worker who is not discouraged by setbacks, but I missed a lot of points for confessing that "my interests change from year to year," and, like so many West Point graduates, I sometimes "set a goal but later choose to pursue a different one." When I was seventeen and positive that I was going to go to the U.S. Air Force Academy to become a pilot and then an astronaut, I probably would have self-assessed at the very top of the Grit Scale. I got all the way to Chicago-area congressman Sidney Yates agreeing to provide a nomination.

But I never did any of that. Instead, at the last minute I changed my mind and went elsewhere to study political science. I took a single poli-sci class, and ended up majoring in Earth and environmental sciences and minoring in astronomy, certain I would become a scientist. I worked in labs during and after college and realized that I was not the type of person who wanted to spend my entire life learning one or two things new to the world, but rather the type who wanted constantly to learn things new to me and share them. I transitioned from science to journalism; my first job was as a midnight-shift street reporter in New York City. (Nothing happy that's going in the *New York Daily News* happens between midnight and 10 a.m.) Growing self-knowledge kept changing my goals and interests until I landed in a career the very lifeblood of which is investigating broad interests. When I later worked at *Sports Illustrated*, determined students would ask me whether it was better to study journalism or English to work at *SI*. I told them I had no clue, but that a statistics or biology course never hurt anyone.

I don't think I have become less passionate or resilient over time, nor do I think that all those former West Point cadets who left the Army lost the drive that got them there in the first place. It makes sense to me that grit would be powerfully predictive for cadets trying to get through their rigorous orientation, or for a sample of schoolchildren or spelling bee contestants. Very young people often have their goals set for them, or at least have a limited menu to choose from, and pursuing them with passion and resilience is the main challenge. The same goes for 800 runners. One of the compelling aspects of sports goals is how straight-forward and easily measurable they are. On the final weekend of the 2018 Winter Olympics, Sasha Cohen, a 2006 silver medalist figure skater, wrote an advice column to retiring athletes. "Olympic athletes need to understand that the rules for life are different from the rules for sports," she wrote. "Yes, striving to accomplish a single overarching goal every day means you have grit, determination and resilience. But the ability to pull yourself together mentally and physically in competi-tion is different from the new challenges that await you. So after you retire, travel, write a poem, try to start your own business, stay out a little too late, devote time to something that doesn't have a clear end goal." In the wider world of work, finding a goal with high match qual-ity in the first place is the greater challenge, and persistence for the sake of persistence can get in the way.

A recent international Gallup survey of more than two hundred thousand workers in 150 countries reported that 85 percent were either "not engaged" with their work or "actively disengaged." In that condi-tion, according to Seth Godin, quitting takes a lot more guts than continuing to be carried along like debris on an ocean wave. The trou-ble, Godin noted, is that humans are bedeviled by the "sunk cost fal-lacy." Having invested time or money in something, we are loath to leave it, because that would mean we had wasted our time or money, even though it is already gone. Writer, psychology PhD, and profes-sional poker player Maria Konnikova explained in her book *The Con-fidence Game* how the sunk cost mindset is so deeply entrenched that conmen know to begin by asking their marks for several small favors or investments before progressing to large asks. Once a mark has in-vested energy or money, rather than walking away from sunk costs he will continue investing, more than he ever wanted to, even as, to any rational observer, disaster becomes imminent. "The more we have invested and even lost," Konnikova wrote, "the longer we will persist in insisting it will all work out."

Steven Naifeh spent a decade researching Van Gogh's life, so I asked him to fill out the grit questionnaire on the painter's behalf. Van Gogh's work ethic stretched belief. He was intoxicated with an image his father had used in a sermon of the sower, who must put in work now so that he can reap later. "Think of all the fields that were turned down by shortsighted people," Dorus van Gogh preached. He invoked that image, Naifeh and Smith wrote, as "a paragon of persistence in the face of adversity." At every job he had, Vincent was convinced that if he outworked everyone around him, he would succeed. But then he would fail. His interests whipsawed constantly. Even once he'd set himself on being an artist, he would devote all his energy to one style or medium only to completely disavow it soon thereafter. Naifeh and Smith used an elegant phrase to describe Van Gogh's pliable passions: his "altered gospel." The Grit Scale statement "I have been obsessed with a certain idea or project for a short time but later lost interest" is Van Gogh in a nutshell, at least up until the final few years of his life when he settled on his unique style and creatively erupted. Van Gogh was an example of match quality optimization, Robert Miller's multi-armed bandit process come to life. He tested options with maniacal intensity and got the maximum information signal about his fit as quickly as possible, and then moved to something else and repeated, until he had zigzagged his way to a place no one else had ever been, and where he alone excelled. Van Gogh's Grit Scale score, according to Naifeh's assessment, was flush with hard work but low on sticking with every goal or project. He landed in the 40th percentile.

Beginning in 2017, to my great honor, I was invited to work with veterans to review applications for the Pat Tillman Foundation, the organization I had begun speaking to in 2015 and that provides scholarships to veterans, active-duty military, and military spouses. A lot of applications come from ambitious West Point alumni.

The essays were fascinating and inspiring. Nearly every single one spoke of some formative lesson learned in Afghanistan, or on a domestic hurricane rescue team, or while translating languages under pressure, or as a spouse moving again and again and arranging services for other military spouses, or even while becoming increasingly frustrated with some aspect of military conflict or bureaucratic dysfunction. The crux was that some unanticipated experience had led to an unexpected new goal or the discovery of an unexplored talent.

Applicants who receive funding join the community of Tillman Scholars, the group of high achievers whose concern about changing directions later than their peers helped inspire this book. Discussing late specialization was practically a catharsis for their anxiety about having taken time to do and learn things they were grateful to have done and learned.

No one in their right mind would argue that passion and perseverance are unimportant, or that a bad day is a cue to quit. But the idea that a change of interest, or a recalibration of focus, is an imperfection and competitive disadvantage leads to a simple, one-size-fits-all Tiger story: pick and stick, as soon as possible. Responding to lived experience with a change of direction, like Van Gogh did habitually, like West Point graduates have been doing since the dawn of the knowledge economy, is less tidy but no less important. It involves a particular behavior that improves your chances of finding the best match, but that at first blush sounds like a terrible life strategy: short-term planning.

CHAPTER 7

Flirting with Your Possible Selves

FRANCES HESSELBEIN GREW UP in the mountains of western Pennsylvania, among families drawn by steel mills and coal mines. "In Johnstown, 5:30 means 5:30," she often says. So if the executives, military officers, and legislators who line up outside the door of her Manhattan office seeking leadership advice want their full hour, they'd better be on time. Even with her hundredth birthday behind her, she is in the office every weekday with more work than she can finish. Hesselbein is fond of telling visitors that she has had four professional positions, all president or CEO, and never applied for one. In fact, she attempted to turn down three of them. When she guessed where life would take her, she was pretty much always wrong.

In high school, she dreamed of a bookish life as a playwright. After graduation, she enrolled in the University of Pittsburgh's Junior College, "Junior Pitt." She loved experimenting with different classes, but her father fell ill during her first year. Hesselbein was seventeen, the oldest of three, stroking her father's cheek in the hospital when he passed away. She kissed him on the forehead and promised to take care of the family. She finished the semester, and then dropped out to work as an adman's assistant at the Penn Traffic Company department store.

Soon she got married, and had a son just in time for her husband, John, to report to the Navy during World War II. John served as a combat aircrew photographer, and upon return set up a studio, doing everything from high school portraits to documentary films. Hesselbein had a protean job she called "helping John." When a customer wanted a photo of a dog to look like a painting, she grabbed oil paints and colored it, voilà.

Hesselbein adored Johnstown's rich diversity, but it afforded some ugly lessons. As part of the newly formed Pennsylvania Human Relations Commission, John responded to acts of discrimination in town, like a barbershop that would not cut black customers' hair. "I don't have the right tools," the barber complained. John's response: "Then you will have to buy the right tools." When John confronted a teacher who kicked two black children off a playground, the teacher called him a "traitor." Hesselbein decided then that a community that valued inclusiveness should answer "yes" to the question, "When they look at us, can they find themselves?"

When Hesselbein was thirty-four, a prominent woman in the community stopped by her home and asked her to lead Girl Scout Troop 17 as a volunteer. The previous leader had left to become a missionary in India, and other neighbors had turned down the request. So did Hesselbein, three times. She had an eight-year-old boy, and professed to know nothing about little girls. Finally, the woman said that the group of thirty ten-year-old girls from modest families who met in a church basement would just have to be disbanded. Hesselbein agreed to stand in for six weeks, until a real leader was found.

In preparation, she read up on the Girl Scouts. She learned that the organization was founded eight years before women could vote in the United States, and that the founder had reminded girls that they could be "a doctor, a lawyer, an aviatrix, or a hot-air balloonist." Hesselbein thought back to second grade, when she announced that she wanted to be a pilot and her classmates laughed. So she showed up in the church basement to start her six weeks. She ended up staying with Troop 17 for eight years, until they graduated high school.

Afterward, Hesselbein kept picking up Girl Scout roles she neither sought nor intended to keep. She was in her midforties when she left the country for the first time, for an international Girl Scout meeting in Greece. More trips followed—India, Thailand, Kenya. Hesselbein realized she loved volunteering.

She was asked to chair the local United Way campaign at a time when that role was as foreign for women as aviatrix had been. It was a volunteer job, so she figured she had nothing to lose. But when she appointed as her vice chairman the president of the local United Steelworkers of America, suddenly the United Way president decided that wasn't such a good idea and he had better check with Bethlehem Steel, a major supporter. Hesselbein stood fast, and managed to get both the company and the union behind her. That year, little Johnstown, Pennsylvania, had the highest per capita giving of any United Way campaign in the country. Of course, it was a temp role as far as Hesselbein was concerned, so the following year she handed it off.

In 1970, a trio of Johnstown business leaders who supported the Girl Scouts invited Hesselbein to lunch. They told her that they had chosen a new executive director of the local Girl Scout council. The previous one had left and the council was in serious financial trouble.

"How wonderful, who is it?" she asked.

"You," they replied.

"I would never take a professional job," she told them. "I am a volunteer."

One of the businessmen was on the United Way board, and he said that if Hesselbein did not take the job and straighten out the finances, the Girl Scouts would lose the United Way partnership. She agreed to fill in for six months only, and then to step aside for an experienced professional. At fifty-four, she began what she calls her first professional job. She devoured management books, and a month in realized that the work fit her. She stayed for four years.

But even as her work was going well, the backdrop was dire. In the late 1960s and early 1970s, society changed dramatically. The Girl Scouts did not. Girls were preparing for college and careers in unprecedented numbers, and they needed information on thorny topics like sex and drugs. The organization was in existential crisis. Membership fell off a cliff. The CEO position went vacant for nearly an entire year. In 1976, the search committee invited Hesselbein to New York City for an interview. Previous Girl Scout CEOs had staggering leadership credentials. Captain Dorothy Stratton had been a psychology professor, university dean, founding director of the U.S. Coast Guard Women's Reserve, and the first personnel director at the International Monetary Fund. The most recent chief executive was Dr. Cecily Cannan Selby, who at sixteen entered Radcliffe College and later used her physical biology PhD from MIT to apply wartime technology to the study of cells. Selby's national leadership positions spanned industry and education. Hesselbein, meanwhile, had been the head of a local Girl Scout council, one of 335 around the country. She planned to spend her life in Pennsylvania, so she politely turned down the interview.

But John accepted it. He said that she could decline the job but he would drive her there to do it in person. Since she was not interested in the job, she felt at ease when the committee asked her what she would do as hypothetical CEO. Hesselbein described the total transformation of an organization steeped in tradition: activities reworked to stay relevant—heavy on math, science, and technology; the hierarchical leadership structure dismantled in favor of "circular management." Rather than rungs on a ladder, staff at all levels would be beads on concentric bracelets, with multiple contacts who could advance ideas from local councils toward the national decision makers at the center. Finally, the organization would be inclusive: when girls of all backgrounds looked at Girl Scouts, they would have to find themselves.

Hesselbein arrived in New York City on July 4, 1976, as CEO of a three-million-member organization. Out went the sacrosanct standard handbook in favor of four handbooks, each targeted at a specific age group. She hired artists and told them that a six-year-old indigenous girl near an ice floe in Alaska who flips through a handbook had better see someone who looks like her in a Girl Scout uniform. She commissioned research on messaging to invite girls of all backgrounds. It culminated in poetic marketing posters. One targeted at Native Americans read, "Your names are on the rivers."

Diversity was great, Hesselbein was told, but it was too much too soon. Fix the organizational problems, and then worry about diversity. But she had decided that diversity *was* the primary organizational problem, so she took it further. She assembled a leadership team that represented her target audience, and modernized everything, from the mission statement to the merit badges. There would now be badges for math and personal computing. She made the gut-wrenching decision to sell campgrounds that volunteers and staff adored from their youth but that were no longer getting enough use.

Hesselbein remained CEO for thirteen years. Under her leadership, minority membership tripled; Girl Scouts added a quarter million members and more than 130,000 new volunteers. The cookie business grew to more than $300 million a year.

In 1990, Hesselbein retired from the Girl Scouts. Revered management expert Peter Drucker proclaimed her the best CEO in the country. "She could manage any company in America," he said. Months later, the CEO of General Motors retired. When *Business Week* asked Drucker who the next head of GM should be, he told them, "I would pick Frances."

The very morning after she retired in 1990, Hesselbein got a surprise call from the chairman of the Mutual of America insurance company asking when she could come see her new office on Fifth Avenue. She was already on the board, and the company decided it wanted her in-house; she could figure out what she wanted to do with the donated office later. By that time, she was fine with proceeding in the absence of a clear long-term plan, since she had been figuring everything out as she went along her entire life.

Hesselbein decided to form a foundation for nonprofit management, to help bring best business practices to social entrepreneurship. She would sit on the board, but had already purchased a home in Pennsylvania, where she would stay put for a while and write a book. The founding team asked Peter Drucker to be honorary chairman. He agreed, on the condition Hesselbein become CEO. So much for book writing in Pennsylvania. Six weeks after leaving the helm of the world's largest organization for girls and women, she was CEO of a foundation with no money or assets, but a free office, which was enough for her to get started. She built a staff, and today is busy running the Frances Hesselbein Leadership Institute.

She never did graduate from college, but her office is festooned with twenty-three honorary doctorates, plus a glistening saber given to her by the U.S. Military Academy for teaching leadership courses—as well as the Presidential Medal of Freedom, the highest civilian award in the United States. When I visited just after her 101st birthday, I brought her a cup of steamed milk, as I had been advised, and right away asked what training had prepared her for leadership. Wrong question. "Oh, don't ask me what my training was," she replied with a dismissing hand wave. She explained that she just did whatever seemed like it would teach her something and allow her to be of service at each moment, and somehow that added up to training. As Steven Naifeh said regarding Van Gogh's life, some "undefinable process of digestion" occurred as diverse experiences accumulated. "I was unaware that I was being prepared," she told me. "I did not intend to become a leader, I just learned by doing what was needed at the time."

In retrospect, Hesselbein can guess at lessons she never recognized when she was going through them. She saw both the power of inclusion and exclusion in diverse Johnstown. She learned resourcefulness as a jack-of-all-trades in the photography business. As a new troop leader with less experience than her charges, she relied on shared leadership. She united stakeholders normally at loggerheads for the United Way campaign. Having never been out of the country until she traveled to international Girl Scout meetings, she learned to quickly find common ground with peers from all over the world.

At the first ever Girl Scout training event Hesselbein attended, she heard another new troop leader complain that she was getting nothing from the session. Hesselbein mentioned it to a dress-factory worker who was also volunteering, and the woman told her, "You have to carry a big basket to bring something home." She repeats that phrase today, to mean that a mind kept wide open will take something from every new experience.

It is a natural philosophy for someone who was sixty when she attempted to turn down an interview for the job that became her calling. She had no long-term plan, only a plan to do what was interesting or needed at the moment. "I never envisioned" is her most popular preamble.

Hesselbein's professional career, which started in her midfifties, was extraordinary. The meandering path, however, was not.

Todd Rose, director of Harvard's Mind, Brain, and Education program, and computational neuroscientist Ogi Ogas cast a broad net when they set out to study unusually winding career paths. They wanted to find people who are fulfilled and successful, and who arrived there circuitously. They recruited high fliers from master sommeliers and personal organizers to animal trainers, piano tuners, midwives, architects, and engineers. "We guessed we'd have to interview five people for each one who created their own path," Ogas told me. "We didn't think it would be a majority, or even a lot."

It turned out virtually every person had followed what seemed like an unusual path. "What was even more incredible is that they all thought they were the anomaly," Ogas said. Forty-five of the first fifty subjects detailed professional paths so sinuous that they expressed embarrassment over jumping from thing to thing over their careers. "They'd add a disclaimer, 'Well, most people don't do it this way,'" Ogas said. "They had been told that getting off their initial path was so risky. But actually we should all understand, this is not weird, it's the norm." Thus the research found a name, the Dark Horse Project, because even as more subjects were added, most perceived themselves as dark horses who followed what seemed like an unlikely path.*

Dark horses were on the hunt for match quality. "They never look around and say, 'Oh, I'm going to fall behind, these people started earlier and have more than me at a younger age,'" Ogas told me. "They focused on, 'Here's who I am at the moment, here are my motivations, here's what I've found I like to do, here's what I'd like to learn, and here are the opportunities. Which of these is the best match *right now*? And maybe a year from now I'll switch because I'll find something better.'"

Each dark horse had a novel journey, but a common strategy. "Short-term planning," Ogas told me. "They all practice it, not long-term planning." Even people who look like consummate long-term visionaries from afar usually looked like short-term planners up close. When Nike cofounder Phil Knight was asked in 2016 about his long-term vision and how he knew what he wanted when he created the company, he replied that he had actually known he wanted to be a professional athlete. But he was not good enough, so he shifted to simply trying to find some way

---

* Bureau of Labor Statistics data shows that the trope of the professionally itinerant Millennial is really just the natural continuation of a knowledge-economy trend. Fifty percent of Late Baby Boomers (born between 1957 and 1964) held at least eleven different jobs between ages eighteen and fifty, and that was pretty similar for women and men of different education levels.

to stay involved with sports. He happened to run track under a college coach who tinkered with shoes and who later became his cofounder. "I feel sorry for the people who know exactly what they're going to do from the time they're sophomores in high school," he said. In his memoir, Knight wrote that he "wasn't much for setting goals," and that his main goal for his nascent shoe company was to fail fast enough that he could apply what he was learning to his next venture. He made one short-term pivot after another, applying the lessons as he went.

Ogas uses the shorthand "standardization covenant" for the cultural notion that it is rational to trade a winding path of self-exploration for a rigid goal with a head start because it ensures stability. "The people we study who are fulfilled do pursue a long-term goal, but they only formulate it after a period of discovery," he told me. "Obviously, there's nothing wrong with getting a law or medical degree or PhD. But it's actually riskier to make that commitment before you know how it fits you. And don't consider the path fixed. People realize things about themselves halfway through medical school." Charles Darwin, for example.

At his father's behest he planned to be a doctor, but he found medical lectures "intolerably dull," and partway through his education he walked out of an operation at the grind of the surgical saw. "Nor did I ever attend again," Darwin wrote, "for hardly any inducement would have been strong enough to make me do so." Darwin was a Bible literalist at the time, and figured he would become a clergyman. He bounced around classes, including a botany course with a professor who subsequently recommended him for an unpaid position aboard the HMS *Beagle*. After convincing his father (with his uncle's help) that he would not become a deadbeat if he took this one detour, Darwin began perhaps the most impactful post-college gap year in history. His father's wishes eventually "died a natural death." Decades later, Darwin reflected on the process of self-discovery. "It seems ludicrous that I once intended to be a clergyman," he wrote. His father, a doctor for more than sixty years, detested the sight of blood. "If his father had given him

any choice," Darwin wrote, "nothing should have induced him to follow it."

Michael Crichton started with medicine too, after learning how few
writers make a living. With medicine, "I would never have to wonder if
the work was worthwhile," he wrote. Except, a few years in he became
disenchanted with medical practice. He graduated from Harvard Medical School, but decided to become a writer. His medical education was
not remotely wasted. He used it to craft some of the most popular stories in the world—the novel *Jurassic Park,* and the TV series *ER,* with
its record-setting 124 Emmy nominations.

Career goals that once felt safe and certain can appear ludicrous,
to use Darwin's adjective, when examined in the light of more self-
knowledge. Our work preferences and our life preferences do not stay
the same, because *we* do not stay the same.

Psychologist Dan Gilbert called it the "end of history illusion." From
teenagers to senior citizens, we recognize that our desires and motivations sure changed a lot in the past (see: your old hairstyle), but believe
they will not change much in the future. In Gilbert's terms, we are
works in progress claiming to be finished.

Gilbert and colleagues measured the preferences, values, and personalities of more than nineteen thousand adults aged eighteen to sixty-
eight. Some were asked to predict how much they would change over
the next decade, others to reflect about how much they had changed in
the previous one. Predictors expected that they would change very little
in the next decade, while reflectors reported having changed a lot in the
previous one. Qualities that feel immutable changed immensely. Core
values—pleasure, security, success, and honesty—transformed. Preferences for vacations, music, hobbies, and even friends were transfigured.
Hilariously, predictors were willing to pay an average of $129 a ticket
for a show ten years away by their current favorite band, while reflec-

tors would only pay $80 to see a show today by their favorite band from ten years ago. The precise person you are now is fleeting, just like all the other people you've been. That feels like the most unexpected result, but it is also the most well documented.

It is definitely true that a shy child is more likely to foreshadow a shy adult, but it is far from a perfect correlation. And if one particular personality trait does not change, others will. The only certainty is change, both on average as a generation ages, and within each individual. University of Illinois psychologist Brent W. Roberts specializes in studying personality development. He and another psychologist aggregated the results of ninety-two studies and revealed that some personality traits change over time in fairly predictable ways. Adults tend to become more agreeable, more conscientious, more emotionally stable, and less neurotic with age, but less open to experience. In middle age, adults grow more consistent and cautious and less curious, open-minded, and inventive.* The changes have well-known impacts, like the fact that adults generally become less likely to commit violent crimes with age, and more able to create stable relationships. The most momentous personality changes occur between age eighteen and one's late twenties, so specializing early is a task of predicting match quality for a person who does not yet exist. It could work, but it makes for worse odds. Plus, while personality change slows, it does not stop at any age. Sometimes it can actually happen instantly.

Thanks to YouTube, the "marshmallow test" could be the most famous scientific experiment in the world. It was actually a series of experiments

---

* For the statistically inclined, the correlation for a particular personality trait between an individual's teen years and that individual's older age is typically around 0.2–0.3, which is on the moderate side. (Assuming no random measurement error, a correlation of 1.0 would mean the personality trait did not change at all relative to one's age-matched peers.) "We are clearly not the same people at seventy-five as fifteen," Roberts told me, but "there are traces that should be recognizable."

starting in the 1960s. The original premise was simple: An experimenter places a marshmallow (or a cookie, or a pretzel) in front of a nursery school child; before leaving, the experimenter tells the child that if she can wait until the experimenter returns, she'll get that marshmallow plus a second one. If the child can't wait, she can eat the marshmallow. The children were not told how long the wait would be (it was fifteen to twenty minutes, depending on age), so they just had to hold out if they wanted the maximum reward.

Psychologist Walter Mischel and his research team followed up with the children years later, and found that the longer a child had been able to wait, the more likely she was to be successful socially, academically, and financially, and the less likely she was to abuse drugs.

The marshmallow test was already a celebrity as scientific experiments go, but it became the Beyoncé of studies when media outlets and parents eager to foretell their child's destiny started posting DIY marshmallow tests online. The videos are by turns adorable and intriguing. Nearly all kids wait at least a little. Some stare at the marshmallow, touch it, sniff it, delicately tap their tongue to it and pull back as if it were hot. Maybe they even put it in their mouth, pull it out, and simulate a big bite. Some tear a barely noticeable piece off for a micro test taste. Before the end of the video, the kids who start by touching it will have eaten the marshmallow. The kids who successfully hold out wield all manner of distraction, from looking away to shoving the plate away, covering their eyes, turning and screaming, singing, talking to themselves, counting, generally thrashing around in the chair, or (boys) hitting themselves in the face. One little boy who spent his time looking in every direction except at the marshmallow is so ravenous when the experimenter returns with his second treat that he mashes them both into his mouth immediately.

The crystal ball allure of the marshmallow test is undeniable, and also misconstrued. Mischel's collaborator Yuichi Shoda has repeatedly made a point of saying that plenty of preschoolers who ate the marsh-mallow turned out just fine.* Shoda maintained that the most exciting aspect of the studies was demonstrating how easily children could learn to change a specific behavior with simple mental strategies, like think-ing about the marshmallow as a cloud rather than food. Shoda's post-marshmallow-test work has been one part of a bridge in psychology between extreme arguments in the debate about the roles of nature and nurture in personality. One extreme suggests that personality traits are almost entirely a function of one's nature, and the other that personality is entirely a function of the environment. Shoda argued that both sides of the so-called person-situation debate were right. And wrong. At a given point in life, an individual's nature influences how they respond to a particular situation, but their nature can appear surprisingly differ-ent in some other situation. With Mischel, he began to study "if-then signatures." *If* David is at a giant party, *then* he seems introverted, but *if* David is with his team at work, *then* he seems extroverted. (True.) So is David introverted or extroverted? Well, both, and consistently so.

Ogas and Rose call this the "context principle." In 2007, Mischel wrote, "The gist of such findings is that the child who is aggressive at home may be less aggressive than most when in school; the man excep-tionally hostile when rejected in love may be unusually tolerant about criticism of his work; the one who melts with anxiety in the doctor's office may be a calm mountain climber; the risk-taking entrepreneur may take few social risks." Rose framed it more colloquially: "If you are conscientious and neurotic while driving today, it's a pretty safe bet you will be conscientious and neurotic while driving tomorrow. At the same time . . . you may *not* be conscientious and neurotic when you are play-ing Beatles cover songs with your band in the context of the local pub." Perhaps that is one reason Daniel Kahneman and his colleagues in the

---

* A replication of the marshmallow test, published in 2018, found that the predictive power for later behaviors was less than in the original study.

military (chapter 1) failed to predict who would be a leader in battle based on who had been a leader in an obstacle course exercise. When I was a college runner, I had teammates whose drive and determination seemed almost boundless on the track, and nearly absent in the classroom, and vice versa. Instead of asking whether someone is gritty, we should ask *when* they are. "If you get someone into a context that suits them," Ogas said, "they'll more likely work hard and it will look like grit from the outside."

Because personality changes more than we expect with time, experience, and different contexts, we are ill-equipped to make ironclad long-term goals when our past consists of little time, few experiences, and a narrow range of contexts. Each "story of me" continues to evolve. We should all heed the wisdom of Alice, who, when asked by the Gryphon in Wonderland to share her story, decided she had to start with the beginning of her adventure that very morning. "It's no use going back to yesterday," she said, "because I was a different person then." Alice captured a grain of truth, one that has profound consequences for the best way to maximize match quality.

Herminia Ibarra, a professor of organizational behavior at London Business School, studied how young consultants and bankers advance (or don't) in firms she described as up-or-out hierarchies. When she followed up a few years later, after her project, she found that some of the budding stars either weren't there anymore, having embarked on new careers, or were hatching escape plans.

Ibarra began another study, this time adding web entrepreneurs, lawyers, doctors, professors, and IT professionals. The focus would be on career switching. Ibarra tracked ambitious professionals, most in their thirties and forties, in the United States, United Kingdom, and France who had traveled a linear career path for a minimum of eight years. Over the course of her work, she watched midcareer professionals move from a flicker of desire for change, to an unsettling period of transition, to the actual jump to a new career. Occasionally she saw the entire process occur twice for the same individual. When she compiled her findings, the central premise was at once simple and profound: we learn who we are only by living, and not before.

Ibarra concluded that we maximize match quality throughout life by sampling activities, social groups, contexts, jobs, careers, and then reflecting and adjusting our personal narratives. And repeat. If that sounds facile, consider that it is precisely the opposite of a vast marketing crusade that assures customers they can alight on their perfect matches via introspection alone. A lucrative career and personality quiz and counseling industry survives on that notion. "All of the strengths-finder stuff, it gives people license to pigeonhole themselves or others in ways that just don't take into account how much we grow and evolve and blossom and discover new things," Ibarra told me. "But people want answers, so these frameworks sell. It's a lot harder to say, 'Well, come up with some experiments and see what happens.'"

If only you fill out this quiz, the promise goes, it will light the way to the ideal career, never mind what psychologists have documented about personal change across time and context. Ibarra criticized conventional-wisdom articles like one in the *Wall Street Journal* on "the painless path to a new career," which decreed that the secret is simply forming "a clear picture of what you want" before acting.

Instead, she told me, in a clever inversion of a hallowed axiom, "First act and then think." Ibarra marshaled social psychology to argue persuasively that we are each made up of numerous possibilities. As she put it, "We discover the possibilities by *doing,* by trying new activities, building new networks, finding new role models." We learn who we are in practice, not in theory.

Think of Frances Hesselbein, who assumed over and over she was just dipping her toe into something new, until she was near the age when her peers were retiring and finally realized she had short-term-planned her way to a vocation. Or Van Gogh, who was certain he found the perfect calling again and again, only to learn in practice that he was mistaken, until he wasn't.

Ibarra documented extreme transitions: Pierre, a thirty-eight-year-old psychiatrist and bestselling author, became a Buddhist monk after a winding road that started with meeting a Tibetan lama at a dinner party. And more quotidian conversions: Lucy, a forty-six-year-old tech manager at a brokerage firm, was floored by the critical personal feedback she got from an organizational development consultant, so she hired the woman as a personal coach. Lucy soon realized she was more inspired to manage people (an area of weakness, the consultant convinced her) than technology. Gradually, she attended classes and conferences and tapped the far-flung fringes of her personal network to get a sense of what was possible. One gig at a time, a weakness became a strength, and she transitioned into an organizational development coach herself.

Themes emerged in the transitions. The protagonists had begun to feel unfulfilled by their work, and then a chance encounter with some world previously invisible to them led to a series of short-term explorations. At first, all career changers fell prey to the cult of the head start and figured it couldn't possibly make sense to dispense with their long-term plans in favor of rapidly evolving short-term experiments. Sometimes they tried to talk themselves out of it. Their confidants advised them not to do anything rash; don't change now, they said, just keep the new interest or talent as a hobby. But the more they dabbled, the more certain they were that it was time for a change. A new work identity did not manifest overnight, but began with trying something temporary, Hesselbein style, or finding a new role model, then reflecting on the experience and moving to the next short-term plan. Some career changers got richer, others poorer; all felt temporarily behind, but as in the *Freakonomics* coin-flip study, they were happier with a change.

Ibarra's advice is nearly identical to the short-term planning the Dark Horse researchers documented. Rather than expecting an ironclad a priori answer to "Who do I really want to become?," their work indicated that it is better to be a scientist of yourself, asking smaller questions that can actually be tested—"Which among my various possible selves should I start to explore now? How can I do that?" Be a flirt with your possible selves.* Rather than a grand plan, find experiments that can be undertaken quickly. "Test-and-learn," Ibarra told me, "not plan-and-implement."

Paul Graham, computer scientist and cofounder of Y Combinator—the start-up funder of Airbnb, Dropbox, Stripe, and Twitch—encapsulated Ibarra's tenets in a high school graduation speech he wrote, but never delivered:

> It might seem that nothing would be easier than deciding what you like, but it turns out to be hard, partly because it's hard to get an accurate picture of most jobs. . . . Most of the work I've done in the last ten years didn't exist when I was in high school. . . . In such a world it's not a good idea to have fixed plans.
>
> And yet every May, speakers all over the country fire up the Standard Graduation Speech, the theme of which is: don't give up on your dreams. I know what they mean, but this is a bad way to put it, because it implies you're supposed to be bound by some plan you made early on. The computer world has a name for this: premature optimization. . . .
>
> . . . Instead of working back from a goal, work forward from promising situations. This is what most successful people actually do anyway.
>
> In the graduation-speech approach, you decide where you want to be in twenty years, and then ask: what should I do now to get

---

* *Grey's Anatomy* and *Scandal* creator Shonda Rhimes flirted in the extreme via what she called her "Year of Yes." Rhimes is introverted and was inclined to turn down every unexpected invitation that came her way. She decided to about-face and say yes to everything for an entire year. She finished the year with a deep understanding of what she wanted to focus on.

there? I propose instead that you don't commit to anything in the future, but just look at the options available now, and choose those that will give you the most promising range of options afterward.

What Ibarra calls the "plan-and-implement" model—the idea that we should first make a long-term plan and execute without deviation, as opposed to the "test-and-learn" model—is entrenched in depictions of geniuses. Popular lore holds that the sculptor Michelangelo would see a full figure in a block of marble before he ever touched it, and simply chip away the excess stone to free the figure inside. It is an exquisitely beautiful image. It just isn't true. Art historian William Wallace showed that Michelangelo was actually a test-and-learn all-star. He constantly changed his mind and altered his sculptural plans as he worked. He left three-fifths of his sculptures unfinished, each time moving on to something more promising. The first line of Wallace's analysis: "Michelangelo did not expound a theory of art." He tried, then went from there. He was a sculptor, painter, master architect, and made engineering designs for fortifications in Florence. In his late twenties he even pushed visual art aside to spend time writing poems (including one about how much he grew to dislike painting), half of which he left unfinished.

Like anyone eager to raise their match quality prospects, Michelangelo learned who he was—and whom he was carving—in practice, not in theory. He started with an idea, tested it, changed it, and readily abandoned it for a better project fit. Michelangelo might have fit well in Silicon Valley; he was a relentless iterator. He worked according to Ibarra's new aphorism: "I know who I am when I see what I do."

Full disclosure: after researching the Dark Horse Project, I got recruited into it, by virtue of a winding career path of short-term plans. The work resonated with me, partly because of my own experiences, but even more so because it describes a roster of people I admire.

The nonfiction writer and filmmaker Sebastian Junger was twenty-nine and working as an arborist, harnessed in the upper canopy of a pine tree, when he tore open his leg with a chainsaw and got the idea to write about dangerous jobs. He was still limping two months later when a fishing vessel out of Gloucester, Massachusetts, where he lived, was lost at sea. Commercial fishing provided his topic; the result was *The Perfect Storm*. Junger stuck with the theme of dangerous jobs, and made the Oscar-nominated war documentary *Restrepo*. "That cut was the best thing that ever could have happened to me," he told me. "It gave me this template for seeing my career. Virtually every good thing in my life I can trace back to a misfortune, so my feeling is you don't know what's good and what's bad when things happen. *You do not know.* You have to wait to find out."

My favorite fiction writers might be darker dark horses still. Haruki Murakami wanted to be a musician, "but I couldn't play the instruments very well," he said. He was twenty-nine and running a jazz bar in Tokyo when he went to a spring baseball game and the crack of the bat—"a beautiful, ringing double," Murakami wrote—gave him the revelation that he could write a novel. Why did that thought come to him? "I didn't know then, and I don't know now." He started writing at night. "The sensation of writing felt very fresh." Murakami's fourteen novels (all feature music prominently) have been translated into more than fifty languages.

Fantasy writer Patrick Rothfuss began studying chemical engineering in college, which "led to a revelation that chemical engineering is boring." He then spent *nine years* bouncing between majors "before being kindly asked to graduate already." After that, according to his official bio, "Patrick went to grad school. He'd rather not talk about it." Meanwhile, he was slowly working on a novel. That novel, *The Name of the Wind* (in which chemistry appears repeatedly), sold millions of copies worldwide and is source material for a potential TV successor to *Game of Thrones*.

Hillary Jordan just happened to live downstairs from me in a Brooklyn apartment building, and told me that she worked in advertising for fifteen years before beginning to write fiction. Her first novel, *Mudbound*, won the Bellwether Prize for socially engaged fiction. The film version was purchased by Netflix and in 2018 received four Oscar nominations.

Unlike Jordan, Maryam Mirzakhani actually expected to be a novelist from the start. She was enchanted by bookstores near her school when she was young and dreamed of writing. She had to take math classes, but "I was just not interested in thinking about it," she said later. Eventually she came to see math as exploration. "It is like being lost in a jungle and trying to use all the knowledge that you can gather to come up with some new tricks, and with some luck, you might find a way out." In 2014, she became the first woman to win the Fields Medal, the most famous math prize in the world.

Of the athletes I met when I worked at *Sports Illustrated,* the one I most admired was British Ironman triathlete (and writer and humanitarian) Chrissie Wellington, who sat atop a road bike for the first time in her life at age twenty-seven. She was working on a sewage sanitation project in Nepal when she found that she enjoyed cycling, and could keep up with Sherpas at altitude in the Himalayas. Two years after returning home, she won the first of four Ironman world championships, and then proceeded to go 13–0 at the Ironman distance over a career that started late and spanned just five years. "My passion for the sport hasn't waned," she said when she retired, "but my passion for new experiences and new challenges is what is now burning the most brightly."

I'm a fan of Irish theater, and my favorite performer is Irish actor Ciarán Hinds, more widely known for his HBO roles—Julius Caesar in

Rome and *Game of Thrones*' Mance Rayder, the "King Beyond the Wall"—and as a star of AMC's *The Terror*. (His voice may be best known as head troll Grand Pabbie in Disney's *Frozen*.) This book gave me an excuse to ask Hinds about his career path, and he recalled having been a "flighty gadabout" unsure of his direction when he enrolled as a law student at Queen's University Belfast. His attention was quickly diverted "due to a keen interest in snooker, poker, and experimental dance," he told me. One of Hinds's class tutors had seen him as a twelve-year-old portraying Lady Macbeth in a school play, and suggested he bag legal studies and apply to drama school. "He also had the goodness to speak to my parents on the matter, who were rather trepidatious," Hinds told me. "Off I went to study at the Royal Academy of Dramatic Art, and my life in the professional theater began."

The Van Gogh biography by Steven Naifeh and his late partner and coauthor Gregory White Smith is one of the best books I have ever read in any genre. Naifeh and Smith met in law school as both were realizing it was not for them. They started cowriting books on an eclectic array of topics, from true crime to men's style, even as an editor told them they needed to pick one genre and stick with it. Their willingness to dive into new areas paid unexpected dividends. When an editor at another publishing house asked them to write a guide to using lawyers' services, it led them to found *Best Lawyers,* which spawned a massive industry of peer-recommendation publications. "If we hadn't taken that idea [to create a reference to help people select lawyers] and run with it," Naifeh told me, "our lives would have been dramatically different, and it wasn't like anything we had done before." They might never have had the means and freedom to spend a decade researching their Van Gogh biography, or their biography of Jackson Pollock that won the Pulitzer Prize.

Pollock, Naifeh told me, "was literally one of the least talented draftsmen at the Art Students League." Naifeh argues that, as with Van Gogh, Pollock's lack of traditional drawing skill was what led him to invent his own rules for making art. As schools offering standardized paths in art have proliferated, "one of the problems is that artists tend to be products of those schools," said Naifeh, an artist himself.

Maybe that has helped fuel an explosion of interest in so-called outsider art, by practitioners who began without a standard path in sight. Of course, there is nothing wrong with coming through the formal talent development system, but if that's the only pipeline that exists, some of the brightest talents get missed. "Outsider artists" are the self-taught jazz masters of visual art, and the originality of their work can be stunning. In 2018, the National Gallery of Art featured a full exhibition dedicated to self-taught artists; art history programs at Stanford, Duke, Yale, and the Art Institute of Chicago now offer seminars in outsider art. Katherine Jentleson, who in 2015 was appointed as a full-time curator of self-taught art at the High Museum of Art in Atlanta, told me that these artists typically started just by experimenting and doing things they liked, while working other jobs. "The majority did not begin their art making in earnest until after retirement," Jentleson said.

She introduced me to the sculptor and painter Lonnie Holley, a prominent self-taught artist who grew up extremely poor in Alabama. In 1979, when he was twenty-nine, his sister's two children died in a fire. The family could not afford gravestones, so Holley gathered discarded sandstone at a nearby foundry and carved them himself. "I didn't even know what art was!" he told me, his eyes wide, as if taken by surprise at his own story. But it felt good. He carved gravestones for other families and started making sculptures out of anything he could find. I was standing with him near the door of an Atlanta gallery featuring his work when he grabbed a paper clip and quickly bent it into an intricate silhouette of a face, which he jabbed decoratively into the eraser of a pencil the woman at the front desk was using. It is hard to imagine a time before he made art, since it seems like he can hardly touch something before his hands begin exploring what else it might become.

Jentleson also pointed me to Paradise Garden, ninety miles north-west of Atlanta, the painting- and sculpture-filled property of the late minister Howard Finster, the Frances Hesselbein of modern art. Finster had long compiled bricolage displays on his land, from collections of tools to assortments of fruit-bearing plants. He was fixing a bicycle one day in 1976, when he was fifty-nine, and saw what looked like a face in a splotch of white paint on his thumb. "A warm feelin' come over my body," he recalled. Finster immediately began an oeuvre of tens of thousands of artworks that filled his property, including thousands of paintings in his unique, semi-cartoonish style, often densely packed with animals and figures—Elvis, George Washington, angels—and set fancifully in apocalyptic landscapes. In short order, he was appearing on Johnny Carson's *Tonight Show* and creating album covers for R.E.M. and Talking Heads. Upon entry to the garden, I was greeted by a giant self-portrait of a smirking Finster in a burgundy suit, affixed to a cinderblock wall. At the bottom are the words "I began painting pictures in Jan-1976—without any training. This is my painting. A person don't know what he can do unless he tryes. Trying things is the answer to find your talent."

CHAPTER 8

The Outsider Advantage

ALPH BINGHAM WILL be the first to admit it: he is hyperspecialized, at least in theory. "My PhD isn't even in chemistry, it's in *organic* chemistry!" he exclaimed. "If there's not a carbon in it, I'm technically not qualified, okay?"

In graduate school in the 1970s, Bingham and his classmates had to devise ways to create particular molecules. "This was a bunch of smart guys and women and we could make these molecules," he told me, "but somehow someone's solution was always cleverer than the others. I was paying attention, and I noticed that the most clever solution always came from a piece of knowledge that was *not* a part of the normal curriculum." One day, he was the cleverest.

He had come up with an elegant solution to synthesize a molecule in four short steps, and the key piece of knowledge involved cream of tartar, a baking ingredient Bingham happened to know from childhood. "You could ask twenty chemists right now what cream of tartar is, and a lot of them would have no idea," he said. "I thought about the process that differentiates solutions, and it wasn't part of any curriculum or on anybody's résumé. I realized there was always going to be this somewhat serendipitous outside thinking that was going to make a solution more clever, cost-effective, efficacious, more on the money than anyone else's. And so I went from that idea, how problems are solved, to 'How does one build an organization that solves problems that way?'" Years later, when Bingham became the VP of research and development strategy at Eli Lilly, he had a chance to try to build his clever organization.

In the spring of 2001, Bingham collected twenty-one problems that had stymied Eli Lilly scientists and asked a top executive if he could post them on a website for anyone to see. The executive would only consider it if the consulting firm McKinsey thought it was a good idea. "McKinsey's opinion," Bingham recalled, "was, 'Who knows? Why don't you launch it and tell us the answer.'" Bingham did, but when the scientists who contributed problems saw them online, "every one of them wrote to the chief scientific officer saying that the problem cannot be released, it's too confidential, 'Why the hell do you think anyone other than us can solve that problem?'" They had a point. If the most highly educated, highly specialized, well-resourced chemists in the world were stuck on technical problems, why would anyone else be able to help? The chief scientific officer (CSO) had every single problem removed from the site.

Bingham lobbied. It was at least worth a try on problems that would definitely not give away a trade secret, and if it didn't work, no harm done. The CSO bought his argument. The site relaunched, and by the fall answers started rolling in. It happened to be the middle of the U.S. anthrax scare, so, Bingham told me, he was the rare mail recipient who was excited to be getting sent white powders. "I'm popping them in a spectrometer," he said, "and going, 'Woohoo, we got another one!'" Strangers were creating substances that had befuddled Eli Lilly chemists. As Bingham had guessed, outside knowledge was the key. "It validated the hypothesis we had going in, but it still surprised me how these knowledge pockets were hidden under other degrees. I wasn't really expecting submissions from attorneys."

One molecular synthesis solution came from a lawyer whose relevant knowledge came from working on chemical patents. The man wrote, "I was thinking of tear gas," when he came up with the solution. It was his version of Bingham's cream of tartar. "Tear gas didn't have anything to do with the problem," Bingham said. "But he saw parallels to the chemical structure of a molecule that we needed."

Bingham had noticed that established companies tended to approach problems with so-called local search, that is, using specialists from a single domain, and trying solutions that worked before. Meanwhile, his invitation to outsiders worked so well that it was spun off as an entirely separate company. Named InnoCentive, it facilitates entities in any field acting as "seekers," paying to post "challenges" and rewards for outside "solvers." A little more than one-third of challenges were completely solved, a remarkable portion given that InnoCentive selected for problems that had stumped the specialists who posted them. Along the way, InnoCentive realized it could help seekers tailor their posts to make a solution more likely. The trick: to frame the challenge so that it attracted a diverse array of solvers. The more likely a challenge was to appeal not just to scientists but also to attorneys and dentists and mechanics, the more likely it was to be solved.

Bingham calls it "outside-in" thinking: finding solutions in experiences far outside of focused training for the problem itself. History is littered with world-changing examples.

Napoleon once fretted that his armies could only carry a few days' worth of provisions. "Hunger is more savage than the sword," a fourth-century Roman military chronicler wrote. The French emperor was a science and technology booster, so in 1795 he offered a reward for research on food preservation. A raft of the world's most formidable minds had been working on the problem for more than a century, including Irish scientist Robert Boyle, the "father of modern chemistry." Where great minds of science failed, Parisian foodie and confectioner Nicolas Appert prevailed.

Appert was a "jack of all trades," according to the Can Manufacturers Institute. He had traversed the gustatory universe as a candy maker, vintner, chef, brewer, pickle maker, and more. His exceptionally wide-ranging culinary wanderings gave him an advantage over scientists who focused on the science of preservation. "Having spent my days in the pantries, the breweries, store-houses, and cellars of Champagne, as well as in the shops, manufactories, and warehouses of confectioners, distillers, and grocers," he wrote in the aptly titled *Art of Preserving All Kinds of Animal and Vegetable Substances for Several Years,* "I have been able to avail myself, in my process, of a number of advantages, which the greater number of those persons have not possessed, who have devoted themselves to the art of preserving provisions." He placed food inside of thick champagne bottles, which he sealed to make airtight and then placed in boiling water for hours. Appert's innovation begat canned food. He preserved a whole sheep in a crock just to show it off. His solution preserved nutrients so well that scurvy, the vitamin C deficiency known as "the sailor's nightmare," went from deadly curse to avoidable nuisance. The main scientific epiphany—heat kills microbes—was still sixty years from being discovered by Louis Pasteur. Appert's method revolutionized public health, and, unfortunately for Napoleon, crossed the English Channel. In 1815, it fed the English troops at Waterloo.

Alph Bingham's critics were aware that clever outsiders and dilettantes had made technical breakthroughs in the past, but they assumed it was purely that, an artifact of the past that would not translate into the era of hyperspecialization. *Help us, an international pharmaceutical giant, conceive and create a molecule that we will use as a stepping-stone to synthesize some other molecule so obscure that we don't mind sharing this information publicly, because we're stuck and nobody outside our walls will have any idea where we're going with this anyway.* Even Bingham's expectations proved too humble when it came to the contributions of outside-in solvers to problems that stumped specialists.

"When a problem NASA worked on for thirty years gets solved," he told me, "I'm definitely still surprised."

Specifically, NASA was unable to predict solar particle storms, radioactive material spewed by the sun that can gravely damage astronauts and the equipment they depend on. Solar physicists were understandably skeptical that outsiders could help, but after three decades of being stuck, there was nothing to lose; NASA posted through InnoCentive in 2009. Within six months, Bruce Cragin, an engineer retired from Sprint Nextel and living in rural New Hampshire, solved the challenge using radio waves picked up by telescopes. Pre-retirement, Cragin had collaborated with scientists, and found that those specialist teams often got mired in working out small details at the expense of practical solutions. "I think it helped me being out of that," he said, "having moved on." A NASA official noted, diplomatically, that "there was some resistance" to Cragin's solution at first, "because it was using a different methodology."

That was exactly the point. Still, Appert and Cragin had some tangentially relevant work experience. Other outside-in solvers thrive because they have none at all.

In 1989, the *Exxon Valdez* oil tanker famously hit a reef and leaked its payload into the Prince William Sound. It was a monumental environmental and commercial fishing disaster. When oil mixes with water, spill workers refer to the resulting goop as "chocolate mousse." Throw in low temperature and spill responders are working with material that has the viscosity of peanut butter. It is devilishly difficult to remove.

Almost twenty years after the *Exxon Valdez* spill, thirty-two thousand gallons of oil remained stubbornly stuck along Alaska's coast. One of the most intractable challenges for oil spill remediation was pumping oil out of recovery barges after it was skimmed from the water. In 2007, Scott Pegau, research program manager at the Alaska-based Oil Spill Recovery Institute, figured he might as well try InnoCentive. He offered a $20,000 reward for a solution to getting cold chocolate mousse out of recovery barges.

Ideas rolled in. Most were too expensive to be practical. And then there was the solution from John Davis, so cheap and simple it made Pegau chuckle. "Everyone kind of looked at it," Pegau told me, "and just said, 'Yep, this should work.'"

Davis, an Illinois-based chemist, had been pondering the oil spill challenge while waiting for flights during work travel. Naturally, he started with chemistry solutions, but made an about-face. "You're already dealing with a chemical pollutant more or less," Davis told me, "so you want to do as little chemistry as possible" in order to avoid adding more pollutants. He abandoned his specialty and turned to a distant analogy. "I visualized the problem as drinking a slushy," he said. "You end up having to whip around the straw to stir it up. How could you make it so you don't have to work so hard to get that slushy out?"

The slushy question in turn reminded Davis of a brief experience in construction. Years earlier, he was enlisted for a day to help build a long flight of concrete steps that ran down from a friend's house to an adjacent lake. "They just needed an extra person to carry the pails or do whatever, grunt work," he told me. "I'm not a super-strong guy, so I wasn't really awesome at that, I'll be honest."

Concrete was unloaded at the top of the hill and sent sluicing down a chute when it was needed at the bottom. Davis was standing at the top, concerned about a massive mound of concrete that was already hardening while it baked in the sun. He alerted his friend's brother. "Watch this," the brother told him. He grabbed a rod attached to a motor and touched it to the mound of concrete. "It fluidized instantly, just like *whoooosh*," Davis recalled. The rod was a concrete vibrator, which is just what it sounds like, a shaking piece of metal that keeps the components of concrete from sticking together. "When it came to my mind it was a eureka moment," Davis told me.

He called a company that sold concrete vibrators to learn a few details, and then made a diagram of how the vibrators could easily attach to a barge and do to "chocolate mousse" what they already do with concrete. Counting diagrams, the solution was a total of three pages.

"Sometimes you just slap your head and go, 'Well why didn't I think of that?' If it was easily solved by people within the industry, it would have been solved by people within the industry," Pegau said. "I think it happens more often than we'd love to admit, because we tend to view things with all the information we've gathered in our industry, and sometimes that puts us down a path that goes into a wall. It's hard to back up and find another path." Pegau was basically describing the Einstellung effect, a psychology term for the tendency of problem solvers to employ only familiar methods even if better ones are available. Davis subsequently earned another cash award in a challenge that sought help with a hair removal product; a memory of rolling chewing gum on his leg as a kid led him to a solution.

When I asked Davis if he was prone to framing problems with distant analogies from random experiences outside his field, he had to ponder it for a moment. Does he do that in his daily chemistry problems, I asked? "You know, I don't, not really," he said. "It's these other puzzles or problems where you have to think outside the box."

InnoCentive works in part because, as specialists become more narrowly focused, "the box" is more like Russian nesting dolls. Specialists divide into subspecialties, which soon divide into sub-subspecialties. Even if they get outside the small doll, they may get stuck inside the next, slightly larger one. Cragin and Davis were outside the box to begin with, and saw straightforward solutions that eluded insiders with seemingly every training and resource advantage. Solvers themselves were often bewildered when they overcame a challenge that stumped entire companies or industries.

"It took me three evenings to write it up," an outside solver told the journal *Science* after he answered Johnson & Johnson's request for help with a production problem in the manufacture of tuberculosis medication. "I think it's strange that a major pharma company cannot solve this kind of problem." Karim Lakhani, codirector of the Laboratory for Innovation Science at Harvard, had InnoCentive solvers rate problems on how relevant they were to their own field of specialization, and found that "the further the problem was from the solver's expertise, the more likely they were to solve it."

As organizational boxes get smaller and smaller, and as outsiders are more easily engaged online, "exploration [of new solutions] now increasingly resides outside the boundaries of the traditional firm," Lakhani and colleagues wrote. Our intuition might be that only hyperspecialized experts can drive modern innovation, but increasing specialization actually creates new opportunities for outsiders.

As Alph Bingham noticed, for difficult challenges organizations tend toward local search. They rely on specialists in a single knowledge domain, and methods that have worked before. (Think about the lab with only *E. coli* specialists from chapter 5.) If those fail, they're stuck. For the most intractable problems, "our research shows that a domain-based solution is often inferior," according to Lakhani. "Big innovation most often happens when an outsider who may be far away from the surface of the problem reframes the problem in a way that unlocks the solution."

Since InnoCentive demonstrated the concept, other organizations have arisen to capitalize on outside-in solvers in normally highly specialized fields. Kaggle is like InnoCentive but specifically for posting challenges in the area of machine learning—artificial intelligence designed to teach itself without human intervention.

Shubin Dai, who lives in Changsha, China, was the top-ranked Kaggle solver in the world as of this writing, out of more than forty thousand contributors. His day job is leading a team that processes data for banks, but Kaggle competitions gave him an opportunity to dabble in machine learning. His favorite problems involve human health or nature conservation, like a competition in which he won $30,000 by wielding satellite imagery to distinguish human-caused from natural forest loss in the Amazon. Dai was asked, for a Kaggle blog post, how important domain expertise is for winning competitions. "To be frank, I don't think we can benefit from domain expertise too much. . . . It's very hard to win a competition just by using [well-known] methods," he replied. "We need more creative solutions."

"The people who win a Kaggle health competition have no medical training, no biology training, and they're also often not real machine learning experts," Pedro Domingos, a computer science professor and machine learning researcher, told me. "Knowledge is a double-edged sword. It allows you to do some things, but it also makes you blind to other things that you could do."

Don Swanson saw it coming—the opportunities for people like Bruce Cragin and John Davis, outsiders who merge strands of disparate knowledge. Swanson earned a physics PhD in 1952, and then worked as an industry computer systems analyst, where he became fascinated with organizing information. In 1963, the University of Chicago took a chance on him as dean of the Graduate Library School. As a thirty-eight-year-old from private industry, he was an oddball. The hiring announcement declared, "Swanson is the first physical scientist to head a professional library school in this country."

Swanson became concerned about increasing specialization, that it would lead to publications that catered only to a very small group of specialists and inhibit creativity. "The disparity between the total quantity of recorded knowledge . . . and the limited human capacity to assimilate it, is not only enormous now but grows unremittingly," he once said. How can frontiers be pushed, Swanson wondered, if one day it will take a lifetime just to reach them in each specialized domain? In 1960, the U.S. National Library of Medicine used about one hundred unique pairs of terms to index articles. By 2010, it was nearing one hundred thousand. Swanson felt that if this big bang of public knowledge continued apace, subspecialties would be like galaxies, flying away from one another until each is invisible to every other. Given that he knew interdisciplinary problem solving was important, that was a conundrum.

In crisis, Swanson saw opportunity. He realized he could make discoveries by connecting information from scientific articles in subspecialty domains that never cited one another and that had no scientists who worked together. For example, by systematically cross-referencing databases of literature from different disciplines, he uncovered "eleven neglected connections" between magnesium deficiency and migraine research, and proposed that they be tested. All of the information he found was in the public domain; it had just never been connected. "Undiscovered public knowledge," Swanson called it. In 2012, the American Headache Society and the American Academy of Neurology reviewed all the research on migraine prevention and concluded that magnesium should be considered as a common treatment. The evidence for magnesium was as strong as the evidence for the most common remedies, like ibuprofen.

Swanson wanted to show that areas of specialist literature that never normally overlapped were rife with hidden interdisciplinary treasures waiting to be connected. He created a computer system, Arrowsmith, that helped other users do what he did—devise searches that might turn up distant but relevant sets of scientific articles, and ignited a field of information science that grapples with connecting diverse areas of knowledge, as specialties that can inform one another drift apart.

Swanson passed away in 2012, so I contacted his daughter, political philosophy professor Judy Swanson, to see if she had ever discussed with him his concerns about specialization. When I reached her, she was at a conference, "as it happens, one related to overspecialization in the social sciences," she told me. From the outside, Judy Swanson looks pretty specialized. Her faculty web page listed forty-four of her articles and books, every single one of which had "Aristotle" in the title. So I asked how she felt about her own specialization, and she seemed surprised. She did not consider herself specialized compared to her peers, she told me, partly because she spends time teaching undergraduates, which requires more than Aristotle. "There is this feeling of frustration," she told me, "that I should be doing something more specialized." Academic departments no longer merely fracture naturally into subspecialties, they elevate narrowness as an ideal.

That is counterproductive. As Karim Lakhani put it after his Inno-Centive research, a key to creative problem solving is tapping outsiders who use different approaches "so that the 'home field' for the problem does not end up constraining the solution." Sometimes, the home field can be so constrained that a curious outsider is truly the only one who can see the solution.

The email subject line caught my eye: "Olympic medalist and muscular dystrophy patient with the same mutation."

I had just written a book on genetics and athleticism, and figured it would point to some journal article I had missed. Instead, it was a note from the muscular dystrophy patient herself, Jill Viles, a thirty-nine-year-old woman in Iowa. She had an elaborate theory connecting the gene mutation that withered her muscles to those of an Olympic sprinter, and she offered to send more info.

I expected a letter, maybe some news clippings. I got a stack of original family photos, a detailed medical history, and a nineteen-page, bound and illustrated packet that referenced gene mutations by their specific DNA locations. She had done some serious homework.

On page 14 there was a photo of Jill in a blue bikini, blonde hair tousled, smiling and sitting in the sand. Her torso looks normal, but her arms are strikingly skinny, like twigs jabbed into a snowman. Her legs did not look like they could possibly hold her, the thigh no wider than her knee joint.

Beside that photo was one of Priscilla Lopes-Schliep, one of the best sprinters in Canadian history. At the 2008 Olympics in Beijing, she won a bronze medal in the 100-meter hurdles. The juxtaposition was breathtaking. Priscilla is midstride, ropes of muscle winding down her legs, veins bursting from her forearms. She's like the vision of a superhero a second grader might draw. I could hardly have imagined two women who looked less likely to share a biological blueprint.

In online pictures of Priscilla, Jill recognized something in her own, vastly scrawnier physique—a familiar pattern of missing fat on her limbs. Her theory was that she and Priscilla have the same mutated gene, but because Priscilla doesn't have muscular dystrophy, her body had found some way "to go around it," as Jill put it, and was instead making gigantic muscles. If her theory was right, Jill hoped, scientists would want to study her and Priscilla to figure out how to help people with muscles like Jill have muscles a little more toward the Priscilla end of the human physique spectrum. She wanted my help convincing Priscilla to get a genetic test.

The idea that a part-time substitute teacher, wielding the cutting-edge medical instrument known as Google Images, would make a discovery about a pro athlete who is examined by doctors as part of her job struck me as somewhere between extremely unlikely and patently nuts. I consulted a Harvard geneticist. He was concerned. "Empowering a relationship between these two women could end badly," he told me. "People go off the deep end when they are relating to celebrities they think they have a connection to."

I hadn't even considered that before; I certainly didn't want to facilitate a stalker. It took time for Jill to convince me that because of her unique life experience, she could see what no specialist could.

———

When Jill was four, a preschool teacher noticed her stumbling. Jill told her mother she was afraid of "witches' fingers" that were grabbing her shins and tripping her. Her pediatrician sent the family to the Mayo Clinic.

Blood tests showed that Jill, her father, and her brother had higher than normal levels of creatine kinase, an enzyme that spills from damaged muscles. Doctors thought some sort of muscular dystrophy might run in the family, but it didn't normally show up that way in little girls, and Jill's brother and father seemed fine.

"They said our family was extremely unique," Jill told me. "That's good in one way because they're being honest. But on the other hand, it was terrifying."

Jill returned to Mayo every summer, and it was always the same. She had stopped falling, but by the time she was eight the fat on her limbs was vanishing. Other kids could wrap their fingers around her arm, and when veins started protruding from her legs, they asked her how it felt to be old. Jill's mother was so worried about her daughter's social life that she clandestinely paid another girl to hang out with her. At twelve, she began struggling to hold her body upright on her bicycle, and had to cling to the railing at a roller skating rink.

Jill began to hunt for answers, kid style. She checked out library books on poltergeists. "It really freaked out my dad," she told me. "He was like, 'Well, are you into the occult, or what?' It was nothing of the sort." She just could not explain what was happening to her, so when she read stories of people with inexplicable afflictions, "Ya know, I believed them."

By the time she left for college, Jill was five foot three and eighty-seven pounds. She hit the library, poring over any scientific journal she could find on muscle disease.

She came upon a paper in *Muscle and Nerve,* on a rare type of muscular dystrophy called Emery-Dreifuss, and was startled by an accompanying photo. *That's my dad's arm,* she thought.

Her dad was thin but his forearm muscles were unusually well defined. Jill called it "Popeye arm" when she was little. Another paper describing Emery-Dreifuss patients actually referred to a Popeye arm deformity. The *Muscle and Nerve* paper reported that Emery-Dreifuss patients have "contractures" that affect joint mobility.

"I'm getting chills reading this," Jill recalled. She described her own contractures as just like a Barbie doll: arms always bent, neck stiff, feet perma-slanted for high heels. The research indicated that Emery-Dreifuss only occurred in males, but Jill was certain she had it, and she was afraid. It comes with heart problems.

She stuffed her bag with articles to bring home over college break. One day, she found her father flipping through them. He had all the symptoms, he told her. "Well, yeah, I know . . . the arm, and the neck," Jill replied. No, he said: the cardiac symptoms.

For years Jill's father had been told that his irregular heart rhythms were due to a virus. "It's not," Jill told him instantly. "We have Emery-Dreifuss." She took her forty-five-year-old father to the Iowa Heart Center and insisted that a cardiologist see him. Nurses demanded a referral, but Jill was so persistent that they relented. The cardiologist put a monitor on her dad that tracked his heart's electrical activity for a day, during which his pulse dropped into the twenties. He was either ready to win the Tour de France or about to drop dead. He was rushed into emergency surgery for a pacemaker. "She saved her dad's life," Jill's mother, Mary, told me.

Still, the Iowa Heart Center could not confirm the family condition. In her reading, Jill came across an Italian research group searching for families with Emery-Dreifuss. They were hoping to locate a gene mutation that caused it.

Nineteen-year-old Jill put on her most imposing navy pantsuit, took her papers to a neurologist in Des Moines, and asked to be connected to the Italian study. "No, you don't have that," she recalled the neurologist saying sternly. She refused even to look at the papers. In fairness, Jill was a teenager self-diagnosing an extremely rare disease known to occur only in men. So in 1995 she wrote to the Italians, and included a picture of herself.

The response she got from the Istituto di Genetica Biochimica ed Evoluzionistica was clearly meant for a scientist. Please send DNA from the entire family, it read. "If you cannot prepare DNA, just send fresh blood." Jill convinced a nurse friend to smuggle needles and test tubes to her house. Fortunately, Italy accepted blood by normal mail.

It would be years before Jill heard from the Italians again, but she had made up her mind. On her annual trip to the Mayo Clinic, against her mother's protestations she took her own pen and wrote "Emery-Dreifuss" on her medical chart.

In 1999, she got an email from Italy. She let the moment sink in, and then clicked. She had a mutation on a gene known as *LMNA,* or the lamin gene, colloquially. Her father did too. So did two brothers and a sister. So did four other families in the study with Emery-Dreifuss. Jill had been right.

The lamin gene carries a recipe for constructing a tangle of proteins at the center of every cell that influences how other genes are switched on or off, like lights, changing how the body builds fat and muscle. Somewhere along the three billion Gs, Ts, As, and Cs in Jill's genome, a single-letter typo just happened to be very poorly placed.

Jill was happy to have helped discover a new disease-causing mutation. And yet "it's almost darkly comical," she told me. "It comes down to a G that was changed to a C."

Jill's father was sixty-three, in 2012, when his heart finally failed.

By then, Jill had transitioned to a motorized scooter, gotten married and had a son, and retired from her medical detective work.

Days after their father passed, her younger sister showed her a picture online of an extremely muscular Olympic sprinter who was conspicuously missing fat. "I took one look at it, and just . . . what?! We don't have that. What are you talking about?" Jill said. Then she got curious.

Jill had actually wondered about fat for a long time. Like muscle, it was noticeably absent from her limbs. More than a decade earlier, when she was twenty-five, a lab director at Johns Hopkins heard about her and, wanting a real-life lamin mutant in the lab, offered her a summer internship perusing journals for any condition caused by a lamin mutation. She came across an incredibly rare disease called partial lipodystrophy, which causes fat on the limbs to disappear, leaving veins and muscles shrink-wrapped in skin. Again, Jill saw her family. Could she have not one, but two ridiculously rare genetic diseases? She pestered doctors at a medical conference with photos. They assured her she did not have lipodystrophy, and diagnosed her with something more common: intern syndrome. "Where you have a medical student introduced to a lot of new diseases," Jill said, "and they keep thinking they have what they're reading about."

It all came flooding back when she Googled images of Priscilla. Not just competition photos, but pictures of her at home, holding her baby daughter. There were the protruding veins, the familiar fall of a shirtsleeve over fatless arms, the visible division between muscles in the hips and butt. "I knew we were cut from the same cloth," Jill said. "A very rare cloth."

It was Jill's third visual lock. First was her own family's Emery-Dreifuss, then when she thought they also had lipodystrophy, and now she saw in Priscilla the same pattern of missing fat. But if they shared a fat condition, how did Priscilla get a double helping of muscle while she got almost none? "This is my kryptonite, but this is her rocket fuel," Jill thought. "We're like comic book superheroes that are just as divergent as can be. I mean, her body has found a way around [muscle loss] somehow." For a year, she pondered how to ask Priscilla to get a genetic test without showing up at a track meet and chasing her in a motorized scooter.

Jill happened to be near her television when I was talking about athletes and genetics on a morning program. "I thought, 'Oh, this is divine providence,'" she told me. She sent the packet, and asked if I would reach out to Priscilla. Priscilla's agent, Kris Mychasiw, and I happened to follow one another on Twitter, so I messaged him. He humored me as I tried to explain the very unlikely idea that these two women were some kind of biological opposites, but also that I was very impressed with Jill's effort. He passed the message to Priscilla.

"He was just like, 'This lady in Iowa. She says she has the same gene as you, and wants to have a conversation,'" Priscilla recalled. "I was kind of like, 'Um, I don't know, Kris.'" He told her just to take my call.

Thanks to her physique, media in Europe openly accused Priscilla of steroid use. Someone posted a picture of her online, straining to the Olympic finish, with a male bodybuilder's head pasted on her body. "That was pretty messed up," Priscilla told me. At the 2009 World Championships in Berlin, she was drug tested minutes before winning the silver medal, even though drug testing was technically not allowed that close to a race. When I called, she was eager to share photos, to show that she was already unusually lean and veiny in high school. One photo showed women in her family flexing. An elderly relative is showing off rippling biceps, a thick cord of vein snaking across her elbow. After our conversation, Priscilla agreed to speak with Jill.

They bonded easily on the phone—over how they'd been teased about their veins as kids—and Priscilla agreed to meet Jill and her mom in a hotel lobby in Toronto. When Priscilla arrived, "Oh my gosh," Jill thought, "it's like seeing family." They retreated to a hotel hallway to compare body parts, vastly different in size but with the same topography exposed by a lack of fat. "There is something real here," Priscilla recalled thinking. "Let's research. Let's find out."

It took a year to find a doctor willing to analyze Priscilla's lamin gene. Finally, Jill went to a medical conference and approached the foremost expert in lipodystrophy, Dr. Abhimanyu Garg, of the University of Texas Southwestern Medical Center. He agreed to do the test, and a lipodystrophy evaluation.

Jill was right again. Not only do she and Priscilla both have lipodystrophy, but they have the exact same rare subcategory of partial lipodystrophy, known as Dunnigan type.

Priscilla's and Jill's typos are neighbors on the same gene. That splinter of distance in location seems to make an extraordinary difference, taking muscle and fat from Jill, but taking only fat from Priscilla while piling on muscle.

Dr. Garg called Priscilla immediately, and caught her at the mall with her kids. "I was just dreaming about getting a juicy burger and fries," Priscilla told me. She asked if she could call him back after lunch. He said that she could not. "He's like, 'You're only allowed to have salad. You're on track for a [pancreatitis] attack.' I was like, 'Say what?'"

Despite an Olympian's training regimen, due to her unmonitored lipodystrophy Priscilla had three times the normal level of fat in her blood. "That was a severe problem," Garg told me. Priscilla had to overhaul her diet immediately, and started medication.

Jill had prolonged her dad's life, and now—wielding Google Images—spurred a life-altering medical intervention for a professional athlete. "You pretty much saved me from having to go to the hospital!" Priscilla told Jill when she called her.

Even Garg was startled by what Jill had done. They were the most extreme cases of muscle development he had ever seen in lipodystrophy patients—on opposite ends of the spectrum, of course. Jill and Priscilla would never have ended up in the same doctor's office under normal circumstances. "I can understand a patient can learn more about their disease," Garg told me. "But to reach out to someone else, and figure out their problem also. It is a remarkable feat."

Jill did not stop there. She came across the work of a French biologist, Etienne Lefai, a hyperspecialist who studies a protein called SREBP1, which helps cells determine whether to use fat from a meal right away or store it for fuel later. Lefai showed that when the protein builds up in animals, it can cause either extreme muscle atrophy or extreme muscle growth. Jill contacted him out of the blue and suggested that he may have uncovered the actual biological mechanism that makes her and Priscilla so different, SREBP1 interacting with lamin.

"Okay, that triggers a kind of reflection from my side saying, 'That's a really good question. That's a really, *really* good question!'" Lefai told me in a thick French accent. He has begun investigating whether a lamin gene mutation can alter the regulation of SREBP1, and in turn cause a simultaneous loss of muscle and fat. "I had no idea of what I can do with genetic diseases before she contacted me," he said. "Now, I have changed the path of my team."

The more information specialists create, the more opportunity exists for curious dilettantes to contribute by merging strands of widely available but disparate information—undiscovered public knowledge, as Don Swanson called it. The larger and more easily accessible the library of human knowledge, the more chances for inquisitive patrons to make connections at the cutting edge. An operation like InnoCentive, which at first blush seems totally counterintuitive, should become even more fruitful as specialization accelerates.

It isn't just the increase in new knowledge that generates opportunities for nonspecialists, though. In a race to the forefront, a lot of useful knowledge is simply left behind to molder. That presents another kind of opportunity for those who want to create and invent but who cannot or simply do not want to work at the cutting edge. They can push forward by looking back; they can excavate old knowledge but wield it in a new way.

CHAPTER 9

Lateral Thinking with Withered Technology

DURING TWO CENTURIES of closed-borders isolation, Japan banned *hanafuda*—"flower cards," so called because the twelve different suits are represented by flowers. The playing cards were associated with gambling and unwanted Western cultural influence. By the late nineteenth century, Japan was reintroducing itself to the world, and the ban was finally lifted. So it was in the fall of 1889 that a young man opened a tiny wooden shop in Kyoto and hung a sign in the window: "Nintendo."

The precise meaning of the Japanese characters is lost to history. They may have meant "leave luck to heaven," but were more likely a poetic way to say "the company that is allowed to sell *hanafuda*." By 1950, there were a hundred workers, and the founder's twenty-two-year-old great-grandson took over. But trouble was coming. As the 1964 Tokyo Olympics approached, Japanese adults were turning to pachinko for gambling, and a bowling craze swallowed entertainment dollars. In a desperate attempt to diversify a company that had survived on *hanafuda* for three-quarters of a century, the young president began scattershot investing. Food would never go out of fashion, so he shifted the company to instant rice and meals branded with cartoon characters. (Popeye noodle soup, anyone?) Then there was the failed taxi fleet venture, and the failed rent-by-the-hour "love hotels," which landed the president in the gossip pages. Nintendo sunk into debt. The president resolved to hire top young university graduates to help him innovate.

That was a nonstarter. Nintendo was a small operation in Kyoto; coveted Japanese students wanted big Tokyo companies. On the bright side, there was still the playing card business, which had become more cost-effective with machine-made cards. In 1965, the president settled for hiring a young local electronics graduate named Gunpei Yokoi, who had struggled through his degree and applied to major electronics manufacturers but gotten no offers. "What will you do at Nintendo?" Yokoi's classmates asked him. He wasn't worried. "I didn't want to leave Kyoto anyway," he said later. "I never had a specific dream for my work, and it was just fine."* His job was to service the card-making machines. There were only a few, so Yokoi was the entire maintenance department.

He had long been an enthusiastic hobbyist: piano, ballroom dancing, choir, skin diving, model trains, working on cars, and most of all *monozukuri*—literally, "thing making." He was a tinkerer. Before car stereos, he connected a tape recorder to his car radio so he could replay content later on. In his first few months at Nintendo, there was so little to do that he spent his time playing with company equipment. One day, he cut crisscrossing pieces of wood and fashioned a simple extendable arm, like the jack-in-the-box kind he had seen in cartoons when a robot's belly opens up and a boxing glove fires out. He stuck a gripping tool on the outer end that closed when he squeezed handles to extend the arm. Now he could lazily retrieve distant objects.

---

* Yokoi's ideas and quotes are from his own writings and interviews, including his coauthored book 横井軍平ゲーム館 (Yokoi Gunpei Gēmu-kan), which translates to *Gunpei Yokoi Game House*. Yokoi's works do not appear in English, so portions were translated for use here.

The company president saw the new hire goofing around with his contraption and called him into his office. "I thought I would be scolded," Yokoi recalled. Instead, the desperate executive told Yokoi to turn his device into a game. Yokoi added a group of colored balls that could be grabbed, and the "Ultra Hand" went to market immediately. It was Nintendo's first toy, and it sold 1.2 million units. The company paid off a chunk of its debt. That was the end of Yokoi's maintenance career. The president assigned him to start Nintendo's first research and development department. The facility that briefly made instant rice was converted into a toy factory.

More toy success followed, but it was an abject failure that first year that profoundly influenced Yokoi. He helped create Drive Game, a tabletop unit where a player used a steering wheel to guide a plastic car along a racetrack, which scrolled beneath the car via electric motor. It was the first Nintendo toy that required electricity, and a complete flop. The internal mechanism was advanced for the time and ended up so complex and fragile that it was expensive and hard to produce, and units were riddled with defects. But the debacle was the seed of a creative philosophy Yokoi would hone for the next thirty years.

Yokoi was well aware of his engineering limitations. As one aficionado of game history put it, "He studied electronics at a time where the technology was evolving faster than the snow melts in sunlight." Yokoi had no desire (or capability) to compete with electronics companies that were racing one another to invent some entirely new sliver of dazzling technology. Nor could Nintendo compete with Japan's titans of traditional toys—Bandai, Epoch, and Takara—on their familiar turf. With that, and Drive Game, in mind, Yokoi embarked on an approach he called "lateral thinking with withered technology." Lateral thinking is a term coined in the 1960s for the reimagining of information in new contexts, including the drawing together of seemingly disparate concepts or domains that can give old ideas new uses. By "withered technology," Yokoi meant tech that was old enough to be extremely well understood and easily available, so it didn't require a specialist's knowledge. The heart of his philosophy was putting cheap, simple technology to use in ways no one else considered. If he could not think more deeply about new technologies, he decided, he would think more broadly about old ones. He intentionally retreated from the cutting edge, and set to *monozukuri*.

He connected a transistor to a cheap, store-bought galvanometer, and noticed he could measure the current flowing through his coworkers. Yokoi imagined a toy that would make it fun for boys and girls to hold hands, risqué at the time in Japan.* The Love Tester was nothing more than two conductive handles and a gauge. Players grasped a handle and joined hands, thereby completing the circuit. The gauge reported electrical current as if it were a measure of the love between participants. The sweatier their palms, the better a couple's conductance. It was a hit among teenagers, and a party prop for adults. Yokoi was encouraged. He committed to using technology that had already become cheap, even obsolete, in new ways.

By the early 1970s, radio-controlled toy cars were popular, but good RC technology could cost a month's salary, so it was a hobby reserved for adults. As he often did, Yokoi pondered a way to democratize RC toys. So he took the tech backward. Expense came from the need for multiple radio control channels. Cars started with two channels, one to control the engine output and one the steering wheel. The more functions a toy had, the more channels it required. Yokoi stripped the technology down to the absolute bare minimum, a single-channel RC car that could only turn left. Product name: Lefty RX. It was less than a tenth the cost of typical RC toys, and just fine for counterclockwise races. Even when it did have to navigate obstacles, kids easily learned how to left-turn their way out of trouble.

One day in 1977, while riding the bullet train back from a business

---

* Twister was a failure in Japan in the late 1960s due to a mismatch with prevailing social norms. It earned the nickname "the eroticism box."

trip in Tokyo, Yokoi awoke from a nap to see a salaryman playing with a calculator to relieve the boredom of his commute. The trend at the time was to make toys as impressively big as possible. What if, Yokoi wondered, there was a game small enough that an adult could play it discreetly while commuting? He sat on the idea for a while, until one day when he was drafted to be the company president's chauffeur. The normal driver had the flu, and thanks to Yokoi's interest in foreign vehicles, he was the only one of Nintendo's hundred employees who had driven a car with the steering wheel on the left, like the president's Cadillac. He floated his miniature game idea from the front seat. "He was nodding along," Yokoi recalled, "but he didn't seem all that interested."

A week later, Yokoi received a surprise visit from executives at Sharp, a calculator manufacturer. At the meeting Yokoi had driven him to, the Nintendo president sat next to the head of Sharp, and relayed his chauffeur's idea. For several years, Sharp had been engaged in calculator wars with Casio. In the early 1970s a calculator cost a few hundred dollars, but as components got cheaper and companies raced for market share, cost plummeted and the market saturated. Sharp was eager to find a new use for its LCD screens.

When Sharp executives heard Yokoi's idea for a video game the size of a business card holder, and that could be held in the lap and played with thumbs, they were intrigued, and skeptical. Was it worth mobilizing a new partnership just to reuse technology that had become dirt cheap? They weren't convinced it was even possible to make a display smooth enough for the game Yokoi proposed, which involved a juggler whose arms move left and right, trying not to drop balls as they speed up. Nonetheless, the Sharp engineers made Yokoi an LCD screen in the appropriate size. Then he hit a severe problem. The electronics in the tiny game were packed in such a thin space that the liquid crystal display element touched a plate in the screen, which created a visual distortion of light and dark bands, known as Newton's rings. Yokoi needed a sliver of space between the LCD and the plate. He took an idea from the credit card industry. With a slight tweak of the old *hanafuda* printing machines, he delicately embossed the screen with hundreds of dots to keep the plate and the display element narrowly separated. As a final flourish, with just a few hours of work, a colleague helped him program a clock into the display. LCD screens were already in wristwatches, and they figured it would give adults an excuse to buy their "Game & Watch."

In 1980, Nintendo released its first three Game & Watch models, with high hopes for one hundred thousand sales. Six hundred thousand copies sold in the first year. Nintendo could not keep up with international demand. The Donkey Kong Game & Watch was released in 1982 and alone sold eight million units. Game & Watch remained in production for eleven years and sold 43.4 million units. It also happened to include another Yokoi invention that would be used laterally: the directional pad, or "D-pad," which allowed a player to move their character in any direction using just a thumb. After the success of the Game & Watch, Nintendo put the D-pad in controllers on its new Nintendo Entertainment System. That home console brought arcade games into millions of homes around the world, and launched a new era of gaming. The combination of successes—the Game & Watch and the NES—also led to Yokoi's lateral-thinking magnum opus, a handheld console that played any game a developer could put on a cartridge: the Game Boy.

From a technological standpoint, even in 1989, the Game Boy was laughable. Yokoi's team cut every corner. The Game Boy's processor had been cutting edge—in the 1970s. By the mid-1980s, home consoles were in fierce competition over graphics quality. The Game Boy was an eyesore. It featured a total of four grayscale shades, displayed on a tiny screen that was tinted a greenish hue somewhere between mucus and old alfalfa. Graphics in fast lateral motion smeared across the screen. To top it off, the Game Boy had to compete with handheld consoles from Sega and Atari that were technologically superior in every way. And it destroyed them.

What its withered technology lacked, the Game Boy made up in user experience. It was cheap. It could fit in a large pocket. It was all but indestructible. If a drop cracked the screen—and it had to be a horrific drop—it kept on ticking. If it were left in a backpack that went in the washing machine, once it dried out it was ready to roll a few days later. Unlike its power-guzzling color competitors, it played for days (or weeks) on AA batteries. Old hardware was extremely familiar to developers inside and outside Nintendo, and with their creativity and speed unencumbered by learning new technology, they pumped out games as if they were early ancestors of iPhone app designers—*Tetris, Super Mario Land, The Final Fantasy Legend,* and a slew of sports games released in the first year were all smash hits. With simple technology, Yokoi's team sidestepped the hardware arms race and drew the game programming community onto its team.

The Game Boy became the Sony Walkman of video gaming, forgoing top-of-the-line tech for portability and affordability. It sold 118.7 million units, far and away the bestselling console of the twentieth century. Not bad for the little company that was allowed to sell *hanafuda.*

Even though he was revered by then, Yokoi had to push and shove internally for his "lateral thinking with withered technology" concept to be approved for the Game Boy. "It was difficult to get Nintendo to understand," he said later. Yokoi was convinced, though, that if users were drawn into the games, technological power would be an afterthought. "If you draw two circles on a blackboard, and say, 'That's a snowman,' everyone who sees it will sense the white color of the snow," he argued.

When the Game Boy was released, Yokoi's colleague came to him "with a grim expression on his face," Yokoi recalled, and reported that a competitor handheld had hit the market. Yokoi asked him if it had a color screen. The man said that it did. "Then we're fine," Yokoi replied.

Yokoi's strategy of finding novel uses for technology, after others had moved on, smacks of exactly what a well-known psychological creativity exercise asks for. In the Unusual (or Alternative) Uses Task, test takers have to come up with original uses for an object. Given the prompt "brick," a test taker will generate familiar uses first (part of a wall, a doorstop, a weapon). To score higher, they have to generate uses that are conceptually distant and rarely given by other test takers, but still feasible. For the brick: a paperweight; a nutcracker; a theatrical coffin at a doll's funeral; a water displacement device dropped in a toilet tank to use less per flush. (In 2015, *Ad Age* awarded "Pro Bono Campaign of the Year" to the cheeky lateral thinkers of the "Drop-A-Brick" project, which manufactured rubber bricks for use in California toilets during a drought.)

There is, to be sure, no comprehensive theory of creativity. But there is a well-documented tendency people have to consider only familiar uses for objects, an instinct known as functional fixedness. The most famous example is the "candle problem," in which participants are given a candle, a box of tacks, and a book of matches and told to attach the candle to the wall such that wax doesn't drip on the table below. Solvers try to melt the candle to the wall or tack it up somehow, neither of which work. When the problem is presented with the tacks *outside* of their box, solvers are more likely to view the empty box as a potential candle holder, and to solve the problem by tacking it to the wall and placing the candle inside. For Yokoi, the tacks were always outside the box.

Unquestionably, Yokoi needed narrow specialists. The first true electrical engineer Nintendo hired was Satoru Okada, who said bluntly, "Electronics was not Yokoi's strong point." Okada was Yokoi's co-designer on the Game & Watch and Game Boy. "I handled more of the internal systems of the machine," he recalled, "with Yokoi handling more of the design and interface aspects." Okada was the Steve Wozniak to Yokoi's Steve Jobs.

Yokoi was the first to admit it. "I don't have any particular specialist skills," he once said. "I have a sort of vague knowledge of everything."

He advised young employees not just to play with technology for its own sake, but to play with ideas. Do not be an engineer, he said, be a producer. "The producer knows that there's such a thing as a semiconductor, but doesn't need to know its inner workings. . . . That can be left to the experts." He argued, "Everyone takes the approach of learning detailed, complex skills. If no one did this then there wouldn't be people who shine as engineers. . . . Looking at me, from the engineer's perspective, it's like, 'Look at this idiot,' but once you've got a couple hit products under your belt, this word 'idiot' seems to slip away somewhere."

He spread his philosophy as his team grew, and asked everyone to consider alternate uses for old technology. He realized that he had been fortunate to come to a playing card company rather than an established electronic toymaker with entrenched solutions, so his ideas were not thwarted because of his technical limitations. As the company grew, he worried that young engineers would be too concerned about looking stupid to share ideas for novel uses of old technology, so he began intentionally blurting out crazy ideas at meetings to set the tone. "Once a young person starts saying things like, 'Well, it's not really my place to say . . .' then it's all over," he said.

Tragically, Yokoi died in a traffic accident in 1997. But his philosophy survived. In 2006, Nintendo's president said that the Nintendo Wii was a direct outgrowth of Yokoi's doctrine. "If I can speak without fear of being misunderstood," the president explained, "I would like to say that Nintendo is not producing next-generation game consoles." The Wii used extremely simple games and technology from a previous console, but motion-based controls were a literal game changer. Given its basic hardware, the Wii was criticized as not innovative. Harvard Business School professor Clayton Christensen argued that it was actually the most important kind of innovation, an "empowering innovation"—one that creates both new customers and new jobs, like the rise of personal computers before it—because it brought video games to an entirely new (often older) audience. Nintendo "simply innovated in a different way," Christensen and a colleague wrote. "It understood that the barrier to new consumers using video game systems was the complexity of game play, not the quality of existing graphics." Queen Elizabeth II of England made headlines when she saw her grandson Prince William playing Wii Bowling and decided to get in on the action herself.

Yokoi's greatest failure came when he departed from his own design tenets. One of his last Nintendo projects was the Virtual Boy, a gaming headset that employed experimental technology. It relied on a processor that produced high radio emissions, and before cell phones, no one knew if that was safe so close to a user's head. A metal plate had to be constructed around the processor, which in turn made the unit too heavy to work as goggles. It was transformed into a device that sat on a table and required the user to assume an unnatural posture to see the screen. It was ahead of its time, but nobody bought it.

Yokoi's greatest triumphs occurred when he thought laterally. He needed specialists, but his concern was that as companies grew and technology progressed, vertical-thinking hyperspecialists would continue to be valued but lateral-thinking generalists would not. "The shortcut [for a lack of ideas] is competition in the realm of computing power," Yokoi explained. "When it comes to that . . . the screen manufacturers and expert graphics designers come out on top. Then Nintendo's reason for existence disappears." He felt that the lateral and vertical thinkers were best together, even in highly technical fields.

Eminent physicist and mathematician Freeman Dyson styled it this way: we need both focused frogs and visionary birds. "Birds fly high in the air and survey broad vistas of mathematics out to the far horizon," Dyson wrote in 2009. "They delight in concepts that unify our thinking and bring together diverse problems from different parts of the landscape. Frogs live in the mud below and see only the flowers that grow nearby. They delight in the details of particular objects, and they solve problems one at a time." As a mathematician, Dyson labeled himself a frog, but contended, "It is stupid to claim that birds are better than frogs because they see farther, or that frogs are better than birds because they see deeper." The world, he wrote, is both broad and deep. "We need birds and frogs working together to explore it." Dyson's concern was that science is increasingly overflowing with frogs, trained only in a narrow specialty and unable to change as science itself does. "This is a hazardous situation," he warned, "for the young people and also for the future of science."

Fortunately, it is possible, even today, even at the cutting edge, even in the most hyperspecialized specialties, to cultivate land where both birds and frogs can thrive.

Andy Ouderkirk laughed as he recalled the story. "It was with three gentlemen who owned the company, and I'll just forever remember them holding up a vial and just looking at me and saying, 'This is a breakthrough in glitter.'"

Standard glitter sparkles; this glitter blazed, as if the vial held a colony of magical prismatic fireflies. Ouderkirk envisioned a lot of applications for multilayer optical film, but glitter was a pleasant surprise. "Here I am, a physical chemist," he told me. "I usually think of breakthroughs as being very sophisticated advanced technologies."

Ouderkirk was an inventor at Minnesota-based 3M, one of twenty-eight "corporate scientists," the highest title among the company's sixty-five hundred scientists and engineers. The road to breakthrough glitter began when he endeavored to challenge the conception of a two-hundred-year-old principle of physics known as Brewster's law, which had been interpreted to mean that no surface could reflect light near perfectly at every angle.

Ouderkirk wondered if layering many thin plastic surfaces on top of one another, each with distinct optical qualities, could create a film that custom-reflected and -refracted various wavelengths of light in all directions. A group of optics specialists he consulted assured him it could not be done, which was exactly what he wanted to hear. "If they say, 'It's a great idea, go for it, makes sense,' what is the chance you're the first person to come up with it? Precisely zero," he told me.

In fact, he was certain it was physically possible. Mother Nature offered proof of concept. The iridescent blue morpho butterfly has no blue pigment whatsoever; its wings glow azure and sapphire from thin layers of scales that refract and reflect particular wavelengths of blue light. There were more pedestrian examples too. The plastic of a water bottle refracts light differently depending on the light's angle. "Everybody knows this, that knows anything about polymers," Ouderkirk said. "It's in front of you literally every day. But nobody ever thought of making optical films out of this."

He formed and led the small team that accomplished just that. In less than the width of a human hair, the film comprises hundreds of polymer layers exquisitely tailored to reflect, refract, or let pass specific wavelengths of light. Unlike typical optical films, or even mirrors, multilayer optical film can reflect light nearly perfectly, and no matter the angle at which it arrives. It can even enhance the light as it bounces around the layers before returning to the viewer. Hence the glitter. Normal glitter doesn't reflect light well in every direction, but the breakthrough glitter dazzled in all directions at once.

The applications of the invention that was supposed to be impossible reached a tad beyond glitter. Inside cell phones and laptops, multilayer optical film reflects and "recycles" light that would normally be absorbed as it travels from a backlight to the screen, thus transmitting more light to the viewer, and drastically reducing the power needed to keep screens bright. It improves efficiency in LED light bulbs, solar panels, and fiber optics. It enhanced the energy efficiency of a projector so dramatically that it only needed a tiny battery for bright video. When a 2010 cave-in trapped thirty-three Chilean gold-and-copper miners a half mile underground for sixty-nine days, pocket-sized projectors with multilayer optical film were lowered through a 4.5-inch hole so that the men could receive messages from their families, safety instructions, and, naturally, a Chile-Ukraine soccer match.

Multilayer optical film is relatively cheap and can be made in large volume. Sitting on spools it could be mistaken for shimmering wrapping paper. It is a multibillion-dollar invention that is good for the environment. So how is it that nobody had looked at a plastic water bottle that way before? A recently published technical book for optics experts "said this technology is not capable of precision," Ouderkirk recalled. "It was written by a real subject matter expert. He's writing a whole book on this topic, so he knew his stuff. The problem is, he didn't know the adjacent stuff."

In 2013, *R&D Magazine* named Ouderkirk Innovator of the Year. Over three decades at 3M, he was named on 170 patents. Along the way, he became fascinated with the ingredients of invention, inventive teams, and individual inventors themselves. He eventually decided to investigate those ingredients systematically. He teamed up with an analytics expert and a professor at Nanyang Technological University in Singapore. They found that it has quite a bit to do with "the adjacent stuff."

Ouderkirk and the other two researchers who set out to study inventors at 3M wanted to know what profile of inventor made the greatest contributions. They found very specialized inventors who focused on a single technology, and generalist inventors who were not leading experts in anything, but had worked across numerous domains.

They examined patents, and with Ouderkirk's internal access to 3M, the actual commercial impact inventors made. The specialists and the generalists, they found, both made contributions. One was not uniformly superior to the other. (They also found inventors who had neither significant depth nor breadth—they rarely made an impact.) The specialists were adept at working for a long time on difficult technical problems, and for anticipating development obstacles. The generalists tended to get bored working in one area for too long. They added value by integrating domains, taking technology from one area and applying it in others. Neither an inventor's breadth nor their depth alone predicted the likelihood that one of their inventions would win the Carlton Award—the "Nobel Prize of 3M."

Ouderkirk's group unearthed one more type of inventor. They called them "polymaths," broad with at least one area of depth. An inventor's depth and breadth were measured by their work history. The U.S. Patent Office categorizes technology into four hundred fifty different classes—exercise devices, electrical connectors, marine propulsion, and myriad more. Specialists tended to have their patents in a narrow range of classes. A specialist might work for years only on understanding a type of plastic composed of a particular small group of chemical elements. Generalists, meanwhile, might start in masking tape, which would lead to a surgical adhesives project, which spawned an idea for veterinary medicine. Their patents were spread across many classes. The polymaths had depth in a core area—so they had numerous patents in that area—but they were not as deep as the specialists. They also had breadth, *even more* than the generalists, having worked across dozens of technology classes. Repeatedly, they took expertise accrued in one domain and applied it in a completely new one, which meant they were constantly learning new technologies. Over the course of their careers, the polymaths' breadth increased markedly as they learned about "the adjacent stuff," while they actually lost a modicum of depth. They were the most likely to succeed in the company and to win the Carlton Award. At a company whose mission is to constantly push technological frontiers, world-leading technical specialization by itself was not the key ingredient to success.

Ouderkirk is a polymath. He had been interested in chemistry since his second-grade teacher showed off a model volcano eruption. He took a winding path from a community college in northern Illinois to a chemistry PhD, to working completely outside of his chemistry background in a laser lab when he arrived at 3M. "What I was taught is to become a world expert in the rate of vibrational energy transfer between [gas-phase] molecules," he said. "What nobody ever told me in my whole career is that, not only is that good, but it's also good to know a little bit about everything else." Ouderkirk's patents range from optics to metal working to dentistry. The patent office frequently registered individual inventions he worked on under several classes at once, because they merged technological domains.

He became so interested in classifying innovators that he wrote a computer algorithm to analyze ten million patents from the last century and learn to identify and classify different types of inventors. Specialist contributions skyrocketed around and after World War II, but more recently have declined. "Specialists specifically peaked about 1985," Ouderkirk told me. "And then declined pretty dramatically, leveled off about 2007, and the most recent data show it's declining again, which I'm trying to understand." He is careful to say that he can't pinpoint a cause of the current trend. His hypothesis is that organizations simply don't need as many specialists. "As information becomes more broadly available, the need for somebody to just advance a field isn't as critical because in effect they are available to everybody," he said. He is suggesting that communication technology has limited the number of hyperspecialists required to work on a particular narrow problem, because their breakthroughs can be communicated quickly and widely to others—the Yokois of the world—who work on clever applications.

Communication technologies have certainly done that in other areas. In the early twentieth century, for example, the state of Iowa alone had more than a thousand opera houses, one for every fifteen hundred residents. They were theaters, not just music venues, and they provided full-time employment for hundreds of local acting troupes and thousands of actors. Fast forward to Netflix and Hulu. Every customer can have Meryl Streep on demand, and the Iowa opera houses are extinct. So much for thousands of fully employed stage actors in Iowa. Ouderkirk's data suggest that something analogous happened for narrowly focused specialists in technical fields. They are still absolutely critical, it's just that their work is widely accessible, so fewer suffice.

It is an extension of the trend that Don Swanson foretold, and it massively increased opportunities for Yokoi-like connectors and polymathic innovators. "When information became more widely disseminated," Ouderkirk told me, "it became a lot easier to be broader than a specialist, to start combining things in new ways."

Specialization is obvious: keep going straight. Breadth is trickier to grow. A subsidiary of PricewaterhouseCoopers that studied technological innovation over a decade found that there was no statistically significant relationship between R&D spending and performance.* (Save for the bottom 10 percent of spenders, which did perform worse than their peer companies.) Seeding the soil for generalists and polymaths who integrate knowledge takes more than money. It takes opportunity.

Jayshree Seth rose to corporate scientist precisely because she was allowed to pinball around different technological domains. Staying in one technical lane isn't her thing. Seth was unenthusiastic enough about the research she did for her master's degree that she ignored warnings and switched labs at Clarkson University for her PhD in chemical engineering. "People said, 'This is going to take too long because you have no fundamental knowledge in this area and you're going to be behind people who have already done their master's there,'" she told me. To clarify: the advice she received was to stick in an area she knew she didn't like because she had already started, even though she wasn't even that far in. It is the sunk cost fallacy embodied.

When she entered the professional world with 3M, she dared to switch

---

* "Performance" included measures of sales growth, profit from innovation, shareholder return, and market capitalization.

focus again, this time away from her PhD research, and for a personal reason: her husband was coming to 3M from the same Clarkson lab, and she didn't want to occupy the spot he might apply for. So she branched out. It worked: Seth has more than fifty patents. She helped create new pressure-sensitive adhesives for stretchable and reusable tapes, and diapers that stay on wiggly babies. She never studied materials science at all, and claimed she is "not that great a scientist." "What I mean," she said, "is I'm not qualified fundamentally to do what I do." She described her approach to innovation almost like investigative journalism, except her version of shoe-leather reporting is going door-to-door among her peers. She is a "T-shaped person," she said, one who has breadth, compared to an "I-shaped person," who only goes deep, an analog to Dyson's birds and frogs. "T-people like myself can happily go to the I-people with questions to create the trunk for the T," she told me. "My inclination is to attack a problem by building a narrative. I figure out the fundamental questions to ask, and if you ask those questions of the people who actually do know their stuff, you are still exactly where you would be if you had all this other knowledge inherently. It's mosaic building. I just keep putting those tiles together. Imagine me in a network where I didn't have the ability to access all these people. That really wouldn't work well."

In his first eight years at 3M, Ouderkirk worked with more than a hundred different teams. Nobody handed him important projects, like multilayer optical film, with potential impact spanning an enormous array of technologies; his breadth helped him identify them. "If you're working on well-defined and well-understood problems, specialists work very, very well," he told me. "As ambiguity and uncertainty increases, which is the norm with systems problems, breadth becomes increasingly important."

Research by Spanish business professors Eduardo Melero and Neus Palomeras backed up Ouderkirk's idea. They analyzed fifteen years of tech patents from 32,000 teams at 880 different organizations, tracking each individual inventor as he or she moved among teams, and then tracking the impact of each invention. Melero and Palomeras measured uncertainty in each technological domain: a high-uncertainty area had a lot of patents that proved totally useless, and some blockbusters; low-uncertainty domains were characterized by linear progression with more obvious next steps and more patents that were moderately useful. In low-uncertainty domains, teams of specialists were more likely to author useful patents. In high-uncertainty domains—where the fruitful questions themselves were less obvious—teams that included individuals who had worked on a wide variety of technologies were more likely to make a splash. The higher the domain uncertainty, the more important it was to have a high-breadth team member. As with the molecular biology groups Kevin Dunbar studied that used analogical thinking to solve problems, when the going got uncertain, breadth made the difference.

Like Melero and Palomeras, Dartmouth business professor Alva Taylor and Norwegian School of Management professor Henrich Greve wanted to examine the creative impact of individual breadth, just in a slightly less technical domain: comic books.

The comic book industry afforded a well-defined era of creative explosion. From the mid-1950s to 1970, comic creators agreed to self-censor after psychiatrist Fredric Wertham convinced Congress that comics were causing children to become deviants. (Wertham manipulated or fabricated aspects of his research.) In 1971, Marvel Comics broke ranks. The U.S. Department of Health, Education, and Welfare asked Marvel editor in chief Stan Lee to create a story that educated readers about drug abuse. Lee wrote a Spider-Man narrative in which Peter Parker's best friend overdosed on pills. The Comics Code Authority, the industry's self-censorship body, did not approve. Marvel published anyway. It was received so well that censorship standards were immediately relaxed, and the creative floodgates swung open. Comic creators developed superheroes with complex emotional problems; *Maus* became the first graphic novel to win a Pulitzer Prize; the avante-garde *Love and Rockets* created an ethnically diverse cast that aged with readers in real time.

Taylor and Greve tracked individual creators' careers and analyzed the commercial value of thousands of comic books from 234 publishers since that time. Each comic required the integration, by one or multiple creators, of narrative, dialogue, art, and layout design. The research duo made predictions about what would improve the average value of comics produced by an individual or team creator, and what would increase the value variance—that is, the chance that a creator would make a comic book that either failed spectacularly compared to their typical work, or that succeeded tremendously beyond their norm.

Taylor and Greve expected a typical industrial production learning curve: creators learn by repetition, so creators making more comics in a given span of time would make better ones on average. They were wrong. Also, as had been shown in industrial production, they guessed that the more resources a publisher had, the better its creators' average product would be. Wrong. And they made the very intuitive prediction that as creators' years of experience in the industry increased, they would make better comics on average. Wrong again.

A high-repetition workload negatively impacted performance. Years of experience had no impact at all. If not experience, repetition, or resources, what helped creators make better comics on average and innovate?

The answer (in addition to not being overworked) was how many of twenty-two different genres a creator had worked in, from comedy and crime, to fantasy, adult, nonfiction, and sci-fi. Where length of experience did not differentiate creators, breadth of experience did. Broad genre experience made creators better on average *and* more likely to innovate.

Individual creators started out with lower innovativeness than teams—they were less likely to produce a smash hit—but as their experience broadened they actually surpassed teams: an individual creator who had worked in four or more genres was more innovative than a team whose members had collective experience across the same number of genres. Taylor and Greve suggested that "individuals are capable of more creative integration of diverse experiences than teams are."

They titled their study *Superman or the Fantastic Four?* "When seeking innovation in knowledge-based industries," they wrote, "it is best to find one 'super' individual. If no individual with the necessary combination of diverse knowledge is available, one should form a 'fantastic' team." Diverse experience was impactful when created by platoon in teams, and even more impactful when contained within an individual. That finding immediately reminded me of my own favorite comics creators. Japanese comics and animated-film creator Hayao Miyazaki may be best known for the dreamlike epic *Spirited Away*, which surpassed *Titanic* as the highest-grossing film ever in Japan, but his comics and animation career before that left almost no genre untouched. He ranged from pure fantasy and fairy tales to historical fiction, sci-fi, slapstick comedy, illustrated historical essays, action-adventure, and much more. Novelist, screenwriter, and comics author Neil Gaiman has a similarly expansive range, from journalism and essays on art to a fiction oeuvre encompassing both stories that can be read to (or by) the youngest readers as well as psychologically complex examinations of identity that have enthralled mainstream adult audiences. Jordan Peele is not a comics creator, but the writer and first-time director of the extraordinarily unique surprise hit *Get Out* struck a similar note when he credited comedy writing for his skill at timing information reveals in a horror film. "In product development," Taylor and Greve concluded, "specialization can be costly."

In kind environments, where the goal is to re-create prior performance with as little deviation as possible, teams of specialists work superbly. Surgical teams work faster and make fewer mistakes as they repeat specific procedures, and specialized surgeons get better outcomes even independent of repetitions. If you need to have surgery, you want a doctor who specializes in the procedure and has done it many times, preferably with the same team, just as you would want Tiger Woods to step in if your life was on the line for a ten-foot putt. They've been there, many times, and now have to re-create a well-understood process that they have executed successfully before. The same goes for airline crews. Teams that have experience working together become exceedingly efficient at delegating all of the well-understood tasks required to ensure a smooth flight. When the National Transportation Safety Board analyzed its database of major flight accidents, it found that 73 percent occurred on a flight crew's first day working together. Like surgeries and putts, the best flight is one in which everything goes according to routines long understood and optimized by everyone involved, with no surprises.

When the path is unclear—a game of Martian tennis—those same routines no longer suffice. "Some tools work fantastically in certain situations, advancing technology in smaller but important ways, and those tools are well known and well practiced," Andy Ouderkirk told me. "Those same tools will also pull you away from a breakthrough innovation. In fact, they'll turn a breakthrough innovation into an incremental one."

University of Utah professor Abbie Griffin has made it her work to study modern Thomas Edisons—"serial innovators," she and two colleagues termed them. Their findings about who these people are should sound familiar by now: "high tolerance for ambiguity"; "systems thinkers"; "additional technical knowledge from peripheral domains"; "repurposing what is already available"; "adept at using analogous domains for finding inputs to the invention process"; "ability to connect disparate pieces of information in new ways"; "synthesizing information from many different sources"; "they appear to flit among ideas"; "broad range of interests"; "they read more (and more broadly) than other technologists and have a wider range of outside interests"; "need to learn significantly across multiple domains"; "Serial innovators also need to communicate with various individuals with technical expertise outside of their own domain." Get the picture?

Charles Darwin "could be considered a professional outsider," according to creativity researcher Dean Keith Simonton. Darwin was not a university faculty member nor a professional scientist at any institution, but he was networked into the scientific community. For a time, he focused narrowly on barnacles, but got so tired of it that he declared, "I am unwilling to spend more time on the subject," in the introduction to a barnacle monograph. Like the 3M generalists and polymaths, he got bored sticking in one area, so that was that. For his paradigm-shattering work, Darwin's broad network was crucial. Howard Gruber, a psychologist who studied Darwin's journals, wrote that Darwin only personally carried out experiments "opportune for experimental attack by a scientific generalist such as he was." For everything else, he relied on correspondents, Jayshree Seth style. Darwin always juggled multiple projects, what Gruber called his "network of enterprise." He had at least 231 scientific pen pals who can be grouped roughly into thirteen broad themes based on his interests, from worms to human sexual selection. He peppered them with questions. He cut up their letters to paste pieces of information in his own notebooks, in which "ideas tumble over each other in a seemingly chaotic fashion." When his chaotic notebooks became too unwieldy, he tore pages out and filed them by themes of inquiry. Just for his own experiments with seeds, he corresponded with geologists, botanists, ornithologists, and conchologists in France, South Africa, the United States, the Azores, Jamaica, and Norway, not to mention a number of amateur naturalists and some gardeners he happened to know. As Gruber wrote, the activities of a creator "may appear, from the outside, as a bewildering miscellany," but he or she can "map" each activity onto one of the ongoing enterprises. "In some respects," Gruber concluded, "Charles Darwin's greatest works represent interpretative compilations of facts first gathered by others." He was a lateral-thinking integrator.

Toward the end of their book *Serial Innovators,* Abbie Griffin and her coauthors depart from stoically sharing their data and observations and offer advice to human resources managers. They are concerned that HR policies at mature companies have such well-defined, specialized slots for employees that potential serial innovators will look like "round pegs to the square holes" and get screened out. Their breadth of interests do not neatly fit a rubric. They are "π-shaped people" who dive in and out of multiple specialties. "Look for wide-ranging interests," they advised. "Look for multiple hobbies and avocations. . . . When the candidate describes his or her work, does he or she tend to focus on the boundaries and the interfaces with other systems?" One serial innovator described his network of enterprise as "a bunch of bobbers hanging in the water that have little thoughts attached to them." *Hamilton* creator Lin-Manuel Miranda painted the same idea elegantly: "I have a lot of apps open in my brain right now."

Griffin's research team noticed that serial innovators repeatedly claimed that they themselves would be screened out under their company's current hiring practices. "A mechanistic approach to hiring, while yielding highly reproducible results, in fact reduces the numbers of high-potential [for innovation] candidates," they wrote. When I first spoke with him, Andy Ouderkirk was developing a class at the University of Minnesota partly about how to identify potential innovators. "We think a lot of them might be frustrated by school," he said, "because by nature they're very broad."

Facing uncertain environments and wicked problems, breadth of experience is invaluable. Facing kind problems, narrow specialization can be remarkably efficient. The problem is that we often expect the hyperspecialist, because of their expertise in a narrow area, to magically be able to extend their skill to wicked problems. The results can be disastrous.

CHAPTER 10

Fooled by Expertise

THE BET WAS ON, and it was over the fate of humanity.

On one side was Stanford biologist Paul Ehrlich. In congressional testimony, on *The Tonight Show* (twenty times), and in his 1968 bestseller *The Population Bomb,* Ehrlich insisted that it was too late to prevent a doomsday apocalypse from overpopulation. On its lower left corner, the book cover bore an image of a fuse burning low, and a reminder that the "bomb keeps ticking." Resource shortages would cause hundreds of millions of starvation deaths within a decade, Ehrlich warned. The *New Republic* alerted the world that the global population had already outstripped the food supply. "The famine has started," it proclaimed. It was cold, hard math: human population was growing exponentially, the food supply was not. Ehrlich was a butterfly specialist, and an accomplished one. He knew full well that nature did not regulate animal populations delicately. Populations exploded, blew past the available resources, and crashed. "The shape of the population growth curve is one familiar to the biologist," he wrote.

Ehrlich played out hypothetical scenarios in his book, representing "the kinds of disasters that *will* occur." In one scenario, during the 1970s the United States and China start blaming one another for mass starvation and end up in a nuclear war. That's the *moderate* scenario. In the bad one, famine rages across the planet. Cities alternate between riots and martial law. The American president's environmental advisers recommend a one-child policy and sterilization of people with low IQ scores. Russia, China, and the United States are dragged into nuclear war, which renders the northern two-thirds of Earth uninhabitable. Pockets of society persist in the Southern Hemisphere, but the environmental degradation soon extinguishes the human race. In the "cheerful" scenario, population controls begin. The pope announces that Catholics should reproduce less, and gives his blessing to abortion. Famine spreads, and countries teeter. By the mid-1980s, the major death wave ends and agricultural land can begin to be rehabilitated. The cheerful scenario only forecast half a billion or so deaths by starvation. "I challenge you to create one more optimistic," Ehrlich wrote, adding that he would not count scenarios involving benevolent aliens with care packages.

Economist Julian Simon took up Ehrlich's challenge to create a more optimistic picture. The late 1960s was the prime of the "green revolution." Technology from other sectors—water control techniques, hybridized seeds, management strategies—moved into agriculture, and global crop yields were increasing. Simon saw that innovation was altering the equation. More people would actually be the solution, because it meant more good ideas and more technological breakthroughs. So Simon proposed a bet. Ehrlich could choose five metals that he expected to become more expensive as resources were depleted and chaos ensued over the next decade. The material stakes were $1,000 worth of Ehrlich's five metals. If, ten years hence, prices had gone down, Ehrlich would have to pay the price difference to Simon. If prices went up, Simon would be on the hook for the difference. Ehrlich's liability was capped at $1,000, whereas Simon's risk had no roof. The bet was made official in 1980.

In October 1990, Simon found a check for $576.07 in his mailbox.

Ehrlich got smoked. The price of every one of the metals declined. Technological change not only supported a growing population, but the food supply per person increased year after year, on every continent. The proportion of people who are undernourished is too high until it is zero, but it has never been so low as it is now. In the 1960s, 50 of every 100,000 global citizens died annually from famine; now that number is 0.5. Even without the pope's assistance, the world's population growth rate began a precipitous decline that continues today. When child mortality declined and education (especially for women) and development increased, birth rates decreased. Humanity will need more innovation as absolute world population continues to grow, but the growth *rate* is declining, rapidly. The United Nations projects that by the end of the century human population will be near a peak—the growth rate approaching zero—or it could even be in decline.

Ehrlich's starvation predictions were almost magically bad. He made them just as technological development was dramatically altering the global predicament, *and* right before the rate of population growth started a long deceleration. And yet, the very same year he conceded the bet, Ehrlich doubled down in another book. Sure, the timeline had been a little off, but "now the population bomb has detonated." Despite one erroneous prediction after another, Ehrlich amassed an enormous following and continued to receive prestigious awards. Simon became a standard-bearer for scholars who felt that Ehrlich had ignored economic principles, and for anyone angry at an incessant flow of dire predictions that did not manifest. The kind of excessive regulations Ehrlich advocated, the Simon camp argued, would quell the very innovation that had delivered humanity from catastrophe. Both men became luminaries in their respective domains. And both were mistaken.

When economists later examined metal prices for every ten-year window from 1900 to 2008, during which time world population quadrupled, they saw that Ehrlich would have won the bet 63 percent of the time. The catch: commodity prices are a bad proxy for population effects, particularly over a single decade. The variable that both men were certain would vindicate their worldviews actually had little to do with them. Commodity prices waxed and waned with macroeconomic cycles, and a recession during the bet brought the prices down. Ehrlich and Simon might as well have flipped a coin and both declared victory.

Both men dug in. Each declared his faith in science and the undisputed primacy of facts. And each continued to miss the value of the other's ideas. Ehrlich was wrong about population (and the apocalypse), but right on aspects of environmental degradation. Simon was right about the influence of human ingenuity on the food and energy supply, but wrong in claiming that improvements in air and water quality also vindicated his predictions. Ironically, those improvements failed to arise naturally from technological initiative and markets, and rather were bolstered through regulations pressed by Ehrlich and others.

Ideally, intellectual sparring partners "hone each other's arguments so that they are sharper and better," Yale historian Paul Sabin wrote. "The opposite happened with Paul Ehrlich and Julian Simon." As each man amassed more information for his own view, each became more dogmatic, and the inadequacies in their models of the world more stark.

There is a particular kind of thinker, one who becomes more entrenched in their single big idea about how the world works even in the face of contrary facts, whose predictions become worse, not better, as they amass information for their mental representation of the world. They are on television and in the news every day, making worse and worse predictions while claiming victory, and they have been rigorously studied.

It started at the 1984 meeting of the National Research Council's committee on American-Soviet relations. Newly tenured psychologist and political scientist Philip Tetlock was thirty years old, by far the most junior committee member. He listened intently as members discussed

Soviet intentions and American policies. Renowned experts confidently delivered authoritative predictions, and Tetlock was struck by the fact that they were often perfectly contradictory to one another, and impervious to counterarguments.

Tetlock decided to put expert predictions to the test. With the Cold War in full swing, he began a study to collect short- and long-term forecasts from 284 highly educated experts (most had doctorates) who averaged more than twelve years of experience in their specialties. The questions covered international politics and economics, and in order to make sure the predictions were concrete, the experts had to give specific probabilities of future events. Tetlock had to collect enough predictions over enough time that he could separate lucky and unlucky streaks from true skill. The project lasted twenty years, and comprised 82,361 probability estimates about the future. The results limned a very wicked world.

The average expert was a horrific forecaster. Their areas of specialty, years of experience, academic degrees, and even (for some) access to classified information made no difference. They were bad at short-term forecasting, bad at long-term forecasting, and bad at forecasting in every domain. When experts declared that some future event was impossible or nearly impossible, it nonetheless occurred 15 percent of the time. When they declared a sure thing, it failed to transpire more than one-quarter of the time. The Danish proverb that warns "It is difficult to make predictions, especially about the future," was right. Dilettantes who were pitted against the experts were no more clairvoyant, but at least they were less likely to call future events either impossible or sure things, leaving them with fewer laugh-out-loud errors to atone for—if, that was, the experts had believed in atonement.

Many experts never admitted systematic flaws in their judgment, even in the face of their results. When they succeeded, it was completely on their own merits—their expertise clearly enabled them to figure out the world. When they missed wildly, it was always a near miss; they had certainly understood the situation, they insisted, and if just one little thing had gone differently, they would have nailed it. Or, like Ehrlich, their understanding was correct; the timeline was just a bit off. Victories were total victories, and defeats were always just a touch of bad luck away from having been victories too. Experts remained undefeated while losing constantly. "There is often a curiously inverse relationship," Tetlock concluded, "between how well forecasters thought they were doing and how well they did."

There was also a "perverse inverse relationship" between fame and accuracy. The more likely an expert was to have his or her predictions featured on op-ed pages and television, the more likely they were always wrong. Or, not always wrong. Rather, as Tetlock and his coauthor succinctly put it in their book *Superforecasting,* "roughly as accurate as a dart-throwing chimpanzee."

Early predictions in Tetlock's research pertained to the future of the Soviet Union. There were experts (usually liberal) who saw Mikhail Gorbachev as an earnest reformer who would be able to change the Soviet Union and keep it intact for a while, and experts (usually conservative) who felt that the Soviet Union was immune to reform, ruinous by its very nature, and losing legitimacy. Both sides were partly right and partly wrong. Gorbachev did bring real reform, opening the Soviet Union to the world and empowering citizens. But those reforms uncorked bottled-up forces in the republics outside of Russia, where the system had lost legitimacy. Starting with Estonia declaring its sovereignty, the forces blew the Soviet Union apart. Both camps of experts were completely taken by surprise at the swift end of the USSR, and their predictions about the course of events were terrible. There was, however, one subgroup within the experts that managed to see more of what was coming.

Unlike Ehrlich and Simon, they were not vested in a single approach. They were able to take from each argument and integrate apparently contradictory worldviews. They agreed that Gorbachev was a real re-former, *and* that the Soviet Union had lost legitimacy outside of Russia. Some of those integrators actually foresaw that the end of the Soviet Union was close at hand, and that real reforms would be the catalyst.

The integrators outperformed their colleagues on pretty much every-thing, but they especially trounced them on long-term predictions. Even-tually, Tetlock conferred nicknames (borrowed from philosopher Isaiah Berlin) that became famous throughout the psychology and intelligence-gathering communities: the narrow-view hedgehogs, who "know one big thing," and the integrator foxes, who "know many little things."

Hedgehog experts were deep but narrow. Some had spent their ca-reers studying a single problem. Like Ehrlich and Simon, they fashioned tidy theories of how the world works through the single lens of their specialty, and then bent every event to fit them. The hedgehogs, accord-ing to Tetlock, "toil devotedly" within one tradition of their specialty, "and reach for formulaic solutions to ill-defined problems." Outcomes did not matter; they were proven right by both successes and failures, and burrowed further into their ideas. It made them outstanding at pre-dicting the past, but dart-throwing chimps at predicting the future. The foxes, meanwhile, "draw from an eclectic array of traditions, and ac-cept ambiguity and contradiction," Tetlock wrote. Where hedgehogs represented narrowness, foxes ranged outside a single discipline or the-ory and embodied breadth.

Incredibly, the hedgehogs performed especially poorly on long-term predictions within their domain of expertise. They actually got worse as they accumulated credentials and experience in their field. The more information they had to work with, the more they could fit any story to their worldview. This did give hedgehogs one conspicuous advantage. Viewing every world event through their preferred keyhole made it easy to fashion compelling stories about anything that occurred, and to tell the stories with adamant authority. In other words, they make great TV.

Tetlock is clearly a fox. He is a professor at Penn, and when I visited his home in Philadelphia I was enveloped in a casual conversation about politics he was having with colleagues, including his wife and collaborator, Barbara Mellers, also a psychologist and eminent scholar of decision making. Tetlock would start in one direction, then interrogate himself and make an about-face. He drew on economics, political science, and history to make one quick point about a current debate in psychology, and then stopped on a dime and noted, "But if your assumptions about human nature and how a good society needs to be structured are different, you would see this completely differently." When a new idea entered the conversation, he was quick with "Let's say for the sake of argument," which led to him playing out viewpoints from different disciplines or political or emotional perspectives. He tried on ideas like Instagram filters until it was hard to tell which he actually believed.

In 2005, he published the results of his long study of expert judgment, and they caught the attention of the Intelligence Advanced Research Projects Activity (IARPA), a government organization that supports research on the U.S. intelligence community's most difficult challenges. In 2011, IARPA launched a four-year prediction tournament in which five researcher-led teams competed. Each team could recruit, train, and experiment however it saw fit. Every day for four years, predictions were due at 9 a.m. Eastern time. The questions were hard. What is the chance that a member will withdraw from the European Union by a target date? Will the Nikkei close above 9,500? What is the likelihood of a naval clash claiming more than ten lives in the East China Sea? Forecasters could update predictions as often as they wanted, but the scoring system rewarded accuracy over time, so a great prediction at the last minute before a question's end date was of limited value.

The team run by Tetlock and Mellers was called the Good Judgment Project. Rather than recruit decorated experts, in the first year of the tournament they made an open call for volunteers. After a simple screening, they invited thirty-two hundred to start forecasting. From those, they identified a small group of the foxiest forecasters—just bright people with wide-ranging interests and reading habits but no particular relevant background—and weighted team forecasts toward them. They destroyed the competition.

In year two, the Good Judgment Project randomly arranged the top "superforecasters" into online teams of twelve, so that they could share information and ideas. They beat the other university-run teams so badly that IARPA dropped those lesser competitors from the tournament. The volunteers drawn from the general public beat experienced intelligence analysts with access to classified data "by margins that remain classified," according to Tetlock. (He has, though, referenced a *Washington Post* report indicating that the Good Judgment Project performed about 30 percent better than a collection of intelligence community analysts.)

Not only were the best forecasters foxy as individuals, they had qualities that made them particularly effective collaborators—partners in sharing information and discussing predictions. Every team member still had to make individual predictions, but the team was scored by collective performance. On average, forecasters on the small superteams became 50 percent more accurate in their *individual* predictions. Superteams beat the wisdom of much larger crowds—in which the predictions of a large group of people are averaged—and they also beat prediction markets, where forecasters "trade" the outcomes of future events like stocks, and the market price represents the crowd prediction.

It might seem like the complexity of predicting geopolitical and economic events would necessitate a group of narrow specialists, each bringing to the team extreme depth in one area. But it was actually the opposite. As with comic book creators and inventors patenting new technologies, in the face of uncertainty, individual breadth was critical. The foxiest forecasters were impressive alone, but together they exemplified the most lofty ideal of teams: they became more than the sum of their parts. A lot more.

A few of the qualities that make the best Good Judgment Project forecasters valuable teammates are obvious from talking to them. They are bright, but so were the hedgehog experts Tetlock started with. They toss around numbers easily, estimating this country's poverty rate or that state's proportion of farmland. And they have range.

Scott Eastman told me that he "never completely fit in one world." He grew up in Oregon and competed in math and science contests, but in college he studied English literature and fine arts. He has been a bicycle mechanic, a housepainter, founder of a housepainting company, manager of a multimillion-dollar trust, a photographer, a photography teacher, a lecturer at a Romanian university—in subjects ranging from cultural anthropology to civil rights—and, most unusually, chief adviser to the mayor of Avrig, a small town in the middle of Romania. In that role, he did everything from helping integrate new technologies into the local economy to dealing with the press and participating in negotiations with Chinese business leaders.

Eastman narrates his life like a book of fables; each experience comes with a lesson. "I think that housepainting was probably one of the greatest helps," he told me. It afforded him the chance to interact with a diverse palette of colleagues and clients, from refugees seeking asylum to Silicon Valley billionaires whom he would chat with if he had a long project working on their homes. He described it as fertile ground for collecting perspectives. But housepainting is probably not a singular education for geopolitical prediction. Eastman, like his teammates, is constantly collecting perspectives anywhere he can, always adding to his intellectual range, so any ground is fertile for him.

Eastman was uncannily accurate at predicting developments in Syria, and surprised to learn that Russia was his weak spot. He studied

Russian and has a friend who was a former ambassador to Russia. "I should have every leg up there, but I saw over a large series of questions, it was one of my weakest areas," he told me. He learned that specializing in a topic frequently did not bear fruit in the forecasts. "So if I know somebody [on the team] is a subject area expert, I am very, very happy to have access to them, in terms of asking questions and seeing what they dig up. But I'm not going to just say, 'Okay, the biochemist said a certain drug is likely to come to market, so he must be right.' Often if you're too much of an insider, it's hard to get good perspective." Eastman described the core trait of the best forecasters to me as: "genuinely curious about, well, really everything."

Ellen Cousins researches fraud for trial lawyers. Her research naturally roams from medicine to business. She has wide-ranging interests on the side, from collecting historical artifacts to embroidery, laser etching, and lock picking. She conducts pro bono research on military veterans who should (and sometimes do) get upgraded to the Medal of Honor. She felt exactly the same as Eastman. Narrow experts are an invaluable resource, she told me, "but you have to understand that they may have blinders on. So what I try to do is take facts from them, not opinions." Like polymath inventors, Eastman and Cousins take ravenously from specialists and integrate.

Superforecasters' online interactions are exercises in extremely polite antagonism, disagreeing without being disagreeable. Even on a rare occasion when someone does say, "'You're full of beans, that doesn't make sense to me, explain this,'" Cousins told me, "they don't mind that." Agreement is not what they are after; they are after aggregating perspectives, lots of them. In an impressively unsightly image, Tetlock described the very best forecasters as foxes with dragonfly eyes. Dragonfly eyes are composed of tens of thousands of lenses, each with a different perspective, which are then synthesized in the dragonfly's brain.

One forecast discussion I saw was a team trying to predict the highest single-day close for the exchange rate between the U.S. dollar and

Ukrainian hryvnia during an extremely volatile stretch in 2014. Would it be less than 10, between 10 and 13, or more than 13? The discussion started with a team member offering percentage predictions for each of the three possibilities, and sharing an *Economist* article. Another team member chimed in with a Bloomberg link and online historical data, and offered three different probability predictions, with "between 10 and 13" favored. A third teammate was convinced by the second's argument. A fourth shared information about the dire state of Ukrainian finances. A fifth addressed the broader issue of how exchange rates change, or don't, in relation to world events. The teammate who started the conversation then posted again; he was persuaded by the previous arguments and altered his predictions, but still thought they were overrating the possibility of "more than 13." They continued to share information, challenge one another, and update their forecasts. Two days later, a team member with specific expertise in finance saw that the hryvnia was strengthening amid events he thought would surely weaken it. He chimed in to inform his teammates that this was exactly the opposite of what he expected, and that they should take it as a sign of something wrong in his understanding. In contrast to politicians, the most adept predictors flip-flop like crazy. The team finally homed in on "between 10 and 13" as the heavy favorite, and they were correct.

In separate work, from 2000 to 2010 German psychologist Gerd Gigerenzer compiled annual dollar-euro exchange rate predictions made by twenty-two of the most prestigious international banks—Barclays, Citigroup, JPMorgan Chase, Bank of America Merrill Lynch, and others. Each year, every bank predicted the end-of-year exchange rate. Gigerenzer's simple conclusion about those projections, from some of the world's most prominent specialists: "Forecasts of dollar-euro exchange rates are worthless." In six of the ten years, the true exchange rate fell outside the entire range of all twenty-two bank forecasts. Where a superforecaster quickly highlighted a change in exchange rate direction that confused him, and adjusted, major bank forecasts missed every single change of direction in the decade Gigerenzer analyzed.

A hallmark of interactions on the best teams is what psychologist Jonathan Baron termed "active open-mindedness." The best forecasters view their own ideas as hypotheses in need of testing. Their aim is not to convince their teammates of their own expertise, but to encourage their teammates to help them falsify their own notions. In the sweep of humanity, that is not normal. Asked a difficult question—for example, "Would providing more money for public schools significantly improve the quality of teaching and learning?"—people naturally come up with a deluge of "myside" ideas. Armed with a web browser, they don't start searching for why they are probably wrong. It is not that we are unable to come up with contrary ideas, it is just that our strong instinct is not to.

Researchers in Canada and the United States began a 2017 study by asking a politically diverse and well-educated group of adults to read arguments confirming their beliefs about controversial issues. When participants were then given a chance to get paid if they read contrary arguments, two-thirds decided they would rather not even *look* at the counterarguments, never mind seriously entertain them. The aversion to contrary ideas is not a simple artifact of stupidity or ignorance. Yale law and psychology professor Dan Kahan has shown that more scientifically literate adults are actually *more* likely to become dogmatic about politically polarizing topics in science. Kahan thinks it could be because they are better at finding evidence to confirm their feelings: the more time they spend on the topic, the more hedgehog-like they become.

In a study during the run-up to the Brexit vote, a small majority of both Remainers and Brexiters were able to correctly interpret made-up statistics about the efficacy of a rash-curing skin cream, but when voters were given the same exact data presented as if it indicated that immigration either increased or decreased crime, hordes of Brits suddenly became innumerate and misinterpreted statistics that disagreed with their political beliefs. Kahan found the same phenomenon in the United States using skin cream and gun control. Kahan also documented a personality feature that fought back against that propensity: science curiosity. Not science knowledge, science *curiosity*.

Kahan and colleagues measured science curiosity cleverly, smuggling relevant questions into what looked like consumer marketing surveys, and tracking how people pursued follow-up information after viewing videos with particular content, some of them science-related. The most science-curious folk always chose to look at new evidence, whether or not it agreed with their current beliefs. Less science-curious adults were like hedgehogs: they became more resistant to contrary evidence and more politically polarized as they gained subject matter knowledge. Those who were high in science curiosity bucked that trend. Their foxy hunt for information was like a literal fox's hunt for prey: roam freely, listen carefully, and consume omnivorously. Just as Tetlock says of the best forecasters, it is not what they think, but how they think. The best forecasters are high in active open-mindedness. They are also extremely curious, and don't merely consider contrary ideas, they proactively cross disciplines looking for them. "Depth can be inadequate without breadth," wrote Jonathan Baron, the psychologist who developed measurements of active open-mindedness.

Charles Darwin must have been one of the most curious and actively open-minded human beings in history. His first four models of evolution were forms of creationism or intelligent design. (The fifth model treated creation as a separate question.) He made a point of copying into his notes any fact or observation he encountered that ran contrary to a theory he was working on. He relentlessly attacked his own ideas, dispensing with one model after another, until he arrived at a theory that fit the totality of the evidence. But before he even started on that life's work, he needed a push from an actively open-minded teammate—or mentor, really. John Stevens Henslow was the priest, geologist, and botany professor who arranged Darwin's place aboard the HMS *Beagle*. Before the ship set sail, he told Darwin to read a controversial new book, *Principles of Geology,* by Charles Lyell. Lyell argued that Earth had changed very gradually over time by processes that continued in the present. Henslow could not accept Lyell's description of geology as entirely separate from theology, warning Darwin "on no account to accept the views therein advocated." But, in foxlike fashion, he set aside his own revulsion and urged his mentee to read the book. It was a revelation. According to science historian Janet Browne, "In one of the most remarkable interchanges in the history of science, Lyell's book taught Darwin how to think about nature."

None of this is to say that hedgehog experts are unnecessary. They produce vital knowledge. Einstein was a hedgehog. He saw simplicity beneath complexity, and found elegant theories to prove it. But he also spent the last thirty years of his life in a rigid quest for a single theory of everything that would explain away the messy apparent randomness inherent to quantum mechanics, a field spawned in part by his own work. As astrophysicist Glen Mackie wrote, "A consensus seems to exist: in later years, Einstein worked with mathematical blinkers, immune to relevant discoveries, and unable to change his method of investigation." God does not play dice with the universe, Einstein asserted, figuratively. Niels Bohr, his contemporary who illuminated the structure of atoms (using analogies to Saturn's rings and the solar system), replied that Einstein should keep an open mind and not tell God how to run the universe.

Beneath complexity, hedgehogs tend to see simple, deterministic rules of cause and effect framed by their area of expertise, like repeating patterns on a chessboard. Foxes see complexity in what others mistake for simple cause and effect. They understand that most cause-and-effect relationships are probabilistic, not deterministic. There are unknowns, and luck, and even when history apparently repeats, it does not do so precisely. They recognize that they are operating in the very definition of a wicked learning environment, where it can be very hard to learn, from either wins or losses.

In wicked domains that lack automatic feedback, experience alone does not improve performance. Effective habits of mind are more important, and they can be developed. In four straight years of forecasting tournaments, Tetlock and Mellers's research group showed that an hour of basic training in foxy habits improved accuracy. One habit was a lot like the analogical thinking that helped the venture capitalists and movie enthusiasts in chapter 5 make better projections of investment returns and film revenues. Basically, forecasters can improve by generating a list of separate events with deep structural similarities, rather than focusing only on internal details of the specific event in question. Few events are 100 percent novel—uniqueness is a matter of degree, as Tetlock puts it—and creating the list forces a forecaster implicitly to think like a statistician.

For example, in 2015, forecasters were asked if Greece would exit the eurozone that year. No country had ever left, so the question seemed totally unique. But there were plenty of examples of international negotiation failures, exits from international agreements, and forced currency conversions that allowed the best forecasters to ground themselves in what usually happens without focusing narrowly on all the unique details of the present situation. Starting with the details—the inside view—is dangerous. Hedgehog experts have more than enough knowledge about the minutiae of an issue in their specialty to do just what Dan Kahan suggested: cherry-pick details that fit their all-encompassing theories. Their deep knowledge works against them. Skillful forecasters depart from the problem at hand to consider completely unrelated events with structural commonalities rather than relying on intuition based on personal experience or a single area of expertise.

Another aspect of the forecaster training involved ferociously dissecting prediction results in search of lessons, especially for predictions that turned out bad. They made a wicked learning environment, one with no automatic feedback, a little more kind by creating rigorous feedback at every opportunity. In Tetlock's twenty-year study, both foxes and hedgehogs were quick to update their beliefs after successful predictions, by reinforcing them even more strongly. When an outcome took them by surprise, however, foxes were much more likely to adjust their ideas. Hedgehogs barely budged. Some hedgehogs made authoritative predictions that turned out wildly wrong, and then updated their theories *in the wrong direction*. They became even more convinced of the original beliefs that led them astray. "Good judges are good belief updaters," according to Tetlock. If they make a bet and lose, they embrace the logic of a loss just as they would the reinforcement of a win.

That is called, in a word: learning. Sometimes, it involves putting experience aside entirely.

CHAPTER 11

Learning to Drop Your Familiar Tools

JAKE, THE ATHLETIC-LOOKING sandy blond, speaks first. He wants to race the car. "What if everybody just agrees?" he asks. "I say, race this thang."

It was early afternoon in fall, and Jake and six of his second-year Harvard Business School classmates found a shady spot where they could eat their lunches and talk.* Their professor had given them three pages containing one of the most famous business school case studies ever created, known as Carter Racing. The crux is whether the fictional Carter Racing team's car should compete in the biggest race of the season, which begins in one hour.

The argument in favor of racing: thanks to a custom turbocharger, Carter Racing has placed in the money (top five) in twelve of twenty-four races. That success secured an oil company sponsorship, and a trial sponsorship from prestigious (and also fictional) Goodstone Tire. Carter Racing won the last race, its fourth win of the season. Today's race will be on national TV, and if Carter Racing finishes in the top five, it will likely draw a $2 million sponsorship from Goodstone. If Carter

---

* Names of students have been changed except for those who gave explicit permission to use a real name.

Racing chooses not to race and withdraws, it would lose part of its entry fee and have to pay back some sponsor money. The team would end a stellar season $80,000 in the hole, and may never get another shot this big. Racing seems like a no-brainer.

The argument against racing: in seven of twenty-four races, the engine failed, each time damaging the car. In the last two races, the mechanics used a new engine-prep procedure and had no trouble, but they aren't sure what caused the problem before. If the engine fails on national TV, the team will lose the oil sponsorship, kiss Goodstone goodbye, and go back to square one, or perhaps out of business. So: race, or don't race?

The group begins with a vote. Three students vote to race, four to sit it out. Now the debate begins.

Even with the engine failures, Jake says, the team has a 50 percent chance of its biggest triumph. The upside of the Goodstone sponsorship is much more money than the team stands to lose if the engine fails and the existing sponsors walk. If Carter Racing withdraws, an excellent season ends with debt, "which, as we all know, is not a sustainable business model."

"I just don't think they can afford not to race," Justin says.

Alexander agrees, and addresses the dissenters: "What's going to change going forward to convince you that now you're ready?" he asks.

Mei, wearing a Harvard hoodie and sitting across the circle, has a calculation to share. "To me, the risk of not racing is about one-third of the downside of [another engine failure]," she says. She adds that she's focusing on loss mitigation, and does not want to race.

The case study says that at the last minute, the team owner, BJ Carter, called his mechanics. Pat, the engine mechanic, dropped out of high school and has no sophisticated engineering training, but he has a decade of race experience. Temperature could be the issue, he suggested. When the turbocharger warms up on a cool day, engine components might expand at different rates and set up failure of the head gasket, a metal seal in the engine. Pat admitted that each engine failure looked different, but all seven had breaks in the head gasket. (Two of the engine failures had multiple breaks in the gasket.) He didn't know what was going on, but couldn't think of anything else on short notice. He was still hyped to race, and jubilant about the new Goodstone uniforms. At 40 degrees, it is the coldest race day of the season. Robin, the chief mechanic, endorsed Pat's idea to look at the temperature data. He plotted it on a graph, but saw no correlation:

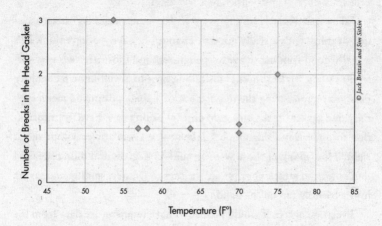

Dmitry, his black hair flopped to one side, is firmly against racing. He agrees that there is no apparent linear relationship between gasket failure and temperature; three gasket breaks occurred on the coolest race day (53 degrees), and two on one of the hottest days (75 degrees). But what if there is an optimal range for the engine, not too cold and not too hot? "If the failures are random, the probability that you both finish and get in the top five is 50 percent," Dmitry says. "But if it's not random, the probability is lower. This day is a very, very low temperature that they haven't experienced before. We don't know if there's a correlation with temperature, but if there is, it's like a sure thing that it fails."

Julia thinks mechanic Pat's temperature idea is "nonsense," but like Dmitry views the engine problem as a black box that does not give the team any information to calculate probability for today's race. She acknowledges that she's being risk averse, and would personally never get involved in car racing at all.

Except for Dmitry, the group agrees that there is "zero correlation at all," as Alexander puts it, between temperature and engine failure. "Am I the only one?" Dmitry asks, to a few giggles.

Jake is particularly unimpressed with engine mechanic Pat's reasoning. "I think Pat's a really good mechanic," he says. "I don't think he's a really good root cause analysis engineer, and those are two very different things." Jake thinks Pat is falling prey to a well-known cognitive bias, overemphasizing the importance of a single, dramatic memory—the three gasket breaks on a cool day. "We don't even have the information to understand this graph," Jake says. "There's twenty-four races, right? How many of those were around 53 degrees and didn't break? I don't mean to attack your point," he says to Dmitry, smiling and giving him a friendly tap on the hand.

Everyone agrees it would be nice to have temperature data from the races with no engine problems, but that they're stuck with what they have. Justin speaks for the entire pro-race side when he says, "I just think you've gotta race, because that's what you're in this business to do."

It seems that the group will finish where they started, voting not to race, until Mei takes another look at her calculations. "I've actually changed my mind," she announces. "I'm voting for yes, race." Comparing the potential financial upside and downside, Mei calculated that Carter Racing needs just a 26 percent chance of finishing in the top five—half their current rate—to make racing a smart bet. Even if the cool temperature changes the odds, "it won't decrease it to 26 percent, so we are still safe." She thinks Dmitry's read of the data is biased; Carter Racing has competed at temperatures from 53 to 82 degrees, with four engine failures below 65 and three above. Dmitry is giving too much credence, Mei says, to the 53-degree data point because it involved three gasket breaks. It's still just one engine failure.

Jake jumps in and says that group members are seeing whatever they want in the temperature chart, so "maybe we table that debate." He likes Mei's expected value argument. "I think that's one concrete thing we can go with, in terms of it's always good to base things on math. . . . If you told me to flip a coin, and if I lose the flip I lose $100 but if I win I get $200, I flip that coin every time." He reminds the group that Carter Racing used a new engine-prep procedure for the last two races, with no problems. "That's a small data point," he says, "but at least it's in the right direction for my argument."

Mei turns to Dmitry. "What is the temperature you feel comfortable to race?" she asks. "We have two engine failures at 70, one at 63, and one at 53. There's no temperature that's safe for us."

Dmitry wants to set limits at exactly the temperatures they have already experienced. Something is not functioning as expected, so anything outside that temperature range is unknown territory. He knows his recommendation comes off as extremely arbitrary.

The group moves to a final tally. With Mei's conversion, it's four to three, they're racing. The students continue to chat as they stuff the case study papers into their backpacks and messenger bags.

Martina quickly reads aloud a part of the case study where team owner BJ Carter asked his chief mechanic, Robin, for his opinion. "The drivers have their lives on the line, I have a career that hangs on every race, and you have every dime tied up in the business," Robin told him. Nobody ever won a race sitting in the pits, he reminded his boss.

Martina has one last question. "This is just about money, right? We're not going to kill anyone if we race, are we?"

A few of the group members look around and laugh, and then they go their separate ways.

When the students arrive in class the next day, they learn that most student groups around the world who have ever been assigned the Carter Racing case chose to race. The professor goes around the room, interrogating their logic for racing or withdrawing.

Teams that decided to race discuss their probability estimates and decision trees. Students are split on whether mid-race engine failure will endanger the driver. A majority of students think the temperature data is a red herring. Heads nod when one woman says, "If we want to make something of ourselves in the business of racing, this is the kind of risk we need to take." Her team was unanimous, 7–0, for race.

Dmitry objects, and the professor grills him ruthlessly. Dmitry contends that every probability decision tree that every group posits is irrelevant if you drop the assumption that engine failures are randomly distributed. He adds that the data are particularly ambiguous because for some reason the chief mechanic didn't plot the race temperatures when the engine didn't fail.

"Okay, so, Dmitry, here comes a quantitative question," the professor says. "How many times did I say yesterday if you want additional information let me know?" Muffled gasps spread across the room. "Four times," the professor answers himself. "Four times I said if you want additional information let me know." Not one student asked for the missing data. The professor puts up a new graph, with every race plotted. It looks something like this:

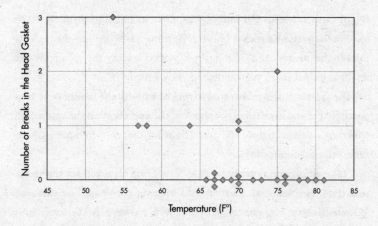

Every single race below 65 degrees had an engine failure. The professor then labels every race either a fail or not fail, and with that binary division runs a simple statistical analysis, familiar to the students, known as a logistic regression. He informs the students that there is a 99.4 percent probability of engine failure at 40 degrees. "Do we have any remaining fans of racing?" he asks. And now he has another surprise.

The temperature and engine failure data are taken exactly from NASA's tragic decision to launch the space shuttle *Challenger*, with the details placed in the context of racing rather than space exploration. Jake's face goes blank. Rather than a broken gasket, *Challenger* had failed O-rings—the rubber strips that sealed joints along the outer wall of the missile-like rocket boosters that propelled the shuttle. Cool temperatures caused O-ring rubber to harden, making them less effective seals.

The characters in the case study are loosely based on managers and engineers at NASA and its rocket-booster contractor, Morton Thiokol, on an emergency conference call the night before the *Challenger* launch. Weather reports on January 27, 1986, predicted unusually cool Florida weather for launch. After the conference call, NASA and Thiokol gave the okay to proceed. On January 28, O-rings failed to properly seal a joint in the wall of a rocket booster. Burning gas shot right through the joint to the outside, and *Challenger* exploded seventy-three seconds into its mission. All seven crew members were killed.

The Carter Racing case study worked exquisitely. It was eerie how precisely the students filled the shoes of the engineers on the emergency conference call who gave the green light for launch. The professor unfurled the lesson masterfully.

"Like all of you, nobody [at NASA or Thiokol] asked for the seventeen data points for which there had been no problems," he explains. "Obviously that data existed, and they were having a discussion like we had. If I was in your situation I would probably say, 'But in a classroom the teacher typically gives us material we're supposed to have.' But it's often the case in group meetings where the person who made the PowerPoint slides puts data in front of you, and we often just use the data people put in front of us. I would argue we don't do a good job of saying, 'Is this the data that we want to make the decision we need to make?'"

The presidential commission that investigated the *Challenger* accident concluded that simply including the nonfailure flights would have revealed the correlation between O-ring damage and temperature. A University of Chicago professor of organizational psychology wrote that the missed data was such a rudimentary mistake that it came down to "a professional weakness shared by all participants" on the conference call. "Arguments against launching at cold temperatures could have been quantified, but were not quantified." The engineers were poorly educated, he declared.

Sociologist Diane Vaughan's book *The Challenger Launch Decision* came to be regarded by NASA as the definitive causal account of the tragedy. "More stunning is the observation that they *did* have the pertinent data," it reads. "There were charts [that several Thiokol engineers who wanted to postpone launch] did not imagine and did not construct that, if created, would have provided the quantitative correlational data required to sustain their position."

Business professors around the world have been teaching Carter Racing for thirty years because it provides a stark lesson in the danger of reaching conclusions from incomplete data, and the folly of relying only on what is in front of you.

And now for one last surprise. They all got it wrong. The *Challenger* decision was not a failure of quantitative analysis. NASA's real mistake was to rely on quantitative analysis too much.

Before ignition, *Challenger*'s O-rings sat squashed in the joints that connected vertical sections of the booster. At ignition, burning gas came shooting down the booster. The metal walls that connected to form a joint pulled apart for a split second, at which point the rubber O-rings immediately expanded to fill the space and keep the joint sealed. When the O-rings got cold, the rubber hardened and could not expand as quickly. The colder the O-ring, the longer the fraction of a second when the joint was not sealed and burning gas could shoot right through the booster wall. Even so, temperature usually did not matter; the O-rings were protected by a special insulating putty meant to block burning gas from reaching them in the first place. On the seventeen flights with no O-ring problems—akin to the seventeen Carter Racing races with no engine problems—the putty worked perfectly. Those flights provided no information whatsoever about how O-rings might fail, no matter the temperature, because the burning gas could not even get to the O-rings to cause a problem. Sometimes, however, small holes formed in the putty when the joints were assembled. On the seven flights that had O-ring issues, burning gas pushed through the holes in the protective putty and reached the O-rings. Only those seven data points were relevant to how the O-rings could be damaged or fail.

And on those seven shuttle flights—unlike gasket breaks in Carter Racing, which was the same problem every time—the O-ring issues came in two different varieties. The first: erosion. On five flights, burning gas that came shooting down the booster at ignition hit the O-rings and eroded the rubber surface. This was not a life-or-death condition. There was more than enough rubber for the O-ring to do its job. And erosion had nothing at all to do with temperature.

The second variety: blow-by. If the rubber ring did not expand instantly to fully seal the joint at ignition, burning gas "blew by" and could potentially shoot right through the booster wall. Blow-by *was* a life-or-death condition and, engineers would later learn, dramatically worsened when cool temperatures hardened the O-ring rubber. Two pre-*Challenger* flights had blow-by, but still returned home safely.

Thiokol engineers who opposed the launch on the emergency pre-launch conference call did not really have twenty-four relevant data points on O-ring failure to work with, as the Carter Racing study indicates. They did not even have seven, like the Harvard students. They had two.

Now what does the chart tell you?

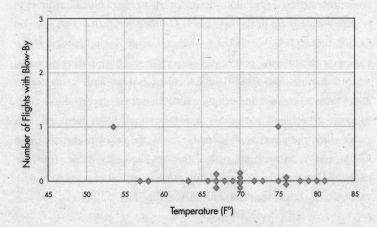

Ironically, Allan McDonald, then director of the rocket-booster project at Morton Thiokol, told me, "Looking only at the relevant data points supported NASA's [prelaunch] position that it was inconclusive." There was no 99.4 percent certainty that was missed. The engineers were not poorly educated.

There was other important information the Thiokol engineers presented that could have helped NASA avert disaster. But it was not quantitative, so NASA managers did not accept it. The Carter Racing study teaches that the answer was available, if only engineers looked at the right numbers. In reality, the right numbers did not contain an answer at all. The *Challenger* decision was truly ambiguous. It was a wicked problem, rife with uncertainty, and outside of previous experience, where demanding more data actually became the problem itself.

The infamous emergency conference call convened thirty-four engineers —every manager was also an engineer—in three locations. Thiokol engineer Roger Boisjoly had personally inspected the joints after both flights with blow-by, and presented photographs from each. Following the 75-degree flight, he found a very thin streak of light gray soot beyond an O-ring in the joint, from a tiny amount of gas that had blown by before the O-ring sealed. It was nowhere close to a catastrophic problem. After the 53-degree flight, he found jet-black soot fanned out across a large swath of the joint. A lot of burning gas had blown past that time. In Boisjoly's opinion, the reason the 53-degree launch looked so much worse was that cool conditions had hardened the O-rings and made them slow to expand and seal at ignition. He was right, but he did not have the data to prove it. "I was asked to quantify my concerns, and I said I couldn't," Boisjoly later testified. "I had no data to quantify it, but I did say I knew that it was away from goodness."

Thanks to an extraordinarily strong technical culture, NASA had developed quantitatively rigorous "flight readiness reviews." They were productively adversarial, like superforecasting team discussions. Managers grilled engineers and forced them to produce data to back up their assertions. The process had worked remarkably. The space shuttle was the most complex machine ever built, and all twenty-four flights had returned safely. But on the emergency conference call, that same quantitative culture led them astray.

On their engineers' advice, McDonald and two Thiokol VPs on the call initially supported a no-launch decision. The *Challenger* had already been cleared, so this was an eleventh-hour reversal. When NASA officials asked Thiokol engineers exactly what temperature range was safe for flight, they recommended setting a limit at 53 degrees, the lower bound of previous experience.

NASA manager Larry Mulloy was flabbergasted. He thought the shuttle was supposed to be cleared to launch from 31 to 99 degrees. A last-minute 53-degree limit was setting an entirely new technical criteria for launches. It had never been discussed, was not backed by quantitative data, and meant that suddenly winter was off-limits for space exploration. Mulloy found it frustrating; he later called it "dumb."

How had the engineers arrived at that number? "They said because they had flown at 53 degrees before," a NASA manager reflected, "which is no reason to me. That's tradition rather than technology." Boisjoly was asked again for data to support his claim, "and I said I have none other than what is being presented."

With the conference call at an impasse, a Thiokol VP asked for a five-minute "offline caucus," during which Thiokol concluded that they had no more data to provide. They returned to the call a half hour later with a new decision: proceed with launch. Their official document read, "temperature data not conclusive on predicting primary O-ring blow-by."

When conference call participants from NASA and Thiokol later spoke with investigators and gave interviews, they repeatedly brought up the "weak engineering position," as one put it. Their statements comprised a repetitive chorus: "Unable to quantify"; "supporting data was subjective";

"hadn't done a good technical job"; "just didn't have enough conclusive data." NASA was, after all, the agency that hung a framed quote in the Mission Evaluation Room: "In God We Trust, All Others Bring Data."

"The engineers' concerns for the most part were just based on a few photographs they took of joints they pulled apart that had soot trapped in there," McDonald told me. "One was at a cool temperature, and one was at a rather warm temperature. Roger Boisjoly thought the difference was absolutely telling a story, but it was a qualitative assessment." NASA's Mulloy later argued that he "would've felt naked" taking Thiokol's argument up the chain of command. Without a solid quantitative case, "I couldn't have defended it."

The very tool that had helped make NASA so consistently successful, what Diane Vaughan called "the original technical culture" in the agency's DNA, suddenly worked perversely in a situation where the familiar brand of data did not exist. Reason without numbers was not accepted. In the face of an unfamiliar challenge, NASA managers failed to drop their familiar tools.

Psychologist and organizational behavior expert Karl Weick noticed something unusual in the deaths of smokejumpers and "hotshot" wilderness firefighters: they held on to their tools, even when ditching equipment would have allowed them to run away from an advancing fire. For Weick, it was emblematic of something larger.

In Montana's 1949 Mann Gulch fire, made famous in Norman Maclean's *Young Men and Fire,* smokejumpers parachuted in expecting to face a "ten o'clock fire," meaning they would have it contained by 10 a.m. the next morning. Until the fire jumped across the gulch from one forested hill slope to the steep slope where the firefighters were, and chased them uphill through dry grass at eleven feet per second. Crew foreman Wagner Dodge yelled at the men to drop their tools. Two did so immediately and sprinted over the ridge to safety. Others ran with their tools and were caught by the flames. One firefighter stopped fleeing and sat down, exhausted, never having removed his heavy pack. Thirteen firefighters died. The Mann Gulch tragedy led to reforms in safety training, but wildland firefighters continued to lose races with fires when they did not drop their tools.

In 1994, on Colorado's Storm King Mountain, hotshots and smoke-jumpers faced a Mann Gulch situation when a fire jumped a canyon and erupted through a stand of gambel oak below them. The sound in the canyon was "like a jet during take off," according to a survivor. Four-teen men and women lost the race with a wall of flame. "[Victim] was still wearing his backpack," reads an analysis from the body recovery operation. "Victim has chainsaw handle still in hand." He was just 250 feet from a safe zone. Survivor Quentin Rhoades had already run nine hundred feet uphill, "then realized I still had my saw over my shoulder! I irrationally started looking for a place to put it down where it wouldn't get burned. . . . I remember thinking I can't believe I'm putting down my saw." Two separate analyses conducted for the U.S. Forest Service and the Bureau of Land Management concluded that the crew would have made it out intact had they simply dropped their tools and run from the start.

In four separate fires in the 1990s, twenty-three elite wildland fire-fighters refused orders to drop their tools and perished beside them. Even when Rhoades eventually dropped his chainsaw, he felt like he was doing something unnatural. Weick found similar phenomena in Navy seamen who ignored orders to remove steel-toed shoes when abandon-ing a ship, and drowned or punched holes in life rafts; fighter pilots in disabled planes refusing orders to eject; and Karl Wallenda, the world-famous high-wire performer, who fell 120 feet to his death when he teetered and grabbed first at his balance pole rather than the wire be-neath him. He momentarily lost the pole while falling, and grabbed it again in the air. "Dropping one's tools is a proxy for unlearning, for adaptation, for flexibility," Weick wrote. "It is the very unwillingness of people to drop their tools that turns some of these dramas into tragedies." For him, firefighters were an example, and a metaphor for what he learned while studying normally reliable organizations that clung to trusty methods, even when they led to bewildering decisions.

Rather than adapting to unfamiliar situations, whether airline accidents or fire tragedies, Weick saw that experienced groups became rigid under pressure and "regress to what they know best." They behaved like a collective hedgehog, bending an unfamiliar situation to a familiar comfort zone, as if trying to will it to become something they actually had experienced before. For wildland firefighters, their tools are what they know best. "Firefighting tools define the firefighter's group membership, they are the firefighter's reason for being deployed in the first place," Weick wrote. "Given the central role of tools in defining the essence of a firefighter, it is not surprising that dropping one's tools creates an existential crisis." As Maclean succinctly put it, "When a firefighter is told to drop his firefighting tools, he is told to forget he is a firefighter."

Weick explained that wildland firefighters have a firm "can do" culture, and dropping tools was not part of it, because it meant they had lost control. Quentin Rhoades's chainsaw was such a part of his firefighting self that he did not even realize he still had it, any more than he realized he still had his arms. When it became utterly ludicrous to carry the saw further, Rhoades still "could not believe" he was parting with it. He felt naked, just as Larry Mulloy said he would have without a quantitative argument for a last-second launch reversal. At NASA, accepting a qualitative argument was like being told to forget you are an engineer.

When sociologist Diane Vaughan interviewed NASA and Thiokol engineers who had worked on the rocket boosters, she found that NASA's own famous can-do culture manifested as a belief that everything would be fine because "we followed every procedure"; because "the [flight readiness review] process is aggressive and adversarial"; because "we went by the book." NASA's tools were its familiar procedures. The rules had always worked before. But with *Challenger* they were outside their usual bounds, where "can do" should have been swapped for what Weick calls a "make do" culture. They needed to improvise rather than throw out information that did not fit the established rubric.

Roger Boisjoly's unquantifiable argument that the cold weather was "away from goodness" was considered an emotional argument in NASA culture. It was based on interpretation of a photograph. It did not conform to the usual quantitative standards, so it was deemed inadmissible evidence and disregarded. The can-do attitude among the rocket-booster group, Vaughan observed, "was grounded in conformity." After the tragedy, it emerged that other engineers on the teleconference agreed with Boisjoly, but knew they could not muster quantitative arguments, so they remained silent. Their silence was taken as consent. As one engineer who was on the *Challenger* conference call later said, "If I feel like I don't have data to back me up, the boss's opinion is better than mine."

Dropping familiar tools is particularly difficult for experienced professionals who rely on what Weick called overlearned behavior. That is, they have done the same thing in response to the same challenges over and over until the behavior has become so automatic that they no longer even recognize it as a situation-specific tool. Research on aviation accidents, for example, found that "a common pattern was the crew's decision to continue with their original plan" even when conditions changed dramatically.

When Weick spoke with hotshot Paul Gleason, one of the best wildland firefighters in the world, Gleason told him that he preferred to view his crew leadership not as decision making, but as sensemaking. "If I make a decision, it is a possession, I take pride in it, I tend to defend it and not listen to those who question it," Gleason explained. "If I make sense, then this is more dynamic and I listen and I can change it." He employed what Weick called "hunches held lightly." Gleason gave decisive directions to his crew, but with transparent rationale and the addendum that the plan was ripe for revision as the team collectively made sense of a fire.

On the night of the *Challenger* conference call, following procedure in the face of uncertainty was so paramount that NASA's Mulloy asked Thiokol to put its final launch recommendation and rationale on paper and sign it. Last-minute sign-off had always been verbal in the past. Thiokol's Allan McDonald was in the room with Mulloy, and refused. One of McDonald's bosses in Utah signed and faxed the document instead. Even Mulloy, who had demanded data, must have felt uneasy with the decision, while at the same time feeling protected by NASA's ultimate tool—its hallowed process. The process culminated with more concern for being able to defend a decision than with using all available information to make the right one. Like the firefighters, NASA managers had merged with their tools. As McDonald said, looking only at the quantitative data actually supported NASA's stance that there was no link between temperature and failure. NASA's normal quantitative standard was a dearly held tool, but the wrong one for the job. That night, it should have been dropped.

It is easy to say in retrospect. A group of managers accustomed to dispositive technical information did not have any; engineers felt like they should not speak up without it. Decades later, an astronaut who flew on the space shuttle, both before and after *Challenger,* and then became NASA's chief of safety and mission assurance, recounted what the "In God We Trust, All Others Bring Data" plaque had meant to him: "Between the lines it suggested that, 'We're not interested in your opinion on things. If you have data, we'll listen, but your opinion is not requested here.'"

Physicist and Nobel laureate Richard Feynman was one of the members of the commission that investigated the *Challenger,* and in one hearing he admonished a NASA manager for repeating that Boisjoly's data did not prove his point. "When you don't have any data," Feynman said, "you have to use reason."

These are, by definition, wicked situations. Wildland firefighters and space shuttle engineers do not have the liberty to train for their most challenging moments by trial and error. A team or organization that is both reliable and flexible, according to Weick, is like a jazz group. There are fundamentals—scales and chords—that every member must overlearn, but those are just tools for sensemaking in a dynamic environment. There are no tools that cannot be dropped, reimagined, or repurposed in order to navigate an unfamiliar challenge. Even the most sacred tools. Even the tools so taken for granted they become invisible. It is, of course, easier said than done. Especially when the tool is the very core of an organization's culture.

As Captain Tony Lesmes described it, his team at Bagram Air Base in northeast Afghanistan only went to work when someone got really unlucky. Lesmes commanded a team of Air Force pararescue jumpers, PJs for short, a division of Special Operations designed for harrowing rescue missions, like parachuting into enemy territory at night to save downed pilots. Cross a soldier, a paramedic, a rescue diver, a firefighter, a mountain rescue specialist, and a parachutist, and you get a PJ. Their emblem depicts an angel with arms wrapped around the world, and the words "That others may live."

There was no typical day for the PJs at Bagram. One day they were rappelling down a mountain to rescue a soldier who fell into an unmarked well. Another day they were rushing to treat Marines injured in a firefight. PJs could accompany units out on missions, but mostly they stayed on twenty-four-hour alert, waiting for a "9-line," a form (with nine lines) that provided basic information about an active emergency. Like one that came in on an autumn day in 2009. It was a category alpha, traumatic injuries. Within minutes, the team would be airborne.

Intel was sparse. A roadside bomb had exploded in the middle of an Army convoy of armored vehicles. The site was approximately a half hour away by helicopter. There were serious injuries, but it was unclear how many or how serious, and whether the bomb was part of a search and rescue trap, where enemies lie in ambush awaiting the rescue team.

The PJs were used to working with cloudy information, but this was ambiguous even for them. Lesmes knew they would have to bring heavy equipment, like the Jaws of Life and a diamond-tipped saw, because "you can't just cut through an armored vehicle like a car door," he told me. Weight was an obstacle, especially at altitude in the mountains. If the choppers were too heavy, they wouldn't grab enough air to stay aloft. Fuel limitations were a challenge. Space was a bigger one. Each PJ came with gear, and each of the two helicopters only had interior space on the order of a large van. They didn't know how many soldiers were injured badly enough to need evacuation, and how much space they would need for them.

Lesmes was certain of just one thing: he wanted to make sure they saved enough room for potential patients so that they would only have to visit the explosion site once. It would take extra time to treat and load severely wounded soldiers. The more time on site, the more likely the operation would draw enemy attention. The rescue team could end up needing a rescue team.

He was twenty-seven, and the previous year had led a stateside hurricane rescue team. Afghanistan was his first extended deployment, and he was directing a team with older members who had had numerous overseas deployments. As usual, Lesmes brought two team members to the operations center to get information and help him make sense of the situation. "Sometimes other guys are able to get really good questions out that I wouldn't normally think of," he told me. "And you want to share as much information as possible, and there isn't a lot of time." But there was little additional intel. "In Hollywood, a drone flies over the site and you get all the information," Lesmes told me. "But that's Hollywood."

He walked out to the helicopters, where PJs were donning their full battle rattle, as he put it. The situation didn't fit the usual decision trees; he laid out the challenges, and asked the men: How do we solve this?

Just move equipment around to cram more stuff into the helicopters, one team member suggested. Another said they could leave a few PJs with the Army convoy if they needed extra helicopter room for patients. One recommended they evacuate the most serious patients, and if a second trip was needed, move the convoy from the explosion site and meet them somewhere less conspicuous. But the bomb had exploded in the middle of a procession of vehicles, in rugged terrain. Lesmes didn't even know how mobile the convoy would be.

"We weren't coming up with any real solution that would give us an advantage. I wanted a speed advantage, and the ability to leverage the weight and space for wounded soldiers," he told me. "The distance and the timeline and the constraints and the unknown of the enemy all started to add up. I just started feeling like we didn't have the setup to be successful in a worst-case scenario. There wasn't that pattern recognition, it was outside of the normal pattern." In others words, he didn't have the definitive intel he would have liked. Based on the information he had, Lesmes guessed there would be more than three serious injuries but fewer than fifteen. An idea started to form, one that could preserve more space for potential patients. He could put aside a tool he had never dropped in this situation: himself.

Lesmes had never not accompanied his team on a mass-casualty category alpha. He was the site conductor. His role was to keep a broad view of the situation while PJs were "heads down" working furiously to save patients, or their limbs. He helped secure the site; communicated with his guys, the base, and helicopter pilots who were circling waiting to pick up patients and go; he radioed planes for backup if a firefight erupted; he coordinated with officers in the area, frequently from other military branches. Emotional chaos was an explosion site certainty. Soldiers watching their shell-shocked teammates suck on fentanyl lollipops, in danger of bleeding out, are desperate to help, but they must be moved. The site had to be managed. This time, as long as there were not many more injuries than Lesmes guessed, he knew his senior enlisted team member could manage leadership on the ground while administering medical aid. Lesmes could help ready the field hospital for returning patients, and coordinate helicopter pickups from the operations center, adjusting as he listened via radio to his guys on the ground. It was a trade-off, but every option was.

Lesmes went to the team with his "hypothesis," as he called it—his hunch held lightly. "I wanted them to disprove it," he told me. He told them he planned to stay at the base to save room for equipment and patients. The helicopter blades were spinning up, moments ticking away in the so-called golden hour, the critical window for saving a severely injured soldier. He told them to talk quickly, and he would consider everything they had to say. A few were quiet. Several objected. Togetherness was their most basic tool, the one they didn't know could be dropped until someone said to drop it. One of the men said flatly that it was the commanding officer's job to come along, and he should do his job. Another got angry. A third reflexively suggested that Lesmes was afraid. He told Lesmes that when it was his time, it was his time, so they should just do what they always did. Lesmes *was* afraid, but not for his life. "If something bad happens, and the officer is not there," he told me, "think about explaining that to ten families."

I was sitting with him at the World War II Memorial in Washington, D.C., when he said that. He had been stoic, and then he started crying. "The whole construct is built on that training and that familiarity and that cohesion," he said. "I totally understand why some guys were upset. It was breaking our standard operating procedure. I mean, my judgment was questioned. But if I go, we might have to go to the rescue site twice." The objections he got were emotional and philosophical, not tactical. They had changed his mind about a plan before, but not this time. He would stay, and it was time for them to go. The helicopters strained into the air as Lesmes returned to the operations center. "I struggled immensely," he said. "I could see what was going on, and if something bad were to happen, I could literally watch the rescue helicopter go down."

The rescue mission, thankfully, was an unqualified success. PJs treated injuries at the explosion site, and seven wounded soldiers had to be loaded into the helicopters. They were packed in like sardines. Several required amputations at the field hospital, but all survived.

When it was over, the senior enlisted man acknowledged it was the right call. Another PJ did not address it for months, and then only to say that he was taken aback that Lesmes had that much trust in them. The soldier who had gotten angry initially remained angry, for a while. Another Bagram PJ I spoke with said, "If I was in that position, I definitely would have said, 'Yeah, we're all going.' It must have been really hard."

"I don't know, man," Lesmes told me. "Sometimes, I still struggle with that decision. Something could've gone wrong and then it would be a bad decision. Maybe it was luck. None of the options at the time looked very optimal."

As we finished talking, I mentioned Weick's work about wilderness firefighters clinging to their tools. Under pressure, Weick explained, experienced pros regress to what they know best. I suggested to Lesmes that maybe his PJs were just reacting emotionally, with a reflex for the familiar. There must be times when even the sacrosanct tool of togetherness should be dropped, right? "Yeah, mmm-hmm." He nodded in agreement. It was, of course, easy for me to say. He paused for a moment. "Yeah," he said, "but everything is built on that."

The *Challenger* managers made mistakes of conformity. They stuck to the usual tools in the face of an unusual challenge. Captain Lesmes dropped a sacred tool, and it worked. Once emotions cooled, several members of his team acknowledged it was the right call. Others never did. Going back over it brought Lesmes to tears. It isn't exactly the fairy-tale ending to a good decision. Had NASA canceled the launch, Allan McDonald told me that engineers who pushed to abort might have been cast as "Chicken Littles." Chicken Little doesn't fare well in the space business. As NASA engineer Mary Shafer once articulated, "Insisting on perfect safety is for people who don't have the balls to live in the real world." It is no wonder that organizations struggle to cultivate experts who are both proficient with their tools and prepared to drop them. But there is an organizational strategy that can help. The strategy, strange as it sounds, is to send a mixed message.

"Congruence" is a social science term for cultural "fit" among an institution's components—values, goals, vision, self-concepts, and leadership styles. Since the 1980s, congruence has been a pillar of organizational theory. An effective culture is both consistent and strong. When all signals point clearly in the same direction, it promotes self-reinforcing consistency, and people like consistency.

Plenty of profiles of individual businesses were written in support of congruence. But in the first study that systematically examined a broad swath of organizations across an industry, researchers who studied cultural congruence at 334 institutions of higher education found that it had no influence on any measure of organizational success whatsoever. Administrators, department heads, and trustees in strongly congruent institutions did have an easier time classifying the culture when asked, but there was no impact at all on performance, from the academic and career development of students to the satisfaction of faculty and the financial health of the college. The researcher who led that work went on to study thousands of businesses. She found that the most effective leaders and organizations had range; they were, in effect, paradoxical. They could be demanding and nurturing, orderly and entrepreneurial, even hierarchical and individualistic all at once. A level of ambiguity, it seemed, was not harmful. In decision making, it can broaden an organization's toolbox in a way that is uniquely valuable.

Philip Tetlock and Barbara Mellers showed that thinkers who tolerate ambiguity make the best forecasts; one of Tetlock's former graduate
students, University of Texas professor Shefali Patil, spearheaded a project with them to show that cultures can build in a form of ambiguity
that forces decision makers to use more than one tool, and to become
more flexible and learn more readily.

In one experiment, subjects played the role of corporate human resources managers who had to predict the performance of job applicants.
The managers were presented with a standard evaluation process that
showed them how a candidate's skills were typically weighted, and then
told that they would be evaluated (and paid) based on how they made
decisions. In a sped-up simulation of real life, after each prediction they
could see how the candidate actually performed according to company
records. In some batches of applications, the candidates performed as the
standard evaluation process predicted; in others, they weren't even close.
Yet, over and over, the individual managers conformed to standard procedure no matter what the results told them, even when it clearly was not
working, and even when a better system was easily discoverable. They
failed to learn with experience. Until a wrinkle was added. Conformist
managers were given fake *Harvard Business Review* research proclaim-
ing that successful groups prioritize independence and dissent. Miracu-
lously, their minds were opened and they started learning. They began to
see when the standard evaluation process clearly needed to be modified
or discarded. They were learning with experience, and their predictions
became more accurate. The managers were benefitting from *incongruence*. The formal, conformist company process rules were balanced out
by an informal culture of individual autonomy in decision making and
dissent from the typical way of doing things.

Incongruence worked in the other direction as well. HR managers
who were given a standard evaluation process but told that only the accuracy of their predictions mattered began by ditching the process and
making up their own rules. They never learned when the standard

process did indeed work. In that case, the cure was fake *Harvard Business Review* research indicating that successful groups prioritize cohesion, loyalty, and finding common ground. Again, the HR managers became learning machines; they suddenly hewed closer to the traditional process when it had value, but continued to deviate readily when it didn't, as NASA should have.

Business school students are widely taught to believe the congruence model, that a good manager can always align every element of work into a culture where all influences are mutually reinforcing—whether toward cohesion or individualism. But cultures can actually be too internally consistent. With incongruence, "you're building in cross-checks," Tetlock told me.

The experiments showed that an effective problem-solving culture was one that balanced standard practice—whatever it happened to be—with forces that pushed in the opposite direction. If managers were used to process conformity, encouraging individualism helped them to employ "ambidextrous thought," and learn what worked in each situation. If they were used to improvising, encouraging a sense of loyalty and cohesion did the job. The trick was expanding the organization's range by identifying the dominant culture and then diversifying it by pushing in the opposite direction.

By the time of the *Challenger* launch, NASA's "can do" culture manifested as extreme process accountability combined with collectivist social norms. Everything was congruent for conformity to the standard procedures. The process was so rigid it spurned evidence that didn't conform to the usual rules, and so sacred that Larry Mulloy felt protected by a signed piece of paper testifying that he had followed the usual process. Dissent was valued at flight readiness reviews, but at the most important moment, the most important engineering group asked for an offline caucus where they found a way, in private, to conform. Like the one engineer said, without data, "the boss's opinion is better than mine."

The more I spoke with Captain Lesmes, the more it seemed to me that he had felt strongly outcome accountable—searching for a solution even if it deviated from standard procedure—within an extraordinarily potent collective culture that ensured he would not make the decision to deviate easily. He had, as Patil, Tetlock, and Mellers wrote, harnessed "the power of cross-pressures in promoting flexible, ambidextrous thought." The subtitle of that paper: "Balancing the Risks of Mindless Conformity and Reckless Deviation."

Superforecasting teams harnessed the same cultural cross-pressure. A team was judged purely by the accuracy of its members' forecasts. But internally the Good Judgment Project incentivized collective culture. Commenting was an expectation; teammates were encouraged to vote for useful comments and recognized for process milestones, like a certain number of lifetime comments.

Prior to *Challenger,* there was a long span when NASA culture harnessed incongruence. Gene Kranz, the flight director when Apollo 11 first landed on the moon, lived by that same mantra, the valorized process—"In God We Trust, All Others Bring Data"—but he also made a habit of seeking out opinions of technicians and engineers at every level of the hierarchy. If he heard the same hunch twice, it didn't take data for him to interrupt the usual process and investigate.

Wernher von Braun, who led the Marshall Space Flight Center's development of the rocket that propelled the moon mission, balanced NASA's rigid process with an informal, individualistic culture that encouraged constant dissent and cross-boundary communication. Von Braun started "Monday Notes": every week engineers submitted a single page of notes on their salient issues. Von Braun handwrote comments in the margins, and then circulated the entire compilation. Everyone saw what other divisions were up to, and how easily problems could be raised. Monday Notes were rigorous, but informal.

On a typed page of notes from two days after the moon landing in

1969, von Braun homed in on a short section in which an engineer guessed why a liquid oxygen tank unexpectedly lost pressure. The issue was already irrelevant for the moon mission, but could come up again in future flights. "Let's pin this down as precisely as possible," von Braun wrote. "We must know whether there's more behind this, that calls for checks or remedies." Like Kranz, von Braun went looking for problems, hunches, and bad news. He even rewarded those who exposed problems. After Kranz and von Braun's time, the "All Others Bring Data" process culture remained, but the informal culture and power of individual hunches shriveled.

In 1974, William Lucas took over the Marshall Space Flight Center. A NASA chief historian wrote that Lucas was a brilliant engineer but "often grew angry when he learned of problems." Allan McDonald described him to me as a "shoot-the-messenger type guy." Lucas transformed von Braun's Monday Notes into a system purely for upward communication. He did not write feedback and the notes did not circulate. At one point they morphed into standardized forms that had to be filled out. Monday Notes became one more rigid formality in a process culture. "Immediately, the quality of the notes fell," wrote another official NASA historian.

Lucas retired shortly after the *Challenger* disaster, but the entrenched process culture persisted. NASA's only other fatal shuttle accident, the space shuttle *Columbia* disintegration in 2003, was a cultural carbon copy of the *Challenger*. NASA clung to its usual process tools in an unusual circumstance. The *Columbia* disaster engendered an even stronger ill-fated congruence between process accountability and group-focused norms. Engineers grew concerned about a technical problem they did not fully understand, but they could not make a quantitative case. When they went to the Department of Defense to request high-resolution photographs of a part of the shuttle they thought was damaged, not only did NASA managers block outside assistance, but they apologized to DoD for contact outside "proper channels." NASA administrators promised the violation of protocol would not happen again. The *Columbia* Accident Investigation Board concluded that NASA's culture "emphasized chain of command, procedure, following the rules, and going by the book. While rules and procedures were essential for coordination, they had an unintended negative effect." Once again, "allegiance to hierarchy and procedure" had ended in disaster. Again, lower ranking engineers had concerns they could not quantify; they stayed silent because "the requirement for data was stringent and inhibiting."

The management and culture aspects of the *Challenger* and *Columbia* disasters were so eerily similar that the investigation board decreed that NASA was not functioning as "a learning organization." In the absence of cultural cross-pressures, NASA had failed to learn, just like the subjects in Patil's work who were placed in strongly congruent cultures.

There were, though, individuals in NASA who learned vital culture lessons, and when the time came, put them to use.

In the spring of 2003, just two months after NASA lost the space shuttle *Columbia,* it had to decide whether to scrap a high-profile project that had been forty years and three-quarters of a billion dollars in the making. Gravity Probe B was a technological marvel designed for a direct test of Einstein's general theory of relativity. It would be launched into space to measure how Earth's mass and rotation warped the fabric of space-time, like a bowling ball twirling in a vat of honey. GP-B had the distinction of being the longest-running project in the history of NASA. That was not a compliment.

It was conceived one year after the founding of NASA itself. The launch was delayed numerous times for technical problems, and the project was nearly cancelled on three separate occasions. There were staff members at NASA who no longer thought its mission was possible, and funding had to be rescued repeatedly by a Stanford physicist with a knack for lobbying Congress.

The technological challenges were immense. The probe required the roundest objects ever manufactured—quartz gyroscope rotors the size of ping-pong balls and so perfectly spherical that if you blew them up to the size of Earth, the highest mountain peak would be eight feet tall. The gyroscopes had to be cooled to −450°F by liquid helium, and the probe required surgically delicate thrusters for precise maneuvering. The technology took twenty years in development before it was ready for a test flight.

Congressional eyes were on NASA. The agency could not afford to launch the probe and have a high-profile failure right after *Columbia*. But if the Gravity Probe B launch had to be delayed once more, it could be the last time. "There was a *huge* amount of pressure to get this thing flown," Rex Geveden, the GP-B program manager, told me. Unfortunately, engineers preparing for the prelaunch flight readiness review found a problem.

The power supply to an electronics box was interfering with a critical scientific instrument. Thankfully, the box only had to work at the beginning of the mission, to get the gyroscopes spinning. It could then be turned off, so it was not a catastrophic issue. But it was unexpected. If there were other flaws that prevented the box from spinning up the gyroscopes to start the experiment, the mission would be a total waste.

The giant Thermos-like container holding the gyroscopes had already been filled with liquid helium, cooled, and sealed for launch. If the box needed inspection, parts that had taken three months to install would have to come off the probe; a launch delay would cost $10–$20 million. Some engineers felt there was more risk in removing and potentially damaging parts than in leaving it all alone. Stanford University was the prime contractor, and the Stanford team leader "was confident that we could succeed," he said, "so I pushed hard that we should go ahead and fly." NASA's chief engineer and head scientist for Gravity

Probe B also both pushed to launch. Plus, the probe had been moved to Vandenberg Air Force Base in California for launch, and a delay would increase the chance of GP-B sitting there when an earthquake struck. So: race, or don't race?

The decision was in Geveden's hands. "My God, I can't even express how stressful it was," he told me. Even before the latest snafu, he had a hunch held lightly—he was uneasy about how the electronics box had been managed. But as long as the box was attached to the probe, there would be no more information forthcoming.

Geveden joined NASA in 1990, and was a keen observer of the culture. "When I was coming through NASA," he said, "I had the intuition that there's a real conformance culture." Early in his tenure, he attended a team-building class offered by the agency. On the very first day the instructor asked the class, rhetorically, for the single most important principle in decision making. His answer: to get consensus. "And I said, 'I don't think the people who launched the space shuttle *Challenger* agree with that point,'" Geveden told me. "Consensus is nice to have, but we shouldn't be optimizing happiness, we should be optimizing our decisions. I just had a feeling all along that there was something wrong with the culture. We didn't have a healthy tension in the system." NASA still had its hallowed process, and Geveden saw everywhere a collective culture that nudged conflict into darkened corners. "You almost couldn't go into a meeting without someone saying, 'Let's take that offline,'" he recalled, just as Morton Thiokol had done for the infamous offline caucus.

Geveden, in his own way, was in favor of balancing the typical, formal process culture with a dose of informal individualism, as Kranz and von Braun once had. "The chain of communication has to be informal," he told me, "completely different from the chain of command." He wanted a culture where everyone had the responsibility to protest if something didn't feel right. He decided to go prospecting for doubts.

He deeply respected Stanford's electronics manager. The manager had worked with the same kind of power supply before, and viewed it as fragile technology. After a formal meeting in which NASA's head engineer and its head scientist on the project both advocated for leaving the box in place, Geveden held informal individual meetings. In one of those, he learned from a member of the NASA team that a manager from Lockheed Martin, which had built the box, was concerned. Like *Challenger*'s O-rings, the known problem with the box was surmountable, but it was unexpected. There were unknown unknowns.

Against the recommendation of the chief engineer and the Stanford team leader, Geveden decided to scrub the launch and pull the box. Once it came off, engineers quickly discovered three other design problems that had not been clear in schematics, including a case of having used the flat-out wrong parts. The surprises prompted Lockheed to go back over every single circuit in the box. They found twenty separate issues.

As if Gravity Probe B was required by the space gods to scale every imaginable obstacle, a month after the box was pulled there was an earthquake near the launch site. The launch vehicle was slightly damaged, but fortunately the probe was intact. Four months later, in April 2004, GP-B finally took off. It was the first direct test to support Einstein's idea that Earth drags the fabric of space-time around with it as it spins. The technology left a greater legacy. Components designed for Gravity Probe B improved digital cameras and satellites; the centimeter-accurate GPS was applied to automatic aircraft landing systems and precision farming.

The following year, a new NASA administrator was appointed by the president. The new administrator demanded the kind of individualism and opinionated debate that could serve as a cross-pressure for NASA's robust process accountability. He made Geveden the associate administrator, essentially the COO of NASA, and the highest position in the agency that is not politically appointed.

In 2017, Geveden took his lessons to a new role as CEO of BWX Technologies, a company whose wide purview includes nuclear propulsion technology that could power a manned Mars mission. Some of BWX Technologies' decision makers are retired military leaders whose dearly held tool is firm hierarchy. So when Geveden became CEO, he wrote a short memo on his expectations for teamwork. "I told them I expect disagreement with my decisions at the time we're trying to make decisions, and that's a sign of organizational health," he told me. "After the decisions are made, we want compliance and support, but we have permission to fight a little bit about those things in a professional way." He emphasized that there is a difference between the chain of command and the chain of communication, and that the difference represents a healthy cross-pressure. "I warned them, I'm going to communicate with all levels of the organization down to the shop floor, and you can't feel suspicious or paranoid about that," he said. "I told them I will not intercept your decisions that belong in your chain of command, but I will give and receive information anywhere in the organization, at any time. I just can't get enough understanding of the organization from listening to the voices at the top."

His description reminded me of Girl Scouts CEO Frances Hesselbein's "circular management." Instead of a ladder, the organizational structure was concentric circles, with Hesselbein in the middle. Information could flow in many directions, and anyone in one circle had numerous entry points to communicate with the next circle, rather than just a single superior who acted as a gate. When she explained it to me, it seemed a lot like the kind of incongruence Geveden worked to engender, and the kind that Captain Lesmes wielded: a differentiated chain of command and chain of communication that produced incongruence, and thus a healthy tension. An occasionally confusing but effective mix of strong formal and informal culture. A trio of psychology and management professors who analyzed a century of Himalayan mountain climbers—5,104 expedition groups in all—found that teams from countries that strongly valued hierarchical culture got more climbers to the summit, but also had more climbers die along the way. The trend did not hold for solo climbers, only teams, and the researchers argued that hierarchical teams benefitted from a clear chain of command, but suffered from a one-way chain of communication that obscured problems. The teams needed elements of both hierarchy and individualism to both excel and survive.

It is a difficult balancing act, cultivating aspects of a culture that seem on their face to push against one another. There are no rules for the qualitative hunches of space shuttle engineers or pararescue jumpers lacking intel. Incongruence, as the experimental research testified, helps people to *discover* useful cues, and to drop the traditional tools when it makes sense.

Karl Weick's tools insight reminded me of an experience I had as a graduate student, working aboard the Research Vessel *Maurice Ewing* in the Pacific Ocean. The ship was bouncing sound waves off the ocean floor to image underwater volcanoes. I got to know a few volcano experts who truly saw the world through volcano-colored glasses. Despite ample evidence that an asteroid impact was either the primary cause of the dinosaur extinction, or at least very important, they insisted that volcanic eruptions were clearly the real culprit. If anything, one told me, the asteroid was really just a lucky knockout punch; volcanoes had already delivered the body blows. He seemed to attribute a whole slew of mass extinctions to volcanoes, some with compelling evidence, others with pretty much none. When all you have is a volcanologist, I learned, every extinction looks like a volcano. That is not necessarily bad for the world. They *should* challenge accepted wisdom, and it drives those narrowly focused experts to find volcano knowledge where no one else is looking. But when entire specialties grow up around devotion to a particular tool, the result can be disastrous myopia.

Interventional cardiologists, for example, specialize in treating chest pain by placing stents—a metal tube that pries open blood vessels. It makes a ton of sense: a patient comes in with chest pain, imaging shows a narrowed artery, a stent is placed to open it and preclude a heart attack. The logic is so compelling that a prominent cardiologist coined the term "oculostenotic reflex," from the Latin for "eye," and stenotic, from the Greek for "narrow," meaning: if you see a blockage, you'll reflexively fix a blockage. Except, repeatedly, randomized clinical trials that compared stents with more conservative forms of treatment show that stents for patients with stable chest pain prevent zero heart attacks and extend the lives of patients a grand total of not at all.

The interventional cardiologists are seeing and treating one tiny part of a complicated system; the cardiovascular system isn't a kitchen sink, and it turns out that treating one blocked pipe often doesn't help. Plus, about one in fifty patients who get a stent will suffer a serious complication or die as a result of the implantation procedure. Despite the bird's-eye evidence, cardiologists who specialize in using that tool reported that they simply cannot believe that stenting doesn't work, even when their compensation was not tied to performing the procedure. Being told to stop using stents was like being told to forget you are an interventional cardiologist. The instinct, often well-meaning, to use interventions that seem logical but that have not been shown to help may explain the finding of a 2015 study: patients with heart failure or cardiac arrest were less likely to die if they were admitted during a national cardiology conference, when thousands of top cardiologists were away. "At large cardiology conventions, my colleagues and I have often joked that the convention center would be the safest place in the world to have a heart attack," cardiologist Rita F. Redberg wrote. "[The conference study] turned that analysis around."

Similarly harrowing findings are now appearing all over medicine, wherever specialties have arisen for the use of a particular tool. One of the most common orthopedic surgeries in the world involves shaving a torn meniscus—a piece of cartilage in the knee—back to its original crescent shape. A patient reports knee pain; an MRI shows a torn meniscus; naturally, a surgeon wants to fix it. When five orthopedic clinics in Finland compared the surgery with "sham surgery"—that is, surgeons took patients with knee pain and a torn meniscus to operating rooms, made incisions, faked surgeries, and sewed them back up and sent them to physical therapy—they found that sham surgery worked just as well. Most people with a torn meniscus, it turns out, don't have any symptoms at all and will never even know. And for those who do have a torn meniscus and knee pain, the tear may have nothing to do with the pain.

Seeing small pieces of a larger jigsaw puzzle in isolation, no matter how hi-def the picture, is insufficient to grapple with humanity's greatest challenges. We have long known the laws of thermodynamics, but struggle to predict the spread of a forest fire. We know how cells work, but can't predict the poetry that will be written by a human made up of them. The frog's-eye view of individual parts is not enough. A healthy ecosystem needs biodiversity.

Even now, even in endeavors that engender specialization unprecedented in history, there are beacons of breadth. Individuals who live by historian Arnold Toynbee's words that "no tool is omnicompetent. There is no such thing as a master-key that will unlock *all* doors." Rather than wielding a single tool, they have managed to collect and protect an entire toolshed, and they show the power of range in a hyperspecialized world.

CHAPTER 12

Deliberate Amateurs

JANUARY 23, 1954, was a Saturday, and Oliver Smithies was in the lab in Toronto, as usual. "Saturday morning experiments," he called them. Nobody was around, and he felt free from the strictures of normal work. On Saturday, he didn't have to weigh things carefully. He could take a pinch of this, a dash of that for an experiment that during the week would be considered a waste of time and equipment. He could try something that intrigued him, but that had little to do with his primary project. One needs to let the brain think about something different from its daily work, he would say. "On Saturday," as Smithies put it, "you don't have to be completely rational."

Smithies worked in a lab studying insulin, and his job was to find an insulin precursor. The work was stuck, literally. The method of separating molecules so they could be studied involved running an electric current through a special type of moist paper. The molecules moved apart as they crossed the paper. But insulin just stuck to it. Smithies had heard that the local children's hospital had tried moist starch grains instead of paper. Starch solved the stickiness problem, but would require him to cut the grains into fifty slices and analyze each one individually to find out where the molecules ended up. That would take forever, so it was a nonstarter. Then he remembered something, from when he was twelve.

Smithies grew up in the town of Halifax in England, and would watch his mother starch his father's work shirts to make the collars firm. She dipped each shirt in gooey hot starch, and then ironed it. To help her tidy up, Smithies disposed of the starch. He noticed that when it cooled, the starch congealed into a jelly.

Smithies had a skeleton key for the building, and went around raiding supply closets for starch grains. He cooked the grains, let them cool into a gel, and tried it in place of the paper. When he applied electrical current, the insulin molecules separated according to size in the gel. "Very promising!" his notebook page from that day reads. In subsequent years, "gel electrophoresis" was refined, and revolutionized biology and chemistry. Individual fragments of DNA and components of human blood serum could be separated and studied.

When I spoke with Smithies in 2016, he was ninety years old and in his lab. He was thinking about how the kidney separates large and small molecules. "At the moment, it's a Saturday morning theoretical experiment," he said.

What struck me as Smithies spoke was his joy in experimentation. Not just in his lab, but in his life. He embodied a number of tenets I set out to explore in this book. From the outside, he looked like the consummate hyperspecialist. He was a molecular biochemist, after all. Except, *molecular biochemist* wasn't really a thing when Smithies was in training. First he studied medicine, until he attended a talk by a professor who was combining chemistry and biology. "He lectured about this new subject which hadn't yet been invented, in a sense," Smithies told me. "It was marvelous, and I thought, 'I'd like to do that. I'd better learn some chemistry.'" He turned on a dime and switched to studying chemistry. He never even thought to feel behind. On the contrary, "that was really very valuable, because at the end I had a good background in biology and wasn't frightened of biology, and then I wasn't frightened of chemistry. That gave me a great deal of power in the early days of molecular biology." What sounds like hyperspecialization today was actually a bold hybrid at the time.

Smithies was a professor at the University of North Carolina when we spoke. He passed away nine months later, at ninety-one. To the end of his life, he encouraged students to think laterally, broaden their experience, and forge their own path in search of match quality. "I try to teach people, 'Don't end up a clone of your thesis adviser,'" he told me. "Take your skills to a place that's not doing the same sort of thing. Take your skills and apply them to a new problem, or take your problem and try completely new skills."

Smithies lived the advice he gave. In his fifties, he took a sabbatical in order to venture a mere two floors away in the same building to learn how to work with DNA. He never did find a precursor to insulin, and by the time he was awarded the Nobel Prize in 2007, it was as a geneticist, for figuring out how to modify disease-causing genes so that they could be studied in animals. In that regard, he was a late specializer. I told Smithies that I had recently talked with the provost of a large research university who was using data analytics to assess contributions and make hires and promotions. The provost told me that chemists reliably fall off a cliff twenty years after they get their PhDs. Smithies laughed. "Yeah, well, my most important paper was published when I was about sixty," he said. A 2016 analysis of ten thousand researchers' careers determined that there is no standard relationship between experience and contribution; an individual's most impactful paper was as likely to be their first as their second, their tenth, or their last. (Researchers did tend to publish more frequently at younger ages, though.)

When I mentioned to Smithies that his starched-shirts memory was an example of lateral thinking with withered technology, he added that in 1990 he shared the Gairdner Award (a sort of pre-Nobel) with Edwin Southern, who also wielded a childhood memory that, on its face, seemed totally unrelated. "His was a memory of cyclostyling," Smithies said, referring to an old document-copying device that used glazed paper and a stencil system. With that in mind, Southern created the "Southern blot," a ubiquitous method for detecting specific DNA molecules. Gunpei Yokoi would have been delighted. And yet those were nothing compared to the withered technology employed by Tu Youyou, who in 2015 became the first (and so far only) Chinese national to win the Nobel Prize in Physiology or Medicine, and the first Chinese woman in any category.

Tu is known as the "professor of the three no's": no membership in the Chinese Academy of Sciences, no research experience outside of China, and no postgraduate degree. Before Tu, other scientists had reportedly tested 240,000 compounds searching for a malaria cure. Tu was interested in both modern medicine and history, and was inspired by a clue in a recipe for medication made from sweet wormwood, written by a fourth-century Chinese alchemist. Technology doesn't get much more withered than that. It led her to experiment (at first on herself) with a sweet wormwood extract known as artemisinin. Artemisinin is now regarded as one of the most profound drug discoveries in medicine. A study on the decline of malaria in Africa attributed 146 *million* averted cases to artemisinin-based therapies between 2000 and 2015. Tu had a lot of disadvantages, but she had an outsider advantage as well that made it easier for her to look in places others would not dare. The kind of advantage Smithies sought on Saturday mornings.

Over his career, Smithies filled and kept 150 notebooks. "That was also Saturday," he repeated, as he walked me through important pages. When I pointed it out, he replied, "Well, I've had people say, 'Why did you come to work any other day!'"

The breakthroughs, of course, were exceptions. One Saturday morning experiment accidentally dissolved an important piece of equipment. In another, Smithies contaminated his shoes with a putrid chemical. He thought he had aired them out sufficiently, until he heard one elderly woman ask another if she smelled a dead body. Smithies could not resist "picking up anything" to experiment with, he said, a habit his colleagues noticed. Rather than throw out damaged equipment, they would leave it for him, with the label NBGBOKFO: "no bloody good, but OK for Oliver."

An enthusiastic, even childish, playful streak is a recurring theme in research on creative thinkers. University of Manchester physicist Andre Geim employs (with no relation to Smithies) "Friday night experiments" (FNEs). It was a Friday night when he began the work that led to his 2000 Ig Nobel Prize. The Ig Nobel is given for work that at first blush seems ridiculous or trivial. The mascot is an image of Rodin's *The Thinker* sculpture, except "The Stinker" has fallen off his pedestal and is lying on his back on the ground. Recipients are asked beforehand if they are willing to accept the award, so they can weigh reputational concerns. Geim won for levitating a frog with strong magnets. (Frogs, and the water they contain, are diamagnetic, or repelled by magnetic fields.)

Needless to say, FNEs are not funded, and most amount to nothing. After the frog, though, another FNE produced "gecko tape," an adhesive inspired by a gecko's feet. And then there was the one that started with using Scotch tape to rip thin layers of graphite, the material that comprises pencil lead. That low-tech affair culminated in the 2010 Nobel Prize in Physics, for Geim and his colleague Konstantin Novoselov's production of graphene, a material one-hundred thousand times thinner than a human hair and two hundred times stronger than steel. It is flexible, more transparent than glass, and an excellent electrical conductor. Spiders fed graphene have spun silk many times tougher than the Kevlar in bulletproof vests. Graphene consists of carbon strips one atom thick, an arrangement previously considered purely theoretical. When Geim and Novoselov submitted their initial work to one of the world's most prestigious journals, one reviewer said it was impossible, and another deemed it not "a sufficient scientific advance."

Art historian Sarah Lewis studies creative achievement, and described

Geim's mindset as representative of the "deliberate amateur." The word "amateur," she pointed out, did not originate as an insult, but comes from the Latin word for a person who adores a particular endeavor. "A paradox of innovation and mastery is that breakthroughs often occur when you start down a road, but wander off for a ways and pretend as if you have just begun," Lewis wrote. When Geim was asked (two years before the Nobel) to describe his research style for a science newsletter, he offered this: "It is rather unusual, I have to say. I do not dig deep—I graze shallow. So ever since I was a postdoc, I would go into a different subject every five years or so. . . . I don't want to carry on studying the same thing from cradle to grave. Sometimes I joke that I am not interested in doing re-search, only search." Deviating from what Geim calls the "straight railway line" of life is "not secure . . . psychologically," but comes with advantages, for motivation and for "questioning things people who work in that area never bother to ask." His Friday evenings are like Smithies's Saturday mornings; they balance the rest of the week's standard practice with wide-roaming exploration. They embrace what Max Delbrück, a Nobel laureate who studied the intersection of physics and biology, called "the principle of limited sloppiness." Be careful not to be too careful, Delbrück warned, or you will unconsciously limit your exploration.

Novoselov was Geim's PhD student, taken on board after Geim's colleague told him that Novoselov "seems to be wasting his life" in another lab. When Novoselov arrived, he found equipment that was similar to that in his previous lab, but "this flexibility and the opportunity to try yourself in different areas which was interesting." A *Science* profile of him bore the section titles "Going for Breadth" and "Spread Thin," which would sound really bad and like he was falling behind if the article wasn't also about how at thirty-six he was the youngest physics Nobel laureate in forty years.

Like Van Gogh or Frances Hesselbein or hordes of young athletes, Novoselov probably looked from the outside like he was behind, until all of a sudden he very much wasn't. He was lucky. He arrived in a workspace that treated mental meandering as a competitive advantage, not a pest to be exterminated in the name of efficiency.

That kind of protection from the cult of the head start is increasingly rare. At some point or other, we all specialize to one degree or another, so the rush to get there can seem logical. Fortunately, there are pioneers who are working to balance the cult of the head start. They want to have it all—the mental meandering along with the wisdom of deep experience; the broad conceptual skills that make use of Flynn's scientific spectacles even within training programs for specialists; and the creative power of interdisciplinary cross-fertilization. They want to reverse the Tiger trend, not just for themselves, but for everyone, and even in domains synonymous with hyperspecialization. The future of discovery, they argue, depends on it.

It only takes a few minutes of conversation to gather that Arturo Casadevall is a beaker-half-full kind of guy. One of the greatest days of his life was when gravitational waves were detected, and that's not his field. "Two black holes collide in space a billion years ago, and for a billion years those gravity waves travel through space-time," he narrated, eyes widening. "When the original signal began, life on Earth was *unicellular,* and in that time humanity manages to build two interferometers and measure it. I mean, what an accomplishment that is." He is also an MD-PhD and a star in his own domains, microbiology and immunology. He has studied AIDS and anthrax, and has illuminated important aspects of how fungal diseases work. His "h-index," a measure of a scientist's productivity and how often they are cited, recently surpassed Albert Einstein's.* So his peers took it seriously when he arrived at the Johns Hopkins Bloomberg School of Public Health in 2015, as chair of

---

* Scientists publish more now than in the past so the comparison isn't entirely fair, but still puts Casadevall in very rare company.

molecular microbiology and immunology, and warned that scientific research is in crisis.

In a lecture to his new colleagues, Casadevall declared that the pace of progress had slowed, while the rate of retractions in scientific literature had accelerated, proportionally outpacing the publication of new studies. "If this continues unabated," he said, "the entire literature will be retracted in a few years." It was science gallows humor, but grounded in data. Part of the problem, he argued, is that young scientists are rushed to specialize before they learn how to think; they end up unable to produce good work themselves and unequipped to spot bad (or fraudulent) work by their colleagues.

The reason Casadevall came to Hopkins, from a comfy post at New York City's Albert Einstein College of Medicine, is that the new gig offered him the chance to create a prototype of what he thinks graduate science education, and eventually *all* education, should be.

Counter to the prevailing trend, Casadevall—with Gundula Bosch, a professor of both biology and education—is despecializing training, even for students who plan to become the most specialized of specialists. The program, known as the R3 Initiative (Rigor, Responsibility, Reproducibility), starts with interdisciplinary classes that include philosophy, history, logic, ethics, statistics, communication, and leadership. A course titled "How Do We Know What Is True?" examines types of evidence through history and across disciplines. In "Anatomy of Scientific Error," students are detectives, hunting for signs of misconduct or poor methods in real research, while also learning how errors and serendipity have led to momentous discoveries.

When Casadevall described his vision of broad education on a professional panel in 2016, a copanelist and editor of the *New England Journal of Medicine* (an extremely prestigious and retraction-prone journal) countered that it would be absurd to add more training time to the already jam-packed curricula for doctors and scientists. "I would say keep the same time, and deemphasize all the other didactic material," Casadevall said. "Do we really need to go through courses with very specialized knowledge that often provides a huge amount of stuff that is very detailed, very specialized, very arcane, and will be totally forgotten in a couple of weeks? Especially now, when all the information is on your phone. You have people walking around with all the knowledge of humanity on their phone, but they have no idea how to integrate it. We don't train people in thinking or reasoning."

Doctors and scientists frequently are not even trained in the basic underlying logic of their own tools. In 2013, a group of doctors and scientists gave physicians and medical students affiliated with Harvard and Boston University a type of problem that appears constantly in medicine:

If a test to detect a disease whose prevalence is 1/1000 has a false positive rate of 5%, what is the chance that a person found to have a positive result actually has the disease, assuming you know nothing about the person's symptoms or signs?

The correct answer is that there is about a 2 percent chance (1.96 to be exact) that the patient actually has the disease. Only a quarter of the physicians and physicians-in-training got it right. The most common answer was 95 percent. It should be a very simple problem for professionals who rely on diagnostic tests for a living: in a sample of 10,000 people, 10 have the disease and get a true positive result; 5 percent, or 500, will get a false positive; out of 510 people who test positive, only 10, or 1.96 percent, are actually sick. The problem is not intuitive, but nor is it difficult. Every medical student and physician has the numerical ability to solve it. So, as James Flynn observed when he tested bright college students in basic reasoning, they must not be primed to use the broader reasoning tools of their trade, even though they are capable.

"I would argue, at least in medicine and basic science where we fill people up with facts from courses, that what is needed is just some background, and then the tools for thinking," Casadevall told me. Currently, "everything is configuring in the wrong way."

He compared the current system to medieval guilds. "The guild system in Europe arose in the Middle Ages as artisans and merchants sought to maintain and protect specialized skills and trades," he wrote with a colleague. "Although such guilds often produced highly trained and specialized individuals who perfected their trade through prolonged apprenticeships, they also encouraged conservatism and stifled innovation." Both training and professional incentives are aligning to accelerate specialization, creating intellectual archipelagos.

There is a growth industry of conferences that invite only scientists who work on a single specific microorganism. Meanwhile, a complete understanding of the body's response to a paper cut was hampered because hyperspecialists in hematology and immunology focus on pieces of the puzzle in isolation, even though the immune response is an integrated system.

"You can do your entire career on one cell type and it's more likely you keep your job by getting grants," Casadevall told me. "There is not even pressure to integrate. In fact, if you write a grant proposal about how the B cell is integrating with the macrophage [a basic interaction of the immune system],* there may be no one to review it. If it goes to the macrophage people, they say, 'Well, I don't know anything about it. Why B cells?' The system maintains you in a trench. You basically have all these parallel trenches, and it's very rare that anybody stands up and actually looks at the next trench to see what they are doing, and often it's related."†

---

* When bacteria enter a cut, the B cell releases antibodies that attach to bacteria and usher them to a macrophage, which destroys them.

† In fact, interdisciplinary research is sometimes looked down upon precisely because it does not signal hyperspecialization. Scientists Diana Rhoten and Stephanie Pfirman wrote in *Inside Higher Ed* that women appear to be more likely to engage in interdisciplinary research, but that they were told to refrain from encouraging junior women to conduct interdisciplinary research "or they'll never be taken seriously."

Substitute a few specific terms, and the system of parallel trenches he described could fit many industries. While I was researching this book, an official with the U.S. Securities and Exchange Commission learned I was writing about specialization and contacted me to make sure I knew that specialization had played a critical role in the 2008 global financial crisis. "Insurance regulators regulated insurance, bank regulators regulated banks, securities regulators regulated securities, and consumer regulators regulated consumers," the official told me. "But the provision of credit goes across all those markets. So we specialized products, we specialized regulation, and the question is, 'Who looks across those markets?' The specialized approach to regulation missed systemic issues."

In 2015, Casadevall showed that biomedical research funding rose exponentially over a recent thirty-five-year period, while discovery slowed down. Life expectancy in countries at the biomedical cutting edge, like the United Kingdom and the United States, recently declined after decades of improvement. The flu annually kills hundreds of thousands of people worldwide while humanity fights it with a cumbersomely produced vaccine from the 1940s. Casadevall's mother is ninety-three, and on five medications that were available when he was a medical resident in the 1980s. "Two of them are older than I am," he said, and two others are barely younger. "I cannot believe we can't do better." He paused for a moment, tilted his head, and leaned forward. "If you write an interdisciplinary grant proposal, it goes to people who are really, really specialized in A or B, and maybe if you're lucky they have the capacity to see the connections at the interface of A and B," he told me. "Everyone acknowledges that great progress is made at the interface, but who is there to defend the interface?"

The interface between specialties, and between creators with disparate backgrounds, has been studied, and it is worth defending.

———

When Northwestern and Stanford researchers analyzed the networks that give rise to creative triumph, they found what they deemed a "universal" setup. Whether they looked at research groups in economics or ecology, or the teams that write, compose, and produce Broadway musicals, thriving ecosystems had porous boundaries between teams.

In professional networks that acted as fertile soil for successful groups, individuals moved easily among teams, crossing organizational and disciplinary boundaries and finding new collaborators. Networks that spawned unsuccessful teams, conversely, were broken into small, isolated clusters in which the same people collaborated over and over. Efficient and comfortable, perhaps, but apparently not a creative engine. "The entire network looks different when you compare a successful team with an unsuccessful team," according to Luís A. Nunes Amaral, a Northwestern physicist who studies networks. Amaral's remark does not compare individual teams, but rather the larger ecosystems that foster the formation of successful teams.

The commercial fate of Broadway during any particular era, be it unusually prosperous or exceptionally flop-ridden, had less to do with specific famous names and more to do with whether collaborators mixed and matched vibrantly. The 1920s featured dozens of shows with Cole Porter, Irving Berlin, George Gershwin, Rodgers and Hammerstein (albeit not yet in collaboration), and also an unusually high overall flop rate of 90 percent for new shows. It was an era of stagnant teams, rife with repeat collaborations and scant boundary crossing.

New collaborations allow creators "to take ideas that are conventions in one area and bring them into a new area, where they're suddenly seen as invention," said sociologist Brian Uzzi, Amaral's collaborator. Human creativity, he said, is basically an "import/export business of ideas."

Uzzi documented an import/export trend that began in both the physical and social sciences in the 1970s, pre-internet: more successful teams tended to have more far-flung members. Teams that included members from different institutions were more likely to be successful than those that did not, and teams that included members based in different countries had an advantage as well.

Consistent with the import/export model, scientists who have worked abroad—whether or not they returned—are more likely to make a greater scientific impact than those who have not. The economists who documented that trend suggested one reason could be migrants' "arbitrage" opportunities, the chance to take an idea from one market and bring it to another where it is more rare and valued.* It echoes Oliver Smithies's advice to bring new skills to an old problem, or a new problem to old skills. The atypical combination of typical forms—say, hip-hop, a Broadway musical, and American historical biography—is not a strategy fluke of showbiz.

Uzzi and a team analyzed eighteen million papers from a variety of scientific domains to see whether atypical knowledge combinations mattered. If a particular paper cited other areas of research that rarely, if ever, appeared together, then it was classified as having used an atypical combination of knowledge. Most papers relied purely on conventional combinations of previous knowledge. That is, they cited work from other journals that often appeared together in other studies' lists of references. The "hit" papers, those that over the next decade were used by a huge number of other scientists, featured ample conventional combinations, but also added an injection of unusual knowledge combinations.

A separate, international team analyzed more than a half million research articles, and classified a paper as "novel" if it cited two other journals that had *never* before appeared together. Just one in ten papers made

---

* When creativity researcher Dean Keith Simonton studied the history of innovation in Japan, which vacillated between being very closed and very open to the rest of the world, he saw that creative explosions in domains from fiction writing and poetry to ceramics and medicine followed bursts of immigration.

a new combination, and only one in twenty made multiple new combinations. The group tracked the impact of research papers over time. They saw that papers with new knowledge combinations were more likely to be published in less prestigious journals, and also much more likely to be ignored upon publication. They got off to a slow start in the world, but after three years, the papers with new knowledge combos surpassed the conventional papers, and began accumulating more citations from other scientists. Fifteen years after publication, studies that made multiple new knowledge combinations were *way* more likely to be in the top 1 percent of most-cited papers.

To recap: work that builds bridges between disparate pieces of knowledge is less likely to be funded, less likely to appear in famous journals, more likely to be ignored upon publication, and then more likely in the long run to be a smash hit in the library of human knowledge.

Casadevall leads by example. A single conversation with him is liable to include *Anna Karenina,* the *Federalist Papers,* the fact that Isaac Newton and Gottfried Leibniz were philosophers as well as scientists, why the Roman Empire wasn't more innovative, and a point about mentoring in the form of a description of the character Mentor from Homer's *Odyssey.* "I work at it," he said, smirking. "I always advise my people to read outside your field, everyday something. And most people say, 'Well, I don't have time to read outside my field.' I say, 'No, you do have time, it's far more important.' Your world becomes a bigger world, and maybe there's a moment in which you make connections."

One of Casadevall's projects was born from a news article he read about a robot sent into the Chernobyl nuclear accident site, still highly contaminated thirty years post-disaster. The article happened to mention that the robot returned with some black mold, a kind that resembled a grotty shower curtain and that had colonized the abandoned reactor. "So, why black mold?" Casadevall asked rhetorically. "And then one thing led to another." He and colleagues made a remarkable find—that the mold was nourishing itself with radiation. Not with radioactive substances—with radiation itself.

Casadevall makes sure to highlight experiences outside the lab and how they contributed to who he is today. His family fled Cuba and arrived in Queens when he was eleven. At sixteen, he got his first job, at McDonald's, and worked there until he was twenty. It's still on his résumé, and he made sure to discuss it in his Johns Hopkins interview. "It was a great, great experience," he told me. "I learned a lot working there." Like handling pressure. His younger brother worked there, too, and was briefly taken hostage during a holdup. "He spent two days on the witness stand where the lawyers made fun of his accent," Casadevall recalled. "He came out ready for law school. Now he's a successful trial lawyer." After McDonald's, Casadevall worked as a bank teller. ("That was held up too!") His father wanted him to have something practical to fall back on, so a community college degree in pest control operations hangs on his office wall, near a certificate of his election into the prestigious National Academy of Medicine.

Casadevall is renowned in his area of expertise. He has no trouble getting research grants, and is frequently one of the scientists who helps determine who else gets grants. He is a winner if the specialization status quo continues. And yet he considers his attempt to shatter it the most important work of his life. The further basic science moves from meandering exploration toward efficiency, he believes, the less chance it will have of solving humanity's greatest challenges.

Laszlo Polgar, in the midst of his chess experiment with his daughters, proclaimed that "the problems of cancer and AIDS" would more likely be solved if his system of narrow specialization and efficient education were used beyond chess, to educate a thousand kids. Casadevall is a student of innovation history. He grew up as a doctor and scientist when HIV/AIDS exploded into an epidemic, and he could hardly disagree more passionately. "When I went to medical school, I was taught that there were no human diseases caused by retroviruses, that retroviruses were a curiosity that occurred in some animal tumors. In 1981, a new disease emerges that nobody knows anything about. In 1984, it's found to be a retrovirus, HIV. In 1987, you have the first therapy. In 1996, you have such effective therapy that people don't have to die of it anymore. How did that happen? Was it because companies all of a sudden rushed to make drugs? No. If you really look back and analyze it, before that time society had spent some of its very hard-earned money to study a curiosity called retroviruses. Just a curiosity in animals. So by the time HIV was found to be a retrovirus, you already knew that if you interfered with the protease [a type of enzyme] that you could deactivate it. So when HIV arrived, society had right off the shelf a *huge* amount of knowledge from investments made in a curiosity that at the time had no use. It may very well be that if you were to take all the research funding in the country and you put it in Alzheimer's disease, you would never get to the solution. But the answer to Alzheimer's disease may come from a misfolding protein in a cucumber. But how are you going to write a grant on a cucumber? And who are you going to send it to? If somebody gets interested in a folding protein in a cucumber and it's a good scientific question, leave them alone. Let them torture the cucumber."

Casadevall's overarching point is that the innovation ecosystem should intentionally preserve range and inefficiency. He is fighting an uphill battle.

In 2006, when I was starting in journalism, I sat in on funding policy hearings of a U.S. Senate subcommittee on science and space, chaired by Texas senator Kay Bailey Hutchison. Hutchison would thumb through a stack of scientists' research proposals and read the titles aloud. If a title did not directly pertain to the creation of a new commercial technology, she whisked it from the stack and asked the room how exactly that sort of thing would help the country get ahead of India and China. Among the disciplines Hutchison classified as distracting from technological innovation were biology, geology, economics, and archaeology. One can only guess how she would have assessed the work of Louis Pasteur (who started as an artist) on chickens with cholera, which led him to lab-created vaccines. Or Einstein's fanciful idea to investigate if time passes differently in high versus low gravity, part of a theory essential to some rather useful technology, like cell phones, which use global positioning satellites with gravitationally adjusted clocks that sync with clocks on Earth.

In 1945, former MIT dean Vannevar Bush, who oversaw U.S. military science during World War II—including the mass production of penicillin and the Manhattan Project—authored a report at the request of President Franklin Roosevelt in which he explained successful innovation culture. It was titled "Science, the Endless Frontier," and led to the creation of the National Science Foundation that funded three generations of wildly successful scientific discovery, from Doppler radar and fiber optics to web browsers and MRIs. "Scientific progress on a broad front results from the free play of free intellects, working on subjects of their own choice," Bush wrote, "in the manner dictated by their curiosity for exploration of the unknown."

A curious phenomenon has appeared in recent years on a near-annual basis when the Nobel Prizes are awarded. Someone who receives one explains that their breakthrough could not have occurred today. In 2016, Japanese biologist Yoshinori Ohsumi closed his Nobel lecture ominously: "Truly original discoveries in science are often triggered by unpredictable and unforeseen small findings. . . . Scientists are increasingly required to provide evidence of immediate and tangible applications of their work." That is head start fervor come full circle; explorers have to pursue such narrowly specialized goals with such hyperefficiency that they can say what they will find before they look for it.

Like Casadevall, Ohsumi knows that applications are the end goal, but the question is how best to get there. There is no shortage of institutions focused tightly on applications. A few appeared in this book. Why specialize the entire research world that way? The "free play" of intellects sounds horribly inefficient, just like the free play of developing soccer players who could always instead be drilling specific skills. It's just that when someone actually takes the time to study how breakthroughs occur, or how the players who grew up to fill Germany's 2014 World Cup winning team developed, "these players performed less organized practice . . . but greater proportions of playing activities."

At its core, all hyperspecialization is a well-meaning drive for efficiency—the most efficient way to develop a sports skill, assemble a product, learn to play an instrument, or work on a new technology. But inefficiency needs cultivating too. The wisdom of a Polgar-like method of laser-focused, efficient development is limited to narrowly constructed, kind learning environments.

"When you push the boundaries, a lot of it is just probing. It *has* to be inefficient," Casadevall told me. "What's gone totally is that time to talk and synthesize. People grab lunch and bring it into their offices. They feel lunch is inefficient, but often that's the best time to bounce ideas and make connections."

When engineer Bill Gore left DuPont to form the company that invented Gore-Tex, he fashioned it after his observation that companies do their most impactful creative work in a crisis, because the disciplinary boundaries fly out the window. "Communication really happens in the carpool," he once said. He made sure that "dabble time" was a cultural staple.

and a baseball analogy doesn't really do it justice. As business writer Michael Simmons put it, "Baseball has a truncated outcome distribution. When you swing, no matter how well you connect with the ball, the most runs you can get is four." In the wider world, "every once in a while, when you step up to the plate, you can score 1,000 runs." It doesn't mean breakthrough creation is luck, although that helps, but rather that it is hard and inconsistent. Going where no one has is a wicked problem. There is no well-defined formula or perfect system of feedback to follow. It's like the stock market that way; if you want the sky highs, you have to tolerate a lot of lows. As InnoCentive founder Alph Bingham told me, "breakthrough and fallacy look a lot alike initially."

The question I set out to explore was how to capture and cultivate the power of breadth, diverse experience, and interdisciplinary exploration, within systems that increasingly demand hyperspecialization, and would have you decide what you should be before first figuring out who you are.

Early in the book, I discussed athletes and musicians, because they are practically synonymous with early specialization. But among athletes who go on to become elite, broad early experience and delayed specialization is the norm. Musicians arrive at greatness via an incredible diversity of paths, but early hyperspecialization is often not necessary for skill development and in the more improvisational forms it is rare—although, as in sports, many adults have an enormous financial interest in making it seem essential. Sviatoslav Richter was one of the greatest pianists of the twentieth century; he started formal lessons at twenty-two. Steve Nash is a relatively normal-sized Canadian who did not get a basketball until he was thirteen years old; he won the NBA MVP award, twice. As I write this, I am listening to a professional violinist who started when she was eighteen. Of course, she was told to stop before she started because she was too old. She now makes a point of teaching beginner adults. The tidy specialization narrative cannot easily fit even these relatively kind domains that have most successfully marketed it.

So, about that one sentence of advice: Don't feel behind. Two Roman historians recorded that when Julius Caesar was a young man he saw a statue of Alexander the Great in Spain and broke down in tears. "Alexander at my age had conquered so many nations, and I have all this time done nothing that is memorable," he supposedly said. Pretty soon, that concern was a distant memory and Caesar was in charge of the Roman Republic—which he turned into a dictatorship before he was murdered by his own pals. It's fair to say that like most youth athletes with highlight reels, he peaked early. Compare yourself to yourself yesterday, not to younger people who aren't you. Everyone progresses at a different rate, so don't let anyone else make you feel behind. You probably don't even know where exactly you're going, so feeling behind doesn't help. Instead, as Herminia Ibarra suggested for the proactive pursuit of match quality, start planning experiments. Your personal version of Friday night or Saturday morning experiments, perhaps.

Approach your own personal voyage and projects like Michelangelo approached a block of marble, willing to learn and adjust as you go, and even to abandon a previous goal and change directions entirely should the need arise. Research on creators in domains from technological innovation to comic books shows that a diverse group of specialists cannot fully replace the contributions of broad individuals. Even when you move on from an area of work or an entire domain, that experience is not wasted.

Finally, remember that there is nothing inherently wrong with specialization. We all specialize to one degree or another, at some point or other. My initial spark of interest in this topic came from reading viral articles and watching conference keynotes that offered early hyperspecialization as some sort of life hack, a prescription that will save you the wasted time of diverse experience and experimentation. I hope I have added ideas to that discussion, because research in myriad areas suggests that mental meandering and personal experimentation are sources of power, and head starts are overrated. As Supreme Court justice Oliver Wendell Holmes wrote a century ago, of the free exchange of ideas, "It is an experiment, as all life is an experiment."

ONE OF THE EARLIEST recorded uses of the phrase "jack of all trades" as an insult dates to 1592. In the New Latin form *"Johannes factotum"*, it was contained in a pamphlet by a playwright criticizing his own industry. The jab refers to a poet with no university education who was apparently involved in various other roles, like copying scripts and bit-part acting, even trying to write plays. The poet on the receiving end of the insult: a young William Shakespeare. The phrase evolved over time, and today it's usually "jack of all trades, master of none." I think it is culturally telling that we habitually hack off the end of the long version: "A jack of all trades is a master of none, but oftentimes better than a master of one."

Lately I've been thinking in a more personal way about the implications of these cultural cues, and of the research in *Range*. Between the time I turned in the final manuscript and the time the hardcover was published, I became a parent. I've been asking myself how, in this new adventure, I might (eventually) wield some of what I learned. That, in turn, led me to a bit of analogical thinking: at the moment, I'm conceiving of my role as akin to the role of a coach-like mentor in the Army's "talent-based branching" program. I realize it might seem odd for me to liken my parenting strategy to a military program—one that I

mentioned only in a footnote on page 140. But this is not a surface analogy: it's a deeper, structural analogy.

The talent-based branching program grew out of the Army's realiza-
tion (discussed in chapter 6) that it had developed a match quality
problem, particularly with West Point and ROTC cadets who received
scholarships. The Army persisted in a traditional model of talent development: assigning future officers to a career path before they knew
much about their own abilities and interests, or much of anything about
the career. Cadets could express preferences, but it amounted to request-
ing a profession they did not know well enough for the person they had
not yet become. And once they chose, they were stuck. In a knowledge
economy, bursting with sampling and lateral mobility, cadets simply left
the service (in droves) if they turned out to have a subpar career match.
The talent-based branching program was designed to help young officers get a better understanding of potential careers earlier in the selection
process, and discover their own interests and talents at the same time.
Essentially, it provides them with a sampling period.

As officers-in-training cycle through classes, internship-like work
experiences, and field training that exposes them to different jobs, they
are encouraged to take part in constant self-reflection, both on their
own (which they can track in an online portal) and with mentors.
(Learning about and reflecting on their own strengths and weaknesses,
according to an Army Strategic Studies Institute monograph, "can
sometimes be a bit of a shock.") The idea is to foster better match quality, and in turn to improve performance, satisfaction, and retention.
When talent-based branching was piloted with West Point cadets,
nearly 90 percent of participating cadets changed at least one of their
top three career preferences. Once again: we learn who we are in practice, not in theory.

I think that's a useful model for parenting. First, I'd like to facilitate
a sampling period for my kid—to expose him to a variety of experiences
and possibilities. (A 2019 OECD report found that children already

significantly narrow their ideas of possible careers by age seven. "We must fight to keep their horizons open," said Andreas Schleicher, OECD's director for education and skills.) And then my role is that of the mentor, supporting my son by helping him get the maximum amount of signal about his own talents, interests, and options from each experience. I hope that will help guide him to good match quality, broaden his toolbox en route, and form a habit of regular reflection reminiscent of the dark horses from chapter 7, who repeatedly say to themselves: "Here's who I am at the moment, here are my motivations, here's what I've found I like to do, here's what I'd like to learn, and here are the opportunities. Which of these is the best match right now? And maybe a year from now I'll switch because I'll find something better."

Shortly after *Range* came out, Ruth Brennan Morrey—a former college soccer captain, pro triathlete, Olympic Trials marathon qualifier, and psychology PhD—tagged me in an apt tweet: "Listening to @DavidEpstein *Range* in the car with twelve-year-old daughter. 'Mom, why do we make "What I want to be when I grow up" signs on the first day of school? We should make "Top 5 things I want to learn about this year" signs.' Smart cookie. :-)" I think I'll borrow the twelve-year-old's idea.

Ultimately, I think the idea of helping individuals get the maximum match quality signal from each zig and zag is a good model, whether one is "managing" kids, mentees, teammates, employees, or, as management scholar Peter Drucker put it twenty years ago in a prophetic *Harvard Business Review* article, "managing oneself." The summary atop the article—which predicts that workers would increasingly have longer and multifaceted careers—reads: "Success in the knowledge economy comes to those who know themselves—their strengths, their values, and how they best perform."

That is often easier said than done. One of the most common questions I received after the hardcover publication of *Range* came from people who viewed themselves as latecomers or generalists; the refrain was that they believe employers will view their varied background as a liability, so they downplay it. They would ask me how to make it a selling point, or at least not a liability.

I get it. Weeks before publication, I had the honor of participating for the second time on the final selection committee for the Pat Tillman Foundation, which awards scholarships to veterans to aid professional development and career changes. I was hyperconscious of the fact that when I began reviewing an application by perusing the candidate's résumé, my first, reflexive impression was sometimes that they appeared a bit scattered. But then I would delve more deeply into their journey, and what appeared scattered at first blush became something completely different. Let's say a hypothetical candidate started work after high school or college. They didn't feel fulfilled, so they joined the military. Once enlisted, they ended up doing something other than what they expected—say, organizing medical care for citizens of a remote village in another country—and during that time they learned something about international relations, or about bureaucratic dysfunction, or about the administration of public health initiatives. Meanwhile, they also learned they were good (or not so good) at and interested in things they had not expected, and they returned to civilian life with new ideas about a field to enter or a business to start. Viewed holistically, what initially looked scattered on a résumé morphed into a journey in which the traveler was responding to lived experience with changes of direction, rather than continuing down an initial path just because they started there. In my experience with the foundation, applicants who win a scholarship are often those who explain a varied path—including stops along the way that sometimes seem far afield—as a series of lessons and subsequent pivots. I think that is a good strategy to keep in mind: rather than hiding diverse experience, explain it.

People who told me that they downplayed their broad backgrounds worried that their online résumés would not serve them well. I think that's a valid concern, and a shame if it holds them back. LinkedIn is the most popular résumé database, and the site's own research has found that one of the strongest predictors of who will eventually become an executive is the number of different job functions an individual has worked across. Based on that analysis, LinkedIn's principal economist, Guy Berger, gave straightforward advice: "My recommendation for those of you who want to become executives is to work across as many job functions as possible." Executives with more varied careers have also been found to be "more likely to have novel strategies . . . which is key to a sustainable competitive advantage," according to Gina Dokko, a professor at the University of California-Davis Graduate School of Management. "Research has established pretty firmly that diverse groups of people are better at innovation and problem solving, but more recent research is finding that diverse career histories within a single person can also benefit performance."

Plus, career-path swerves are now common. Separate LinkedIn research found that nearly half of professionals who switch jobs move to a different industry—up about 10 percent from a decade ago—and 60 percent move to a completely new job function. So perhaps it would be a good idea for sites that host résumés, and organizations that review them, to include some function that allows users the chance to share their résumé as a narrative journey in which they can explain the lessons of their zigs and zags, rather than just list them as bullet points. In my mind, a system that leads people to downplay previous experiences, as if they were entirely wasted, is a counterproductive one. We shouldn't be ashamed of broad experience, or of needing time to find match quality. Take it from Angela Duckworth, the researcher whose work popularized the psychological construct of "grit."

Two days before *Range* was published, an edition of Duckworth's weekly email was titled, "Summer is for Sampling." "Many parents ask me for advice on how to get their kids to stick to one thing for years and years like the paragons of grit I study," Duckworth wrote. "I can empathize. In the decade of adult life it took me to commit to becoming a psychologist, I was desperate for direction to match my determination."

Duckworth added that it is neither "necessary nor healthy" for children to be directed toward one career before they can make that decision themselves—a decision that, again, took her years of adulthood. "So what does grit look like early in life?" she wrote. "A young child who decides today that she wants to become a doctor but thinks tomorrow that she'd rather build houses. A teenager who decides, no, she won't go out for track this year and instead will see what it's like to write for the school newspaper." Specialization has benefits, she added, "but before specialization comes sampling, the exploration of possibilities that, really, you cannot know anything about until you try them . . . *Don't* confuse the healthy development of a work ethic with the premature commitment to a singular passion."

As one researcher suggested to me: "When you get fit, it will look like grit." That is, if you help someone find a good fit, they are more likely to display the characteristics of grit—like sticking with something—even if they didn't before.

Needless to say, most people aren't going to be Tillman Scholars, executives, or William Shakespeare. And while many of the stories in *Range* portray uncommon achievements, I hoped those would serve as memorable portals of engagement into research that applies to a much broader swath of humanity.

In fact, international research that studied thousands of workers— more than three-quarters of whom did not have tertiary education— produced findings that resonate with a major theme of the book: *that sometimes the actions that provide a head start will undermine long-term development*, whether that is choosing a career or a course of study, or simply developing a skill or learning new material.

A 2017 study published by four economists in the U.S., Germany, and China, analyzed education and employment data in eleven countries with large vocational education or apprenticeship programs, comparing people within each country who had similar backgrounds—including test scores, family background, and years of education—but differed in whether they received career-focused or broader, general education. Naturally, there was considerable variation between countries and certainly between individuals, but the general pattern was: people who got narrow, career-focused education were more likely to be employed right out of school and earned more right away, but over time both advantages evaporated; decades later, they had spent less overall time in the labor market and had lower lifetime earnings. The early specializers often won in the short term, and lost in the long run. Workers who received general education, the economists concluded, were better positioned to adapt to change in a wicked world where work next year might not look like work last year.

The pattern was particularly pronounced in two countries with famously extensive apprenticeship programs—Denmark and Germany—an important finding given that, over the last decade, U.S. politicians on both sides of the aisle have advocated for a move toward the German apprenticeship model. In 2017, President Trump issued an executive order to expand apprenticeship programs to prepare workers for "today's rapidly changing economy". The economists, on the other hand, concluded that the more rapidly a nation's economy is changing, the greater the long-term advantage of general education. Of the three countries with widespread apprenticeship programs—Denmark, Germany, Switzerland—early specialization only resulted in a lifetime earnings advantage in Switzerland, which has had easily the slowest growing economy of those three nations in recent decades. "This comparison is consistent with the idea that those with general education are more adaptable to changed economic demands," two of the economists wrote. "Vocational education has been promoted largely as a way of improving the transition from schooling to work, but it also appears to reduce the adaptability of workers to technological and structural change in the economy."

Does that mean we should have no early vocational training or apprenticeships at all? I certainly don't think so, and one of the economists who did this work pointed out that apprenticeships still work well in specific areas, like the building trades, but also that those trades are a small portion of unfilled jobs. In my opinion, we should preserve a variety of pathways, to fit a variety of life circumstances. But I also think we need to be aware of how easy it is to be fooled by head starts, assuming that they represent terminally stable trajectories, whether the head start be for child athletes, college students learning math, or workers entering the labor force. "The advantages of vocational training in smoothing entry into the labor market," the economists wrote, "have to be set against disadvantages later in life, disadvantages that are likely to be more severe as we move more into being a knowledge economy."

The question of how broad or specialized to be is important to just about everyone at some point or another, but usually only discussed with intuition. Like any complex question that involves human beings, there is no one-size-fits-all answer. My hope was to make discussions about that crucial topic more interesting and productive.

I'm a science writer, so in doing that, I wanted to rely heavily on scientific research that bears on the question from various angles. In talking with readers after the hardcover publication, though, I've increasingly felt that the stories of late starts or zig-zagging career paths have a specific importance. The "availability heuristic" is a well-known cognitive bias in which we tend to rely on the first example that comes to mind when making a decision or judging an idea. Tiger stories have supplied millions of brains with availability-heuristic ammo when they think of specialization. I hope some of the stories in this book—from

Federer and Van Gogh to Frances Hesselbein (now 104, still work-ing)—might stick in readers' minds and surface when the Tiger stories do, adding much needed balance to how we consider the topic.

When I was allotted this space for an afterword to the paperback edition, I first thought I should stuff it with research that I had to cut from the hardcover due to space constraints. (My editor talked me off that cliff.) Instead, I'd like to share one more memorable story.

When asked, Titus Kaphar reflexively says that nobody in his family went to college. His mother didn't go to college. His father went to prison, but not to college. Neither his grandmother nor his grandfather went to college. Nobody went to college. Except—he corrects him-self—a distant cousin went to college. Kaphar himself certainly wasn't going to college. He often didn't even go to high school, hence the 0.65 GPA.

And yet, in his twenties, he decided to enroll in a few junior college classes. Allow him to explain: he wanted to date a soon-to-be teacher; she was four years older, contemplating grad school, and not impressed that he had no plans for his future.

"So I just went over to the junior college," Kaphar told me, "kind of as a joke, not really taking it seriously, because, you know, I'm not an academic. I'm not a person who does really well in school." He picked a few classes more or less at random. He came back and told the object of his affection. They had a quick laugh about it.

One class was art history. Why? "I probably read the word 'art' and thought, 'art should be easy,'" Kaphar told me. In an unexpected way, it was. Kaphar realized that he could remember details of paintings—not just remember what he had seen, but associate the painting with the style of a particular artist or artistic movement. "I remember one day we were talking about Van Gogh," he recalled, "and I remember seeing the image and being very aware of where the painting sat in the history of art, where it sat in the timeline the professor was trying to lay out for us." He began to contribute to class discussions. His confidence grew, and he got a B in the class.

"That was a new experience for me," he told me, "a B overall in the class at something that was academic. It made me go, 'Hold up, wait a minute.' I realized this was, in fact, something that I was enjoying, and I could feel myself wanting to push harder. When it became difficult, that grit became more apparent." He took more classes, and tested strategies until he found something that worked, like dictating essays into a recorder for his first draft, and studying for history tests by focusing on connecting the images in a book to the surrounding material. Suddenly, college didn't seem like such a crazy idea.

Kaphar proceeded to San José State University to study fine arts. In an art history survey course, to his dismay, the professor skipped over the section on black painters. So Kaphar decided to compile his own syllabus on the topic. "I think to some degree, it was like being a reporter doing an investigation," he said. A friend's grandmother was a sculptor, and gave him books. The first was on the Harlem Renaissance. "That sort of opened the floodgates," he recalled. He realized that the traditional artistic canon used in class was not some magical pantheon, but just another syllabus assembled by humans. He collected more books, and introduced new names into class discussion.

Eventually, he took an actual painting class, but the teacher told the class that he didn't believe in painting anymore, so he gave no instruction whatsoever on technique. Instead, Kaphar started looking over other students' shoulders and self-teaching. "It was like, last semester I painted an apple, and it looked like a cannonball," he told me. "This semester that actually looks like an apple. Now, it's loose, a child could do the same thing, but it looks like an apple. Awesome, let's keep going." He began to study paintings and then try to reverse-engineer them. When he noticed that shadows in Velázquez paintings didn't look flat, he experimented to find out why. It turned out he could get the effect by painting on a canvas that had a particular weave, and then scraping the paint back with a palette knife so that the weave itself broke up the brushstroke. "That right there is how I learned to paint, by looking a lot." He spent hours in the studio, forgetting to eat because he was so engaged with the work. He considered himself an extreme extrovert, but for the first time was finding fulfilment in an activity that he did quietly, in a corner, by himself. And he got better, a lot better.

He got so much better that a professor told him he should apply to the master of fine arts program at Yale. "What's Yale?" he asked. The professor chuckled and showed him a pamphlet. Kaphar applied, and got rejected. The next year, he applied to Yale and a bunch of other grad schools. He got rejected from all of them. He resolved to apply to Yale every year. By that point, whether he got in or not was a secondary consideration. He had found his work identity. "I'm an artist," he said. "I'm a maker, so I'm going to make."

The resulting body of work eventually got him into Yale, where he was one of the oldest students in his class. Yale was not a place to learn technique, but by then he was used to self-teaching. At Yale he learned that some art critics had pronounced painting dead as an important medium. "I don't understand how something that's dead can make me feel so alive," Kaphar said. So he kept making, churning out paintings, sculptures, and painting/sculpture combinations.

In 2011, Kaphar was researching his father's prison history, and was surprised to find ninety-seven men with the same name who had been incarcerated. That spawned his "Jerome Project," in which he used mugshots to paint portraits of the men on wood panels with gold leaf backgrounds, (evocative of Byzantine portraits of St. Jerome), and with tar covering a portion of each face to represent a life scarred by prison. His work has now been featured in venues from the Museum of Modern Art and the National Portrait Gallery to the pages of *Time* magazine.

Today, Kaphar lives in New Haven, Connecticut, with his two kids and his wife—a.k.a. the older woman he wanted to impress by taking junior college classes. In 2015, Kaphar and a colleague founded NXTHVN (pronounced "Next Haven"), an art space created in a former manufacturing plant, and where early-career artists can apply for a stipend and studio space. Those artists in turn mentor local high school students who are paid to serve as their studio assistants. For most of the high school students, it is their first job of any kind. Kaphar wants to diversify the entry points into the art pipeline, because imagine who we miss if we force every Titus Kaphar to find his vocation by chance alone.

In 2018, Kaphar won a MacArthur Foundation fellowship, colloquially known as a "genius grant." He doesn't love that moniker, however. He doesn't really like the word "genius" at all. It makes it seem as if someone was plopped on Earth magically knowing what to do and how to do it. It doesn't seem like it could encompass someone who took a junior college class hoping for a date, and accidentally found his path.

"In that class," Kaphar told me, "I realized that I had a visual intelligence that no one had ever asked me to use."

———

Diversifying the entry points into a given path, I think, is a productive strategy. That includes allowing for early specialization, when it makes sense, as one of many possibilities.

In late 2019, I had a chance to talk with Serena Williams. I hadn't researched her childhood at all, but I had heard that it was a Tiger story. I was only slightly surprised when she complicated that notion. Her father was ahead of his time, she told me. She participated in ballet, gymnastics, taekwondo and track and field. She and Venus threw a football to develop the motion for a powerful serve, a habit they continued as professionals.

I certainly don't share that to suggest that pure Tiger stories do not exist. After all, the literal Tiger story opened this book. But we may be telling even that one slightly wrong. As Woods said in 2000: "To this day, my dad has never asked me to go play golf. I ask him. It's the child's desire to play that matters, not the parent's desire to have the child play."

Mozart's childhood might be the second most influential story of development. In researching Mozart's childhood, I came across a letter to Mozart's sister from a musician and Mozart family friend; it recounted Mozart's father, Leopold, shooing little Wolfgang away when he asked to play violin with the adults. "Papa [Leopold] refused him this foolish request, because he had not yet had the least instruction in the violin, and Papa thought that he could not possibly play anything," the letter read. Little Wolfgang cried, and then proceeded to play the violin in front of his awestruck father.

There is no evidence that parents can simply manufacture what psychologist Ellen Winner calls the "rage to master" evident in prodigies like Woods and Mozart. For both Tiger and Mozart, it seems that their famous fathers were initially responding to the son's very unusual display of both interest and prowess in a highly structured activity. Even if the goal were to create as many Tigers and Mozarts as possible, I expect that the best strategy would be exposing children to an array of activities and seeing if one happens to light their fire.

On the other hand, you have people like me, who aren't quite sure what they're going to be when they grow up, only—as the twelve-year-old recommended—a list of things they'd like to learn about this year. I recently came across a quote from Christopher Nolan—writer and director of films like *Inception*, *Interstellar*, and *The Dark Knight*—on finding a next project. "For me, it's all about trying new things," he said. "If you're going to write, you want to read a lot before you write, without any purpose." Of course, the purpose is to find something that stimulates you but that you couldn't have known to look for—an interest you didn't know you had. I think I'll take that advice.

ACKNOWLEDGMENTS

I VIEW BOOK WRITING as kind of like running the 800—torture in the middle, but if you PR or give a supreme effort, pretty soon you look back and say, "Well, that wasn't *so* bad." It was, but still you should do it again.

All sorts of cool things transpired while I worked on this book. For example: I learned a ton. Also, one day while my brain was overheating, a cardinal, a blue jay, and an oriole appeared near my windowsill— that's all the eponymous birds of Major League Baseball teams. That never happens.

Thank you, first, to the entire team at Riverhead, especially my editor, Courtney Young. Courtney spooked me a little when we first agreed to go about this book project together by saying something like, "I'd be worried if I weren't familiar with you." [Gulp]. She then proceeded to respond like a great coach developing an athlete; she let me engage in broad, self-directed activity, and when I resurfaced two years later with a manuscript that was too long, she switched gears and responded to my desire for fast and frequent feedback as I cut it down to size and shape. When the time came, she gave feedback that made a wicked learning environment a bit more kind ("Yes, I like it; now he sounds like less of a magical gnome." —Courtney's feedback on what may have been an overwritten description.). Appropriately, she has range; she almost became an engineer.

Thank you to my agent, Chris Parris-Lamb, who finished 235th in the New York City Marathon, which is important, but not so important as his animating mission, which, as far as I can tell, is to help writers earn their freedom. To use a sports analogy, my strategy for working with an agent was to draft the best athlete available and get out of the way.

Thank you to everyone who took part in my tortuous fact-checking process, but especially Emily Krieger and Drew Bailey, and the interviewees who gave their time (again . . . and sometimes again) so that I could pester them about things they had already told me. Thanks to Masaharu Kawamata and Tyler Walker for help with Japanese translation.

Thanks to Malcolm Gladwell. The first time we met was for a debate at the MIT Sloan Sports Analytics Conference, framed as "10,000-hours vs. The Sports Gene." (It's on YouTube.) It turned into a great discussion, and I think we both took new thoughts home. He invited me for an interval workout the next day, and then again, and we got to talking (only during warmup) about that whole "Roger vs. Tiger" idea. The discussion was filed away somewhere in my head and surfaced when I interacted with Tillman Scholars. I'm not sure I would have explored the topic without it. As psychologist Howard Gruber wrote, "Ideas are not really lost, they are reactivated when useful."

This book was the greatest organizational challenge I've faced; figuring out how to gather information, what to include, and then where to put it overwhelmed me many times. A quote kept coming to mind: "It's a little like wrestling a gorilla. You don't quit when you're tired, you quit when the gorilla's tired." Whatever the reception, I'm proud I kept coming back for more. And I thank the friends and family who supported me and accepted my answer of "hopefully next year" to so many questions. Believe me, it's not that I didn't want tickets to that thing I like. It's just that, as any Westerosi knows, my house words are: "When my book is done." Those supporters: My brother, Daniel (whose enthusiastic response to my rambling about ideas in chapter 4 convinced me to write about them); sister, Charna (she may have purchased all the copies of my last book); my parents, Mark and Eve, who always waited until after I did something ridiculous to weigh in, rather than prohibiting it beforehand. It makes for a vibrant sampling period. Thanks to "Prince Andrei," you'll know who you are when you read this; and to my niece Sigalit Koufax (yes, that Koufax) Epstein-Pawar, and her dad Ameya; and to Andrea and John for moral and caloric support, and the whole Weiss and Green families. Special thanks to Liz O'Herrin and Mike Christman for getting me involved with the Tillman Foundation; to Steve Mesler for getting me involved with Classroom Champions; to my late friend Kevin Richards, without whom I probably would not have become a science writer; and to my friend Harry Mbang, who is never not up for a midnight run to a certain bookstore. Thanks to the entire Chalkbeat family—keep swimming.

Special thanks to Toru Okada, Alice, Natasha Rostova, Katurian K. Katurian, Petter and Mona Kummel, Nate River, Gbessa, Benno von Archimboldi, Tony Webster, Sonny's brother, Tony Loneman, the trio of Tommy, Doc, and Maurice, Braiden Chaney, Stephen Florida, and many other characters who insist on teaching me about writing. I hope those of you I'm forgetting will forgive me.

I feel a little like Inigo Montoya after he finally got revenge: What now?? But I'm about a million times more excited and less fearful about "What now?" than I would have been before I did the research that went into this book. I closed the acknowledgments of my last book with a note about Elizabeth: "If I ever write another book, I'm sure that one will be dedicated to her too." (Even though she was waffling between me and John Dewey for her book dedication.) At the close of my second book, I think it's safe to say that if I ever write another book, I'm sure that one will be dedicated to her too.

For space considerations, here I present copious but not comprehensive citations. I intend these notes as both a trail of reporting that went into this book as well as a detailed entry point into primary sources for anyone interested in some Friday night (or Saturday morning) exploration. The vast majority of spoken quotes in the book are from interviews I conducted. When that is not the case, the source is identified in the text or here. In the interest of packing as many citations in the available space as I could, I removed subtitles of books and papers in some of the references below.

INTRODUCTION: ROGER VS. TIGER

1   the boy could balance on his father's palm: G. Smith, "The Chosen One," *Sports Illustrated*, December 23, 1996. (Additionally, Earl Woods included a photograph of this in the source cited below.)

1   "It is very difficult to communicate how to putt": The primary source on Tiger's childhood in this section is: E. Woods (with P. McDaniel, foreword by Tiger Woods), *Training a Tiger: Raising a Winner in Golf and Life* (New York: Harper Paperbacks, 1997).

2   taught psychological warfare: J. Benedict and A. Keteyian, *Tiger Woods* (New York: Simon & Schuster, 2018).

2   "He has a larger forum than any of them": Smith, "The Chosen One."

3   "I was always very much more interested"; "We had no plan A": R. Jacob, "Ace of Grace," *Financial Times*, January 13, 2006, online ed.

3   "became unbearable"; "he would have just upset me anyway": R. Stauffer, *The Roger Federer Story: Quest for Perfection* (Chicago: New Chapter Press, 2007 [Kindle ebook]).

3   **"pully"; "if they nudged him"; "just don't cheat"; *"Mehr CDs"*:** J. L. Wertheim,
        Strokes of Genius (New York: Houghton Mifflin Harcourt, 2009 [Kindle ebook]).

4   **"being invincible"; "His story is completely different":** Stauffer, *The Roger Fe-
        derer Story.*

5   **study of thirty violinists:** K. A. Ericsson, R. T. Krampe, and C. Tesch-Römer,
        "The Role of Deliberate Practice in the Acquisition of Expert Performance," *Psy-
        chological Review* 100, no. 3 (1993): 363–406.

6   **"we have to check":** A. Gawande, *The Checklist Manifesto* (New York: Metro-
        politan Books, 2010).

6   **"slow bakers":** For an excellent look at how Great Britain altered its talent pipe-
        lines, see: O. Slot, *The Talent Lab* (London: Ebury Press, 2017).

7   **ramp up technical practice in one area:** Examples of studies—including those
        cited in the introduction—from a range of sports and countries documenting the
        trend of sampling and delayed specialization include (the first paper here is the
        source for data in the charts showing practice hours): K. Moesch et al., "Late Spe-
        cialization: The Key to Success in Centimeters, Grams, or Seconds (CGS) Sports,"
        Scandinavian Journal of Medicine and Science in Sports 21, no. 6 (2011): e282–
        90; K. Moesch et al., "Making It to the Top in Team Sports: Start Later, Inten-
        sify, and Be Determined!," *Talent Development and Excellence* 5, no. 2 (2013):
        85–100; M. Hornig et al., "Practice and Play in the Development of German
        Top-Level Professional Football Players," *European Journal of Sport Science* 16,
        no. 1 (2016): 96–105 (epub ahead of print, 2014); A. Güllich et al., "Sport Ac-
        tivities Differentiating Match-Play Improvement in Elite Youth Footballers—A
        2-Year Longitudinal Study," *Journal of Sports Sciences* 35, no. 3 (2017): 207–15
        (epub ahead of print, 2016); A. Güllich, "International Medallists' and Non-
        medallists' Developmental Sport Activities—A Matched-Pairs Analysis," *Jour-
        nal of Sports Sciences* 35, no. 23 (2017): 2281–88; J. Gulbin et al., "Patterns of
        Performance Development in Elite Athletes," *European Journal of Sport Science*
        13, no. 6 (2013): 605–14; J. Gulbin et al., "A Look Through the Rear View Mir-
        ror: Developmental Experiences and Insights of High Performance Athletes,"
        Talent Development and Excellence 2, no. 2 (2010): 149–64; M. W. Bridge and
        M. R. Toms, "The Specialising or Sampling Debate," *Journal of Sports Sciences*
        31, no. 1 (2013): 87–96; P. S. Buckley et al., "Early Single-Sport Specialization,"
        Orthopaedic Journal of Sports Medicine 5, no. 7 (2017): 2325967117703944;
        J. P. Difiori et al., "Debunking Early Single Sports Specialization and Reshaping
        the Youth Sport Experience: An NBA Perspective," *British Journal of Sports
        Medicine* 51, no. 3(2017): 142–43; J. Baker et al., "Sport-Specific Practice and
        the Development of Expert Decision-Making in Team Ball Sports," *Journal of
        Applied Sport Psychology* 15, no. 1 (2003): 12–25; R. Carlson, "The Socializa-
        tion of Elite Tennis Players in Sweden: An Analysis of the Players' Backgrounds
        and Development," *Sociology of Sport Journal* 5 (1988): 241–56; G. M. Hill,
        "Youth Sport Participation of Professional Baseball Players," *Sociology of Sport
        Journal* 10 (1993): 107–14.; F. G. Mendes et al., "Retrospective Analysis of

Accumulated Structured Practice: A Bayesian Multilevel Analysis of Elite Brazilian Volleyball Players," *High Ability Studies* (advance online publication, 2018); S. Black et al., "Pediatric Sports Specialization in Elite Ice Hockey Players," *Sports Health: A Multidisciplinary Approach* (advance online publication, 2018). (France, which won the 2018 World Cup, overhauled its youth development decades ago to emphasize unstructured play at the expense of formal competitions, and to make room for late bloomers. A top youth footballer in France might play half as many formal games as an American peer. When French kids in the national development system do have formal games, coaches are barred from talking for most of the competition so that they cannot micromanage young players. "There is no remote [control] for the players. . . . Let them play," as Ludovic Debru, who helped design the youth system, put it at the 2018 edition of the Aspen Institute's Project Play Summit.)

8   **"In an era of sports specialization":** J. Brewer, "Ester Ledecka Is the Greatest Olympian at the Games, Even If She Doesn't Know It," *Washington Post,* February 24, 2018, online ed.

9   **"I was doing so many different sports":** J. Drenna, "Vasyl Lomachenko: 'All Fighters Think About Their Legacy. I'm No Different,'" *Guardian,* April 16, 2018, online ed.

11   **"young people are just smarter":** M. Coker, "Startup Advice for Entrepreneurs from Y Combinator," *VentureBeat,* March 26, 2007.

11   **a tech founder who is fifty:** P. Azoulay et al., "Age and High-Growth Entrepreneurship," NBER Working Paper No. 24489 (2018).

12   **"No one imagined silos like that":** G. Tett, *The Silo Effect: The Peril of Expertise and the Promise of Breaking Down Barriers* (New York: Simon & Schuster, 2015 [Kindle ebook]).

12   **if they were admitted during a national cardiology meeting:** A. B. Jena et al., "Mortality and Treatment Patterns Among Patients Hospitalized with Acute Cardiovascular Conditions During Dates of National Cardiology Meetings," *JAMA Internal Medicine* 175, no. 2 (2015): 237–44. See also: R.F. Redberg, "Cardiac Patient Outcomes during National Cardiology Meetings," *JAMA Internal Medicine* 175, no.2 (2015): 245.

CHAPTER 1: THE CULT OF THE HEAD START

15   **go along with the plan:** The lives of the Polgar sisters have been chronicled in a number of books and articles. For the details in this chapter, in addition to an interview with Susan Polgar, the most useful sources were: Y. Aviram (director), *The Polgar Variant* (Israel: Lama Films, 2014); S. Polgar with P. Truong, *Breaking Through: How the Polgar Sisters Changed the Game of Chess* (London: Everyman Chess, 2005); C. Flora, "The Grandmaster Experiment," *Psychology Today,* July 2005, online ed.; P. Voosen, "Bringing Up Genius: Is Every Healthy Child a Potential Prodigy?," *Chronicle of Higher Education,* November 8, 2015, online ed.; C. Forbes, *The Polgar Sisters* (New York: Henry Holt, 1992).

15   **"met a very interesting person":** Polgar with Truong, *Breaking Through.*

16   **"gray average mass":** *People* staff, "Nurtured to Be Geniuses, Hungary's Polgar Sisters Put Winning Moves on Chess Masters," *People,* May 4, 1987.

16   **"Chess is very objective":** L. Myers, "Trained to Be a Genius, Girl, 16, Wallops Chess Champ Spassky for $110,000," *Chicago Tribune,* February 18, 1993.

17   **"absolute category":** Aviram, *The Polgar Variant.*

18   **problems like cancer and AIDS:** W. Hartston, "A Man with a Talent for Creating Genius," *Independent,* January 12, 1993.

20   **"complete lack of connection":** "Daniel Kahneman—Biographical," Nobelprize .org, Nobel Media AB 2014. I had the pleasure of discussing Kahneman's life and work with him over lunch in December 2015. Additional detail can be found in his book *Thinking, Fast and Slow* (New York: Farrar, Straus & Giroux, 2011).

20   **impressed him "enormously":** The still-relevant book that impressed Kahneman is: Paul E. Meehl, *Clinical Versus Statistical Prediction* (Minneapolis: University of Minnesota Press, 1954). Meehl sparked an enormous amount of research showing that experts often gain confidence but not skill with experience. An excellent review of some of that work is: C. F. Camerer and E. J. Johnson, "The Process-Performance Paradox in Expert Judgment: How Can Experts Know So Much and Predict So Badly?," in *Toward a General Theory of Expertise,* ed. K. A. Ericsson and Jacqui Smith (Cambridge: Cambridge University Press, 1991).

20   **In 2009, Kahneman and Klein:** D. Kahneman and G. Klein, "Conditions for Intuitive Expertise: A Failure to Disagree," *American Psychologist* 64, no. 6 (2009): 515–26.

21   **"kind" learning environments:** Robin Hogarth's fantastic book on learning environments is *Educating Intuition* (Chicago: University of Chicago Press, 2001).

22   **"a more productive carrier":** L. Thomas, *The Youngest Science* (New York: Penguin, 1995), 22.

22   **In a 1997 showdown:** Kasparov was on the cover of the May 5, 1997, *Newsweek,* with the headline, "The Brain's Last Stand."

22   **"Today the free chess app":** Kasparov and his aide-de-camp Mig Greengard were kind enough to answer my questions. Additional information came from a lecture Kasparov gave at Georgetown University on June 5, 2017, and Kasparov and Greengard's book *Deep Thinking* (New York: PublicAffairs, 2017).

22   **"you can get a lot further":** S. Polgar and P. Truong, *Chess Tactics for Champions* (New York: Random House Puzzles & Games, 2006), x.

23   **"Human creativity was even more paramount"; "My advantage in calculating":** Kasparov and Greengard, *Deep Thinking.*

23   **"freestyle chess":** For an excellent discussion of human-computer chess partnerships, see: T. Cowen, *Average is Over* (New York: Dutton, 2013).

23   **His teammate, Nelson Hernandez:** Hernandez kindly engaged in an extended back-and-forth, explaining to me the nuances of freestyle chess and providing me

with documentation about tournaments. He estimated that Williams's Elo rating in traditional chess would be about 1800.

24 **In 2007, National Geographic TV:** The program was "My Brilliant Brain."

24 **The first took place in the 1940s:** A. D. de Groot, *Thought and Choice in Chess* (Amsterdam: Amsterdam University Press, 2008).

25 **added a wrinkle: Chase and Simon's chunking theory:** W. G. Chase and H. A. Simon, "Perception in Chess," *Cognitive Psychology* 4 (1973): 55–81.

26 **if rigorous training had not begun by age twelve:** F. Gobet and G. Campitelli, "The Role of Domain-Specific Practice, Handedness, and Starting Age in Chess," *Developmental Psychology* 43 (2007): 159–72. For the different rates at which individuals progress, see: G. Campitelli and F. Gobet, "The Role of Practice in Chess: A Longitudinal Study," *Learning and Individual Differences* 18, no. 4 (2007): 446–58.

27 **Treffert studied savants:** Treffert shared with me videos from his library of documentation on savants. His book *Islands of Genius* (London: Jessica Kingsley Publishers, 2012) is a great account of his research.

27 **"What I heard seemed so unlikely":** A. Ockelford, "Another Exceptional Musical Memory," in *Music and the Mind,* ed. I. Deliège, and J. W. Davidson (Oxford: Oxford University Press, 2011). Other sources on savants and atonal music: L. K. Miller, *Musical Savants* (Hove, East Sussex: Psychology Press, 1989); B. Hermelin et al., "Intelligence and Musical Improvisation," *Psychological Medicine* 19 (1989): 447–57.

27 **when artistic savants are briefly shown pictures:** N. O'Connor and B. Hermelin, "Visual and Graphic Abilities of the Idiot-Savant Artist," *Psychological Medicine* 17 (1987): 79–90. (Treffert has helped replace the term "idiot-savant" with "savant syndrome.") See also: E. Winner, *Gifted Children: Myths and Realities* (New York: BasicBooks, 1996), ch. 5.

28 **AlphaZero programmers touted:** D. Silver et al., "Mastering Chess and Shogi by Self-Play with a General Reinforcement Learning Algorithm," *arXiv* (2017): 1712.01815.

29 **"In narrow enough worlds":** In addition to an interview with Gary Marcus, I used video of his June 7, 2017, lecture at the AI for Good Global Summit in Geneva, as well as several of his papers and essays: "Deep Learning: A Critical Appraisal," *arXiv*: 1801.00631; "In Defense of Skepticism About Deep Learning," *Medium,* January 14, 2018; "Innateness, AlphaZero, and Artificial Intelligence," *arXiv*: 1801.05667.

29 **IBM's Watson:** For a balanced take on Watson's challenges in healthcare—from one critic calling it "a joke," to others suggesting it falls far short of the original hype but does indeed have value—see: D. H. Freedman, "A Reality Check for IBM's AI Ambitions," *MIT Technology Review,* June 27, 2017, online ed.

29 **"The difference between winning at *Jeopardy!*":** The oncologist is Dr. Vinay Prasad. He said this to me in an interview, and also shared it on Twitter.

29 **a report in the esteemed journal** *Nature*: J. Ginsberg et al., "Detecting Influenza Epidemics Using Search Engine Query Data," *Nature* 457 (2009): 1012–14.

30 **double the prevalence:** D. Butler, "When Google Got Flu Wrong," *Nature* 494 (2013): 155–56; D. Lazer et al., "The Parable of Google Flu: Traps in Big Data Analysis," *Science* 343 (2014): 1203–5.

30 **"the essence of their job":** C. Argyris, "Teaching Smart People How to Learn," *Harvard Business Review,* May–June 1991.

31 **subtitle of Schwartz's paper:** B. Schwartz, "Reinforcement-Induced Behavioral Stereotypy: How Not to Teach People to Discover Rules," *Journal of Experimental Psychology: General* 111, no. 1 (1982):23–59.

32 **"Big-C creator":** E. Winner, "Child Prodigies and Adult Genius: A Weak Link," in *The Wiley Handbook of Genius,* ed. D. K. Simonton (Malden, MA: John Wiley & Sons, 2014).

32 **Accountants and bridge and poker players:** A useful source, in addition to Kahneman and Klein's "adversarial collaboration" paper, and Hogarth's *Educating Intuition,* is: J. Shanteau, "Competence in Experts: The Role of Task Characteristics," *Organizational Behavior and Human Decision Processes* 53 (1992): 252–62.

32 **"robust statistical regularities":** Kahneman, *Thinking, Fast and Slow.*

32 **research in the game of bridge:** P. A. Frensch and R. J. Sternberg, "Expertise and Intelligent Thinking: When Is It Worse to Know Better?" in *Advances in the Psychology of Human Intelligence,* vol. 5, ed. R. J. Sternberg (New York: Psychology Press, 1989).

32 **experienced accountants; "cognitive entrenchment"; "having one foot outside":** E. Dane, "Reconsidering the Trade-Off Between Expertise and Flexibility," *Academy of Management Review* 35, no. 4 (2010): 579–603. For a general discussion of expert flexibility and inflexibility: P. J. Feltovich et al., "Issues of Expert Flexibility in Contexts Characterized by Complexity and Change," in *Expertise in Context,* ed. P. J. Feltovich et al. (Cambridge, MA: AAAI Press/MIT Press, 1997); and F. Gobet, *Understanding Expertise* (Basingstoke: Palgrave Macmillan, 2016).

33 **Nobel laureates are at least:** R. Root-Bernstein et al., "Arts Foster Scientific Success: Avocations of Nobel, National Academy, Royal Society and Sigma Xi Members," *Journal of Psychology of Science and Technology* 1, no. 2 (2008): 51–63; R. Root-Bernstein et al., "Correlations Between Avocations, Scientific Style, Work Habits, and Professional Impact of Scientists," *Creativity Research Journal* 8, no. 2 (1995): 115–37.

33 **"To him who observes them from afar":** S. Ramón y Cajal, *Precepts and Counsels on Scientific Investigation* (Mountain View, CA: Pacific Press Publishing Association, 1951).

33 **those who did not make a creative contribution:** A. Rothenberg, *A Flight from Wonder: An Investigation of Scientific Creativity* (Oxford: Oxford University Press, 2015).

33 **"rather than obsessively focus[ing]":** D. K. Simonton, "Creativity and Expertise: Creators Are Not Equivalent to Domain-Specific Experts!," in *The Science of Expertise,* ed. D. Hambrick et al. (New York: Routledge, 2017 [Kindle ebook]).

33 **"When we were designing":** Steve Jobs's 2005 commencement address at Stanford: https://news.stanford.edu/2005/06/14/jobs-061505.

34 **"no one else was familiar":** J. Horgan, "Claude Shannon: Tinkerer, Prankster, and Father of Information Theory," *IEEE Spectrum* 29, no. 4 (1992): 72–75. For more depth on Shannon, see J. Soni and R. Goodman, *A Mind at Play* (New York: Simon & Schuster, 2017).

34 **"career streams"; "traveled on an eight-lane highway":** C. J. Connolly, "Transition Expertise: Cognitive Factors and Developmental Processes That Contribute to Repeated Successful Career Transitions Amongst Elite Athletes, Musicians and Business People" (PhD thesis, Brunel University, 2011).

CHAPTER 2: HOW THE WICKED WORLD WAS MADE

37 **a thirty-year-old paper:** R. D. Tuddenham, "Soldier Intelligence in World Wars I and II," *American Psychologist* 3, no. 2 (1948): 54–56.

38 **Should Martians alight on Earth:** J. R. Flynn, *Does Your Family Make You Smarter?* (Cambridge: Cambridge University Press, 2016), 85.

38 **"cradle to the grave":** J. R. Flynn, *What Is Intelligence?* (Cambridge: Cambridge University Press, 2009).

39 **When Flynn published his revelation:** J. R. Flynn, "The Mean IQ of Americans: Massive Gains 1932 to 1978," *Psychological Bulletin* 95, no. 1 (1984): 29–51; J. R. Flynn, "Massive IQ Gains in 14 Nations," *Psychological Bulletin* 101, no. 2 (1987): 171–91. For an excellent primer on the Flynn effect and response, see I. J. Deary, *Intelligence: A Very Short Introduction* (Oxford: Oxford University Press, 2001).

39 **tests that gauged material:** In addition to interviews with Flynn, his books were helpful—particularly the hundred pages of appendices in *Are We Getting Smarter?* (Cambridge: Cambridge University Press, 2012).

39 **both separate day from night:** M. C. Fox and A. L. Mitchum, "A Knowledge-Based Theory of Rising Scores on 'Culture-Free' Tests," *Journal of Experimental Psychology* 142, no. 3 (2013): 979–1000.

39 **When a group of Estonian researchers:** O. Must et al., "Predicting the Flynn Effect Through Word Abstractness: Results from the National Intelligence Tests Support Flynn's Explanation," *Intelligence* 57 (2016): 7–14. I first saw these results in St. Petersburg, Russia, at the 2016 annual conference of the International Society for Intelligence Research. The ISIR invited me to give the annual Constance Holden Memorial Address. Four attempts at getting a visa later, I arrived. The event was full of vigorous but civil debate, including over the Flynn effect, and was an excellent background resource.

39 **"The huge Raven's gains":** J. R. Flynn, *What Is Intelligence?*

40   **Even in countries:** E. Dutton et al., "The Negative Flynn Effect," *Intelligence* 59 (2016): 163–69. And see Flynn's *Are We Getting Smarter?* on, for example, trends in Sudan.

41   **Alexander Luria:** Luria's fascinating book is the major source for this section: *Cognitive Development: Its Cultural and Social Foundations* (Cambridge, MA: Harvard University Press, 1976).

41   **He learned the local language:** E. D. Homskaya, *Alexander Romanovich Luria: A Scientific Biography* (New York: Springer, 2001).

43   **"eduction":** Flynn's *Does Your Family Make You Smarter?* and chap. 22 of R. J. Sternberg and S. B. Kaufman, eds., *The Cambridge Handbook of Intelligence* (Cambridge: Cambridge University Press, 2011).

44   **forest for the trees:** An in-depth description of the "seeing the trees" phenomenon in a different context can be found in sections about "weak central coherence" in U. Frith, *Autism: Explaining the Enigma* (Malden, MA: Wiley-Blackwell, 2003).

44   **The Kpelle people:** S. Scribner, "Developmental Aspects of Categorized Recall in a West African Society," *Cognitive Psychology* 6 (1974): 475–94. For more on work that extended Luria's findings, see: M. Cole and S. Scribner, *Culture and Thought* (New York: John Wiley & Sons, 1974).

44   **The word "percent":** Google Books Ngram Viewer search for "percent." See also: J. B. Michel et al., "Quantitative Analysis of Culture Using Millions of Digitized Books," *Science* 331 (2011): 176–82.

44–45   **They do very well on Raven's:** Flynn, *Does Your Family Make You Smarter?*

45   **provides peace of mind:** S. Arbesman, *Overcomplicated* (New York: Portfolio, 2017), 158–60.

45   **"cognitively flexible":** C. Schooler, "Environmental Complexity and the Flynn Effect," in *The Rising Curve*, ed. U. Neisser (Washington, DC: American Psychological Association, 1998). And see: A. Inkeles and D. H. Smith, *Becoming Modern: Individual Change in Six Developing Countries* (Cambridge, MA: Harvard University Press, 1974).

45   **"No historian who takes in the sweep of human history":** S. Pinker, *The Better Angels of our Nature* (New York: Penguin, 2011).

46   **more slowly for women:** Flynn, *Are We Getting Smarter?*.

48   **"the traits that earn good grades":** Flynn, *How to Improve Your Mind* (Malden, MA: Wiley-Blackwell, 2012). Flynn kindly provided me with the test and answer key.

48   **econ professors have been shown:** R. P. Larrick et al., "Teaching the Use of Cost-Benefit Reasoning in Everyday Life," *Psychological Science* 1, no. 6 (1990): 362–70; R. P. Larrick et al., "Who Uses the Cost-Benefit Rules of Choice?," *Organizational Behavior and Human Decision Processes* 56 (1993): 331–47. (Hogarth's "what strikes me" quote in the footnote is from his Educating Intuition, p. 222).

48   **Chemists, on the other hand:** J. F. Voss et al., "Individual Differences in the Solving of Social Science Problems," in *Individual Differences in Cognition*, vol. 1, ed.

R. F. Dillon and R. R. Schmeck (New York: Academic Press, 1983); D. R. Lehman et al., "The Effects of Graduate Training on Reasoning," *American Psychologist* 43, no. 6 (1988): 431–43.

49   **"is intended as an introduction":** "The College Core Curriculum," University of Chicago, https://college.uchicago.edu/academics/college-core-curriculum.

50   **registration filled up in the first minute:** M. Nijhuis, "How to Call B.S. on Big Data: A Practical Guide," *The New Yorker,* June 3, 2017, online ed.

50   **"Computational thinking is using abstraction":** J. M. Wing, "Computational Thinking," *Communications of the ACM* 49, no. 3 (2006): 33–35.

50   **narrow vocational training:** B. Caplan, *The Case Against Education* (Princeton, NJ: Princeton University Press, 2018), 233–35.

50–51   **a career unrelated to their major:** J. R. Abel and R. Deitz, "Agglomeration and Job Matching among College Graduates." *Regional Science and Urban Economics* 51 (2015): 14–24.

51   **"No tool is omnicompetent":** A. J. Toynbee, *A Study of History,* vol. 12, *Reconsiderations* (Oxford: Oxford University Press, 1964), 42.

51   **"Everyone is so busy doing research":** Center for Evidence-Based Medicine video, "Doug Altman—Scandal of Poor Medical Research," https://www.youtube.com/watch?v=ZwDNPldQO1Q.

52   **like Fermi-izing, can go a long way:** In addition to the Larrick and Lehman studies above, see: D. F. Halpern, "Teaching Critical Thinking for Transfer Across Domains," *American Psychologist* 53, no. 4 (1998): 449–55; W. Chang et al., "Developing Expert Political Judgment," *Judgment and Decision Making* 11, no. 5 (2016): 509–26.

53   **"how Fermi estimation can cut":** "Case Studies: Bullshit in the Wild," Calling Bullshit, https://callingbullshit.org/case_studies.html.

CHAPTER 3: WHEN LESS OF THE SAME IS MORE

55   The citations for this chapter will be extensive but necessarily abbreviated. Explanation: The most extensive research on life and music at the *ospedali* was conducted by Jane L. Baldauf-Berdes. Some of her work can be found in books, like *Women Musicians of Venice* (Oxford: Oxford University Press, 1996), which she barely completed before she died of cancer. She was still very much in the thick of her work. In the course of reporting, I learned that she left her research files to the David M. Rubenstein Rare Book and Manuscript Library at Duke University. Thanks to the library and its staff, I had access to forty-eight boxes full of Baldauf-Berdes's research material, from translations of original documents and photographs of antique instruments, to rosters of musicians and correspondence with other historians. Her passion for the topic bursts from those boxes. A few details in this chapter that come from her research are, I believe, published here for the first time. I only hope she would be glad that some curious writer came along and made a little use of it. I would like to dedicate this chapter to Jane L. Baldauf-Berdes.

55 **exploding from its traditional bounds:** J. Kerman and G. Tomlinson, *Listen (Brief Fourth Edition).* (Boston: Bedford/St. Martin's, 2000), chaps. 7 and 9. (Vivaldi as "undisputed champion" is from p. 117.)

56 **full weight of entertainment:** This is from pp. 118–38 of the modern publication of a contemporaneous account that provided an important source throughout the chapter on eighteenth-century music in Europe: P. A. Scholes, ed., *Dr. Burney's Musical Tours in Europe,* vol. 1, *An Eighteenth-Century Musical Tour in France and Italy* (Oxford: Oxford University Press, 1959).

56 **dominated for a century:** E. Selfridge-Field, "Music at the Pietà Before Vivaldi," *Early Music* 14, no. 3 (1986): 373–86; R. Thackray, "Music Education in Eighteenth Century Italy," reprint from *Studies in Music* 9 (1975): 1–7.

56 **"Only in Venice":** E. Arnold and J. Baldauf-Berdes, *Maddalena Lombardini Sirmen* (Lanham, MD: Scarecrow Press, 2002).

56 **reserved for men:** J. Spitzer and N. Zaslaw, *The Birth of the Orchestra* (Oxford: Oxford University Press, 2004), 175. Also: Scholes, ed., *Burney's Musical Tours in Europe,* vol. 1, 137.

56 **"They sing like angels":** A. Pugh, *Women in Music* (Cambridge: Cambridge University Press, 1991).

56 **"The sight of girls":** Hester L. Piozzi, *Autobiography, Letters and Literary Remains of Mrs. Piozzi (Thrale)* (Tradition Classics, 2012 [Kindle ebook]).

56 **"feminine instruments"; "first of her sex":** Arnold and Baldauf-Berdes, *Maddalena Lombardini Sirmen.*

56 **"angelic Sirens":** Coli's writing appeared in 1687 in *Pallade Veneta,* a (largely forgotten) periodical that carried commentary in letter form. The best source on the periodical is: E. Selfridge-Field, *Pallade Veneta: Writings on Music in Venetian Society, 1650–1750* (Venice: Fondazione Levi, 1985).

56 **"the premier violinist in Europe"; "unsurpassed":** J. L. Baldauf-Berdes, "Anna Maria della Pietà: The Woman Musician of Venice Personified," in *Cecilia Reclaimed,* ed. S. C. Cook and J. S. Tsou (Urbana: University of Illinois Press, 1994).

56 **An expense report:** This is from another remarkable source, a book of scanned original documents compiled by Micky White, a British former sports photographer and Vivaldi enthusiast who moved to Venice and made it her mission to pore over the Pietà's immense archives: M. White, *Antonio Vivaldi: A Life in Documents (with CD-ROM)* (Florence: Olschki, 2013), 87.

57 **ordered by the Senate:** Baldauf-Berdes, "Anna Maria della Pietà."

57 **"I had brought with me":** Rousseau was a musical autodidact. His quotes come from his famous autobiographical work, *The Confessions.*

58 **"Missing are the fingers":** The anonymous poem (c. 1740) was translated by Baldauf-Berdes and M. Civera from R. Giazotto, *Vivaldi* (Turin: ERI, 1973).

58 **"My request was granted":** Lady Anna Riggs Miller, *Letters from Italy Describing the Manners, Customs, Antiquities, Paintings, etc. of that Country in the Years MDCCLXX and MDCCLXXI,* vol. 2 (Printed for E. and C. Dilly, 1777), 360–61.

59   **some trinket left:** D. E. Kaley, "The Church of the Pietà" (Venice: International Fund for Monuments, 1980).

59   **An eighteenth-century roster:** From one of the many lists of musicians and instruments that Baldauf-Berdes compiled from archival research. This particular one is in Box 1 of 48 in the Baldauf-Berdes collection at Duke's Rubinstein Library.

60   **"penitential mood":** Baldauf-Berdes, *Women Musicians of Venice* (Oxford: Oxford University Press, 1996).

61   **"It was really curious":** Scholes, ed., *Burney's Musical Tours in Europe,* vol. 1.

61   **"acquiring skills not expected of my sex":** Arnold and Baldauf-Berdes, *Maddalena Lombardini Sirmen.*

61   **Pelegrina della Pietà:** One of the many orphans listed on a Pietà roster, she is also expertly discussed by Micky White in a BBC Four film called *Vivaldi's Women.*

62   **"all styles":** R. Rolland, *A Musical Tour Through the Land of the Past* (New York: Henry Holt, 1922).

62   **"Vivaldi had at his disposal":** M. Pincherle, "Vivaldi and the 'Ospitali' of Venice," *Musical Quarterly* 24, no. 3 (1938): 300–312.

63   **"might never have been composed at all":** D. Arnold. "Venetian Motets and Their Singers," *Musical Times* 119 (1978): 319–21. (The specific piece discussed is *Exsultate, jubilate,* but the author uses it as representative of Mozart's sacred music.)

63   **Napoleon's troops:** Arnold and Baldauf-Berdes, *Maddalena Lombardini Sirmen.*

63   **went entirely unidentified:** In a research proposal written for the Gladys Krieble Delmas Foundation in 1989, Baldauf-Berdes chronicled this and other instances of the *figlie* being forgotten. The series she intended to publish, unfortunately, was one of those she was never able to complete.

63   **left the world having been:** Baldauf-Berdes, "Anna Maria della Pietà."

64   **"able indigents":** G. J. Buelow, ed., *The Late Baroque Era* (Basingstoke: Macmillan, 1993).

65   **"how to choose":** R. Lane, "How to Choose a Musical Instrument for My Child," Upperbeachesmusic.com, January 5, 2017.

65   **he didn't really like the first two instruments:** M. Steinberg, "Yo-Yo Ma on Intonation, Practice, and the Role of Music in Our Lives," *Strings,* September 17, 2015, online ed.

66   **A study of music students:** J. A. Sloboda et al., "The Role of Practice in the Development of Performing Musicians," *British Journal of Psychology* 87 (1996): 287–309. See also: G. E. McPherson et al., "Playing an Instrument," in *The Child as Musician,* ed. G. E. McPherson (Oxford: Oxford University Press, 2006) ("[I]t was discovered some of the most successful young learners were those who had been through a range of musical instruments"); and J. A. Sloboda and M. J. A. Howe, "Biographical Precursors of Musical Excellence," *Psychology of Music* 19 (1991): 3–21 ("The exceptional children practiced much less than the average children on their first chosen instrument but much more than the average children on their third instrument").

66 "a mismatch between the instruments": S. A. O'Neill, "Developing a Young Musician's Growth Mindset," in *Music and the Mind*, ed. I. Deliège and J. W. Davidson (Oxford: Oxford University Press, 2011).

66 "It seems very clear": Sloboda and Howe, "Biographical Precursors of Musical Excellence."

67 A study that followed up: A. Ivaldi, "Routes to Adolescent Musical Expertise," in *Music and the Mind*, ed. Deliège and Davidson.

69 "Despite the ever-increasing number": P. Gorner, "Cecchini's Guitar Truly Classical," *Chicago Tribune*, July 13, 1968. (Studs Terkel interviewed Cecchini the day before the performance. That fantastic conversation about music can be found here: http://jackcecchini.com/Interviews.html).

70 "There was no connection": T. Teachout, *Duke: A Life of Duke Ellington* (New York: Gotham Books, 2013).

70 America's preeminent composer: Kerman and Tomlinson, *Listen*, 394.

70 "John played anything": L. Flanagan, *Moonlight in Vermont: The Official Biography of Johnny Smith* (Anaheim Hills, CA: Centerstream, 2015).

71 "I got a wonderful piano teacher": F. M. Hall, *It's About Time: The Dave Brubeck Story*. (Fayetteville: University of Arkansas Press, 1996).

72 "with a drawn knife"; "I wonder if": M. Dregni, *Django: The Life and Music of a Gypsy Legend* (Oxford: Oxford University Press, 2004 [Kindle ebook]). Two other sources provided particularly important details about Django's life: C. Delaunay, *Django Reinhardt* (New York: Da Capo, 1961) (on the back cover, James Lincoln Collier, author of *The Making of Jazz*, identifies Django as "without question, the single most important guitarist"); and a special Django issue of *Guitar Player* magazine (November 1976) devoted to legendary musicians recounting their time with him.

73 creativity erupted: The 5-CD set "Django Reinhardt—Musette to Maestro 1928–1937: The Early Work of a Guitar Genius" (JSP Records, 2010) includes recordings of a young Reinhardt both before and after his injury.

73 Jimi Hendrix, who kept an album of Django's: Jacob McMurray, senior curator at Seattle's Museum of Pop Culture, kindly confirmed this with the museum's permanent collection.

74 sepia-toned YouTube clip: "Django Reinhardt Clip Performing Live (1945)," YouTube, www.youtube.com/watch?v=aZ308aOOX04. (The date on the YouTube video is incorrect. The clip is from the 1938 short film "Jazz 'Hot.'")

74 "one of osmosis" (and other Berliner quotes): P. F. Berliner, *Thinking in Jazz* (Chicago: University of Chicago Press, 1994).

75 "as if the brain turned off": C. Kalb, "Who Is a Genius?," *National Geographic*, May 2017.

75 "Well, I can't read either": *Guitar Player*, November 1976.

76 "a concept that went against conservatory training": Dregni, *Django*.

76   **"I can't improvise at all"**: A. Midgette, "Concerto on the Fly: Can Classical Musicians Learn to Improvise," *Washington Post,* June 15, 2012, online ed.

76   **"My complete self-taught technique"** and detail about hitting siblings with violins: S. Suzuki, *Nurtured by Love,* trans. W. Suzuki (Alfred Music, 1993 [Kindle ebook]).

77   **household rules:** J. S. Dacey, "Discriminating Characteristics of the Families of Highly Creative Adolescents," *Journal of Creative Behavior* 23, no. 4 (1989): 263–71. (Grant referenced the study in: "How to Raise a Creative Child. Step One: Back Off," *New York Times*, Jan. 30, 2016.)

CHAPTER 4: LEARNING, FAST AND SLOW

79   **"Okay? You're going to an Eagles game":** The classroom scene is from video, transcript, and analysis from the Trends in International Mathematics and Science Study (TIMSS). The particular video is "M-US2 Writing Variable Expressions."

80   **"three dollars for a hot dog":** The teacher briefly misspoke and said "two." It is corrected for clarity.

82   **"using procedures"; "making connections":** J. Hiebert et al., "Teaching Mathematics in Seven Countries," National Center for Education Statistics, 2003, chap. 5.

84   *bansho*: E.R.A. Kuehnert et al. "Bansho: Visually Sequencing Mathematical Ideas," *Teaching Children Mathematics* 24, no. 6 (2018):362–69.

84   **"Students do not view mathematics as a *system*":** L. E. Richland et al., "Teaching the Conceptual Structure of Mathematics," *Educational Psychology* 47, no. 3 (2012): 189–203.

85   **tested sixth graders in the South Bronx:** N. Kornell and J. Metcalfe, "The Effects of Memory Retrieval, Errors and Feedback on Learning," in *Applying Science of Learning in Education*, V.A. Benassi et al., ed. (Society for the Teaching of Psychology, 2014); J. Metcalfe and N. Kornell, "Principles of Cognitive Science in Education," *Psychonomic Bulletin and Review* 14, no. 2 (2007): 225–29.

86   **"hypercorrection effect":** T. S. Eich et al., "The Hypercorrection Effect in Younger and Older Adults," *Neuropsychology, Development and Cognition. Section B, Aging, Neuropsychology and Cognition* 20, no. 5 (2013): 511–21; J. Metcalfe et al., "Neural Correlates of People's Hypercorrection of Their False Beliefs," *Journal of Cognitive Neuroscience* 24, no. 7 (2012): 1571–83.

86   **Oberon and Macduff:** N. Kornell and H. S. Terrace, "The Generation Effect in Monkeys," *Psychological Science* 18, no. 8 (2007): 682–85.

88   **"Like life":** N. Kornell et al., "Retrieval Attempts Enhance Learning, but Retrieval Success (Versus Failure) Does Not Matter," *Journal of Experimental Psychology: Learning, Memory, and Cognition* 41, no. 1 (2015): 283–94.

88   **Spanish vocabulary learners:** H. P. Bahrick and E. Phelps, "Retention of Spanish Vocabulary over 8 Years," *Journal of Experimental Psychology: Learning, Memory, and Cognition* 13, no. 2 (1987): 344–49.

88–89   **Iowa State researchers read:** L. L. Jacoby and W. H. Bartz, "Rehearsal and Transfer to LTM," *Journal of Verbal Learning and Verbal Behavior* 11 (1972): 561–65.

89   **"produce misleadingly high levels":** N. J. Cepeda et al., "Spacing Effects in Learning," *Psychological Science* 19, no. 11 (2008): 1095–1102.

89   **In 2007, the U.S. Department of Education:** H. Pashler et al., "Organizing Instruction and Study to Improve Student Learning," National Center for Education Research, 2007.

90   **an extraordinarily unique study:** S. E. Carrell and J. E. West, "Does Professor Quality Matter?," *Journal of Political Economy* 118, no. 3 (2010): 409–32.

92   **A similar study was conducted at Italy's Bocconi University:** M. Braga et al., "Evaluating Students' Evaluations of Professors," *Economics of Education Review* 41 (2014): 71–88.

92   **"desirable difficulties":** R. A. Bjork, "Institutional Impediments to Effective Training," in *Learning, Remembering, Believing: Enhancing Human Performance,* ed. D. Druckman and R. A. Bjork (Washington, DC: National Academies Press, 1994), 295–306.

92   **"Above all, the most basic message":** C. M. Clark and R. A. Bjork, "When and Why Introducing Difficulties and Errors Can Enhance Instruction," in *Applying the Science of Learning in Education,* ed. V. A. Benassi et al. (Society for the Teaching of Psychology, 2014 [ebook]).

92   **said in national surveys:** C. Rampell, "Actually, Public Education is Getting Better, Not Worse," *Washington Post,* September 18, 2014.

92–93   **School has not gotten worse; "jobs that pay well":** G. Duncan and R. J. Murnane, *Restoring Opportunity* (Cambridge, MA: Harvard Education Press, 2014 [Kindle ebook]).

94   **In a study using college math problems:** D. Rohrer and K. Taylor, "The Shuffling of Mathematics Problems Improves Learning," *Instructional Science* 35 (2007): 481–98.

95   **butterfly species identification to psychological-disorder diagnosis:** M. S. Birnbaum et al., "Why Interleaving Enhances Inductive Learning," *Memory and Cognition* 41 (2013): 392–402.

95   **naval air defense simulations:** C. L. Holladay and M.A. Quiñones, "Practice Variability and Transfer of Training," *Journal of Applied Psychology* 88, no. 6 (2003): 1094–1103.

95   **In one of Kornell and Bjork's interleaving studies, 80 percent of students:** N. Kornell and R. A. Bjork, "Learning Concepts and Categories: Is Spacing the 'Enemy of Induction'?," *Psychological Science* 19, no. 6 (2008): 585–92.

95   **a particular left-hand jump across fifteen keys:** M. Bangert et al., "When Less of the Same Is More: Benefits of Variability of Practice in Pianists," *Proceedings of the International Symposium on Performance Science* (2013): 117–22.

96 **O'Neal should practice from a foot in front:** Bjork makes this suggestion in Daniel Coyle's *The Talent Code* (New York: Bantam, 2009).

96 **hallmark of expert problem solving:** See, for example: M.T.H. Chi et al., "Categorization and Representation of Physics Problems by Experts and Novices," *Cognitive Science 5*, no. 2 (1981): 121–52; and J. F. Voss et al., "Individual Differences in the Solving of Social Science Problems," in *Individual Differences in Cognition,* vol. 1, ed. R. F. Dillon and R. R. Schmeck (New York: Academic Press, 1983).

96 **reviewed sixty-seven early childhood education programs:** D. Bailey et al., "Persistence and Fadeout in Impacts of Child and Adolescent Interventions," *Journal of Research on Educational Effectiveness* 10, no. 1 (2017): 7–39.

97 **The motor-skill equivalent:** S. G. Paris, "Reinterpreting the Development of Reading Skills," *Reading Research Quarterly* 40, no. 2 (2005): 184–202.

CHAPTER 5: THINKING OUTSIDE EXPERIENCE

99 **Giordano Bruno:** A. A. Martinez, "Giordano Bruno and the Heresy of Many Worlds," *Annals of Science* 73, no. 4 (2016): 345–74.

99 **Johannes Kepler inherited:** Sources that give excellent background on the worldviews that Kepler inherited, and his transformative analogies, are: D. Gentner et al., "Analogical Reasoning and Conceptual Change: A Case Study of Johannes Kepler," *Journal of the Learning Sciences* 6, no. 1 (1997): 3–40; D. Gentner, "Analogy in Scientific Discovery: The Case of Johannes Kepler," in *Model-Based Reasoning: Science, Technology, Values,* ed. L. Magnani and N. J. Nersessian (New York: Kluwer Academic/Plenum Publishers, 2002), 21–39; D. Gentner et al., "Analogy and Creativity in the Works of Johannes Kepler," in *Creative Thought: An Investigation of Conceptual Structures and Processes,* ed. T. B. Ward et al. (Washington, DC: American Psychological Association, 1997).

101 **maybe the planets were like magnets:** D. Gentner and A. B. Markman, "Structure Mapping in Analogy and Similarity," *American Psychologist* 52, no. 1 (1997): 45–56. Also, Kepler read a new publication on magnetism: A. Caswell, "Lectures on Astronomy," *Smithsonian Lectures on Astronomy,* 1858 (British Museum collection).

101 **"the moon's dominion over the waters":** J. Gleick, *Isaac Newton* (New York: Vintage, 2007).

102 **no concept of gravity as a force; "Ye physicists" :** A. Koestler, *The Sleepwalkers: A History of Man's Changing Vision of the Universe* (New York: Penguin Classics, 2017).

102 **"I especially love analogies":** B. Vickers, "Analogy Versus Identity," in: *Occult and Scientific Mentalities in the Renaissance,* ed. B. Vickers (Cambridge: Cambridge University Press, 1984).

103 "action at a distance": Gentner et al., "Analogy and Creativity in the Works of Johannes Kepler."; E. McMullin, "The Origins of the Field Concept in Physics," *Physics in Perspective* 4, no. 1 (2002): 13–39.

104 Suppose you are a doctor: M. L. Gick and K. J. Holyoak, "Analogical Problem Solving," *Cognitive Psychology* 12 (1980): 306–55.

105–107 There once was a general; small-town fire chief; "might well have supposed"; "ill-defined" problems: M. L. Gick and K. J. Holyoak, "Schema Induction and Analogical Transfer," *Cognitive Psychology* 15 (1983): 1–38.

107 An experiment on Stanford international relations students; college football coaches: T. Gilovich, "Seeing the Past in the Present: The Effect of Associations to Familiar Events on Judgments and Decisions," *Journal of Personality and Social Psychology* 40, no. 5 (1981): 797–808.

108 Kahneman had a personal experience: Kahneman's story is in his *Thinking, Fast and Slow* (New York: Farrar, Straus & Giroux, 2011). With background on the inside and outside views, it is also in D. Kahneman and D. Lovallo, "Timid Choices and Bold Forecasts," *Management Science* 39, no. 1 (1993): 17–31.

109 investors from large private equity firms: D. Lovallo, C. Clarke, and C. Camerer, "Robust Analogizing and the Outside View," *Strategic Management Journal* 33, no. 5 (2012): 496–512.

110 qualities of the specific horse: M. J. Mauboussin, *Think Twice: Harnessing the Power of Counterintuition* (Boston: Harvard Business Review Press, 2009).

110 the more internal details: L. Van Boven and N. Epley, "The Unpacking Effect in Evaluative Judgments: When the Whole Is *Less* Than the Sum of Its Parts," *Journal of Experimental Social Psychology* 39 (2003): 263–69.

110 "natural causes": A. Tversky and D. J. Koehler, "Support Theory," *Psychological Review* 101, no. 4 (1994): 547–67.

110 90 percent of major infrastructure projects: B. Flyvbjerg et al., "What Causes Cost Overrun in Transport Infrastructure Projects?" *Transport Reviews* 24, no. 1 (2004): 3–18.

111 a massive underestimate: B. Flyvbjerg, "Curbing Optimism Bias and Strategic Misrepresentation in Planning," *European Planning Studies* 16, no. 1 (2008): 3–21. The £1 billion price tag: S. Brocklehurst, "Going off the Rails," *BBC Scotland*, May 30, 2014, online ed.

111 the movie business: Lovallo, Clarke, and Camerer, "Robust Analogizing and the Outside View."

111 Netflix came to a similar conclusion: T. Vanderbilt, "The Science Behind the Netflix Algorithms That Decide What You'll Watch Next," Wired.com, August 7, 2013; and C. Burger, "Personalized Recommendations at Netflix," Tastehit .com, February 23, 2016.

112 Lovallo and Dubin gave some students: F. Dubin and D. Lovallo, "The Use and Misuse of Analogies in Business," Working Paper (Sydney: University of Sydney, 2008).

113 **In 2001, the Boston Consulting Group:** A short discussion about the impetus for BCG's exhibits is: D. Gray, "A Gallery of Metaphors," *Harvard Business Review,* September 2003.

114 **Gentner and colleagues gave the Ambiguous Sorting Task:** B. M. Rottman et al., "Causal Systems Categories: Differences in Novice and Expert Categorization of Causal Phenomena," *Cognitive Science* 36 (2012): 919–32.

115 **In one of the most cited studies:** M. T. H. Chi et al., "Categorization and Representation of Physics Problems by Experts and Novices," *Cognitive Science* 5, no. 2 (1981): 121–52.

115 **"What matters to me":** Koestler, *The Sleepwalkers.*

116 **1 percent of the national budget:** N. Morvillo, *Science and Religion: Understanding the Issues* (Malden, MA: Wiley-Blackwell, 2010).

116 **"If I had believed we could ignore these eight minutes":** Koestler, *The Sleepwalkers.*

117 **When Dunbar started:** An excellent background source on Dunbar's work is: K. Dunbar, "What Scientific Thinking Reveals About the Nature of Cognition," in *Designing for Science,* ed. K. Crowley et al. (Mahwah, NJ: Lawrence Erlbaum Associates, 2001).

119 **"When all the members":** K. Dunbar, "How Scientists Really Reason," in *The Nature of Insight,* ed. R. J. Sternberg and J. E. Davidson (Cambridge, MA: MIT Press, 1995), 365–95.

CHAPTER 6: THE TROUBLE WITH TOO MUCH GRIT

121 **The boy's mother appreciated:** Details of Van Gogh's life come from several main sources, including translated letters written by and to Van Gogh. More than nine hundred letters (that is, every surviving one) are available at the incredible Vincent van Gogh: The Letters website (vangoghletters.org), courtesy of the Van Gogh Museum and the Huygens Institute for the History of the Netherlands. Without another incredible source, I would not have known which letters to read: Steven Naifeh and Gregory White Smith, *Van Gogh: The Life* (New York: Random House, 2011). Naifeh and Smith took the extraordinary step of creating a searchable database of sources at vangoghbiography.com/notes.php. It was extremely helpful. Two other written sources that were helpful: N. Denekamp et al., *The Vincent van Gogh Atlas* (New Haven, CT: Yale University Press and the Van Gogh Museum, 2016); and J. Hulsker, *The Complete Van Gogh* (New York: Harrison House/H. N. Abrams, 1984). Finally, two exhibitions: "Van Gogh's Bedrooms" at the Art Institute of Chicago (2016), and the impressionism and post-impressionism collections at the Hermitage Museum in St. Petersburg, Russia.

122 **"None of it registered":** Naifeh and Smith, *Van Gogh: The Life.*

122 **"absolutely *nothing* of them":** Van Gogh letter to brother Theo, June 1884.

123 "own desires"; "happier and calmer"; "push on": Naifeh and Smith, *Van Gogh: The Life*.

123 "must sit up": Van Gogh letter to brother Theo, September 1877.

124 "up in Hell": Émile Zola, *Germinal*, trans. R. N. MacKenzie (Indianapolis: Hackett Publishing, 2011).

124 "the bars of his cage": Van Gogh letter to brother Theo, June 1880.

124 "I'm writing to you while drawing": Van Gogh letter to brother Theo, August 1880.

125 *Guide to the ABCs of Drawing*: Naifeh and Smith, *Van Gogh: The Life*.

125 "you are no artist"; "you started too late": Van Gogh letter to brother Theo, March 1882 (trans. Johanna van Gogh-Bonger).

126 "[He] made an astonishing discovery": Naifeh and Smith, *Van Gogh: The Life*.

126 "Painting has proved less difficult": Van Gogh letter to brother Theo, August 1882. The painting that Van Gogh made that day is *Beach at Scheveningen in Stormy Weather*. The painting was stolen from the Van Gogh Museum in 2002, but recovered more than a decade later.

127 An ecstatic review: The review, by G.-Albert Aurier, was titled "*Les isolés:* Vincent van Gogh."

128 life expectancy in the Netherlands: The exact figure is 39.84 and comes from the online publication *Our World in Data* (ourworldindata.org).

128 Gauguin . . . at the age of thirty-five: *The Great Masters* (London: Quantum Publishing, 2003).

128 "failed on an epic scale": J. K. Rowling, text of speech, "The Fringe Benefits of Failure, and the Importance of Imagination," *Harvard Gazette*, June 5, 2008, online ed.

129 Nobel laureate economist Theodore Schultz: T. W. Schultz, "Resources for Higher Education," *Journal of Political Economy* 76, no. 3 (1968): 327–47.

129 found a natural experiment: O. Malamud, "Discovering One's Talent: Learning from Academic Specialization," *Industrial and Labor Relations* 64, no. 2 (2011): 375–405.

130 Scots quickly caught up: O. Malamud, "Breadth Versus Depth: The Timing of Specialization in Higher Education," *Labour* 24, no. 4 (2010): 359–90.

130 more mistakes: D. Lederman, "When to Specialize?," *Inside Higher Ed*, November 25, 2009.

130 "The benefits to increased match quality": Malamud, "Discovering One's Talent."

131 Steven Levitt . . . leveraged his readership: S. D. Levitt, "Heads or Tails: The Impact of a Coin Toss on Major Life Decisions and Subsequent Happiness," NBER Working Paper No. 22487 (2016).

131 "the willingness to jettison": Levitt, in the September 30, 2011, *Freakonomics Radio* program, "The Upside of Quitting."

132 **"Teachers tend to leave schools"**: C. K. Jackson, "Match Quality, Worker Productivity, and Worker Mobility: Direct Evidence from Teachers," *Review of Economics and Statistics* 95, no. 4 (2013): 1096–1116.

132 **Psychologist Angela Duckworth conducted the most famous study**: A. L. Duckworth et al., "Grit: Perseverance and Passion for Long-Term Goals," *Journal of Personality and Social Psychology* 92, no. 6 (2007): 1087–1101. (The entire incoming class comprised 1,223 freshman cadets, so Duckworth surveyed nearly every one.) Table 3 gives a nice summary of the amount of variance accounted for by grit in results from West Point, the Scripps National Spelling Bee, Ivy League students' grades, and adult educational attainment. Additionally, Duckworth made her work very accessible in her book, *Grit: The Power of Passion and Perseverance* (New York: Scribner, 2016).

133 **Duckworth learned that:** An incisive piece on grit and the Whole Candidate Score is: D. Engber, "Is 'Grit' Really the Key to Success?," *Slate,* May 8, 2016.

134 **"I worry I've contributed"**: A. Duckworth, "Don't Grade Schools on Grit," *New York Times,* March 26, 2016.

135 **"necessarily limited"**: Duckworth et al., "Grit: Perseverance and Passion for Long-Term Goals."

135 **32 of 1,308**: M. Randall, "New Cadets March Back from 'Beast Barracks' at West Point," *Times Herald-Record*, August 8, 2016.

136 **"young and foolish"**: R. A. Miller, "Job Matching and Occupational Choice," *Journal of Political Economy* 92, no. 6 (1984): 1086–1120.

136 **"tasks we don't have the guts to quit"**: S. Godin, *The Dip: A Little Book That Teaches You When to Quit (and When to Stick)* (New York: Portfolio, 2007 [Kindle ebook]).

137 **twenty-year mark**: G. Cheadle (Brig. Gen. USAF [Ret.]), "Retention of USMA Graduates on Active Duty," white paper for the USMA Association of Graduates, 2004.

137–138 **A 2010 monograph; "institution that taught its cadets"**: This monograph is one in a six-part series about officer development and retention: C. Wardynski et al., "Towards a U.S. Army Officer Corps Strategy for Success: Retaining Talent," Strategic Studies Institute, 2010.

140 **Ash Carter visited West Point**: A. Tilghman, "At West Point, Millennial Cadets Say Rigid Military Career Tracks Are Outdated," *Military Times,* March 26, 2016.

140 **talent-based branching**: D. Vergun, "Army Helping Cadets Match Talent to Branch Selection," *Army News Service*, March 21, 2017.

141 **American adults at large**: You can compare your grit score to other adults at https://angeladuckworth.com/grit-scale/.

143 **"Olympic athletes need to understand"**: S. Cohen, "Sasha Cohen: An Olympian's Guide to Retiring at 25," *New York Times,* February 24, 2018.

143 **A recent international Gallup survey**: Gallup's *State of the Global Workplace* report, 2017.

CHAPTER 7: FLIRTING WITH YOUR POSSIBLE SELVES

147 **Frances Hesselbein grew up:** Information about Hesselbein's life comes from multiple interviews with her, as well as her books, and corroboration from others who know her. Her book, *My Life in Leadership* (San Francisco: Jossey-Bass, 2011), was a particularly useful source and contains the "a doctor, a lawyer, an aviatrix" quote.

151 **"any company in America":** E. Edersheim, "The Woman Drucker Said Was the Best CEO in America," *Management Matters Network*, April 27, 2017.

151 **"I would pick Frances":** J. A. Byrne, "Profiting from the Nonprofits," *Business Week*, March 26, 1990.

152 **Presidential Medal of Freedom:** When President Bill Clinton presented the medal to Hesselbein, he made a humorous point of asking her to come "forward" to receive the award, as she did not like the use of hierarchical words like "up" and "down."

154 **Phil Knight:** *Good Morning America*, April 26, 2016.

155 **"wasn't much for setting goals":** Phil Knight, *Shoe Dog* (New York: Scribner, 2016).

155 **"Nor did I ever attend again":** These and other details of Darwin's life can be found in *The Autobiography of Charles Darwin*. A free version with annotation can be found at Darwin-online.org.uk.

155 **recommended him for an unpaid position:** There is a wealth of information, like the invitation from professor J. S. Henslow (in a letter on August 24, 1831), publicly available at the University of Cambridge's Darwin Correspondence Project (www.darwinproject.ac.uk).

155–156 **"died a natural death"; "It seems ludicrous"; "If his father had given him any choice":** *The Autobiography of Charles Darwin*.

156 **"I would never have to wonder":** Bio at www.michaelcrichton.com.

156 **"end of history illusion":** J. Quoidbach, D. T. Gilbert, and T. D. Wilson, "The End of History Illusion," *Science* 339, no. 6115 (2013): 96–98.

157 **the results of ninety-two studies:** B.W. Roberts et al., "Patterns of Mean-Level Change in Personality Traits Across the Life Course," *Psychological Bulletin* 132, no. 1 (2006): 1-25. See also: B. W. Roberts and D. Mroczek, "Personality Trait Change in Adulthood," *Current Directions in Psychological Science* 17, no. 1 (2009): 31–35. For a nice (and free) review of personality research intended for a broad audience, see M. B. Donnellan, "Personality Stability and Change," in *Noba Textbook Series: Psychology,* ed. R. Biswas-Diener and E. Diener (Champaign, IL: DEF Publishers, 2018), nobaproject.com.

158 **Psychologist Walter Mischel and his research team:** W. Mischel, *The Marshmallow Test* (New York: Little, Brown, 2014 [Kindle ebook]).

158–159 **Shoda has repeatedly made a point:** Shoda used the occasion of winning a research award to make the point again. A June 2, 2015, press release from the University of Washington announcing the award noted, "While pleased by the honor, Shoda expressed concern about media coverage of the study over the years, and the incorrect notion that parents could predict their children's fate by doing the study themselves." He added that "the relationships we are finding are far from perfect. And there is a lot of room for change."

159 **"if-then signatures"; "The gist of such findings":** Y. Shoda et al., eds., *Persons in Context: Building a Science of the Individual* (New York: Guilford Press, 2007 [Kindle ebook]).

159 **"If you are conscientious":** T. Rose, *The End of Average: How We Succeed in a World That Values Sameness* (New York: HarperOne, 2016 [Kindle ebook]).

159 **a replication of the marshmallow test:** T. W. Watts et al., "Revisiting the Marshmallow Test," *Psychological Science* 29, no. 7 (2018): 1159–77.

160–161 **Ibarra began; "We discover the possibilities":** H. Ibarra, *Working Identity* (Boston: Harvard Business Review Press, 2003).

161 **"painless path to a new career":** P. Capell, "Taking the Painless Path to a New Career," *Wall Street Journal Europe*, January 2, 2002.

163 **Paul Graham . . . high school graduation speech:** "What You'll Wish You'd Known," www.paulgraham.com/hs.html.

164 **William Wallace showed:** W. Wallace, "Michelangelo: Separating Theory and Practice," in *Imitation, Representation and Printing in the Italian Renaissance*, ed. R. Eriksen and M. Malmanger (Pisa and Rome: Fabrizio Serra Editore, 2009).

164 **grew to dislike painting; half . . . left unfinished:** *The Complete Poems of Michelangelo*, trans. J. F. Nims (Chicago: University of Chicago Press, 1998): poem 5 (painting); p. 8 (half unfinished).

165 **"I couldn't play the instruments":** "Haruki Murakami, The Art of Fiction No. 182." *The Paris Review*, 170 (2004).

165 **"ringing double":** H. Murakami, "The Moment I Became a Novelist," *Literary Hub*, June 25, 2015.

165 **"led to a revelation":** Bio at patrickrothfuss.com.

166 **"I was just not interested in thinking about it":** Interview with Maryam Mirzakhani, *Guardian*, August 12, 2014, republished with permission of the Clay Mathematics Institute.

166 **"It is like being lost in a jungle":** A. Myers and B. Carey, "Maryam Mirzakhani, Stanford Mathematician and Fields Medal Winner, Dies," *Stanford News*, July 15, 2007.

166 **"My passion for the sport":** "A new beginning," Chrissiewellington.org, March 12, 2012.

169 **"A warm feelin' come over my body":** H. Finster, as told to T. Patterson, *Howard Finster: Stranger from Another World* (New York: Abbeville Press, 1989).

CHAPTER 8: THE OUTSIDER ADVANTAGE

173 **more than one-third:** K. R. Lakhani, "InnoCentive.com (A)," HBS No. 9-608-170, Harvard Business School Publishing, 2009. See also: S. Page, *The Difference* (Princeton, NJ: Princeton University Press, 2008).

173 **"more savage":** T. Standage, *An Edible History of Humanity* (New York: Bloomsbury, 2009).

173 **offered a reward:** "Selected Innovation Prizes and Rewards Programs," Knowledge Ecology International, KEI Research Note, 2008: 1.

174 **a whole sheep:** J. H. Collins, *The Story of Canned Foods* (New York: E. P. Dutton, 1924).

174 **fed the English troops at Waterloo:** Standage, *An Edible History of Humanity.*

175 **"I think it helped me":** Cragin's presentation at *Collaborative Innovation: Public Sector Prizes,* June 12, 2012, Washington, D.C., The Case Foundation and The Joyce Foundation.

177 **"three evenings":** J. Travis, "Science by the Masses," *Science* 319, no. 5871 (2008): 1750–52.

178 **"the further the problem was":** C. Dean, "If You Have a Problem, Ask Everyone," *New York Times,* July 22, 2008. See also: L. Moise interview with K. Lakhani, "5 Questions with Dr. Karim Lakhani," *InnoCentive Innovation Blog,* Jul 25, 2008.

178 **"exploration [of new solutions]":** K. R. Lakhani et al., "Open Innovation and Organizational Boundaries," in A. Grandori, ed., *Handbook of Economic Organization* (Cheltenham: Edward Elgar, 2013).

178 **"our research shows":** S. Joni, "Stop Relying on Experts for Innovation: A Conversation with Karim Lakhani," *Forbes,* October 23, 2013, online ed.

179 **"need more creative solutions":** Kaggle Team, "Profiling Top Kagglers: Bestfitting, Currently #1 in the World," No Free Hunch (official Kaggle blog), May 7, 2018.

179 **"Swanson is the first physical scientist":** Copy of University of Chicago Office of Public Relations memo (No. 62-583) for December 17, 1962.

179 **"The disparity between the total quantity":** D. R. Swanson, "On the Fragmentation of Knowledge, the Connection Explosion, and Assembling Other People's Ideas," *Bulletin of the American Society for Information Science and Technology* 27, no. 3 (2005): 12–14.

179–180 **In 1960, the U.S. National Library of Medicine:** K. J. Boudreau et al., "Looking Across and Looking Beyond the Knowledge Frontier," *Management Science* 62, no. 10 (2016): 2765–83.

180 **"eleven neglected connections":** D. R. Swanson, "Migraine and Magnesium: Eleven Neglected Connections," *Perspectives in Biology and Medicine* 31, no. 4 (1988): 526–57.

181 **"'home field'":** L. Moise interview with K. Lakhani, "5 Questions with Dr. Karim Lakhani."

183 **She came upon a paper:** the paper was F. Deymeer et al., "Emery-Dreifuss Muscular Dystrophy with Unusual Features," *Muscle and Nerve* 16 (1993): 1359–65.

185 **In 1999, she got an email from Italy:** The Italian research team soon published their results (and thanked Jill): G. Bonne et al., "Mutations in the Gene Encoding

Lamin A/C Cause Autosomal Dominant Emery-Dreifuss Muscular Dystrophy," *Nature Genetics* 21, no. 3 (1999): 285–88.

CHAPTER 9: LATERAL THINKING WITH WITHERED TECHNOLOGY

191 **During two centuries of closed-borders isolation:** Several sources on the history of Nintendo were of particular importance: F. Gorges with I. Yamazaki, *The History of Nintendo,* vol. 1, *1889–1980* (Triel-sur-Seine: Pix'N Love, 2010). F. Gorges with I. Yamazaki, *The History of Nintendo,* vol. 2, *1980–1991* (Triel-sur-Seine: Pix'N Love, 2012); E. Voskuil, *Before Mario: The Fantastic Toys from the Video Game Giant's Early Days* (Châtillon: Omaké Books, 2014); J. Parish, *Game Boy World 1989* (Norfolk, VA: CreateSpace, 2016); D. Sheff, *Game Over: How Nintendo Conquered the World* (New York: Vintage, 2011).

192 **"I didn't want to leave Kyoto":** For source note on Yokoi's quotes, see footnote on p. 192.

193 **"snow melts in sunlight":** Gorges with Yamazaki, *The History of Nintendo, vol.* 2, 1980–1991.

193 **"lateral thinking":** E. de Bono, *Lateral Thinking: Creativity Step by Step* (New York: HarperCollins, 2010).

196 **delicately embossed the screen:** Yokoi's often simple patents are a treasure trove of invention history. This patent (U.S. no. 4398804) and others can be found using Google Patents.

197 **118.7 million units:** B. Edwards, "Happy 20th b-day, Game Boy," *Ars Technica,* April 21, 2009.

197 **"It was difficult"; "'snowman'"; "grim expression":** shmuplations.com (translation), "Console Gaming Then and Now: A Fascinating 1997 Interview with Nintendo's Legendary Gunpei Yokoi," techspot.com, July 10, 2015.

198 **the "candle problem":** For an excellent description, see D. Pink, *Drive* (New York: Riverhead, 2011).

198 **"Electronics was not Yokoi's strong point":** Satoru Okada's foreword in *Before Mario.*

198 **"design and interface":** IGN staff, "Okada on the Game Boy Advance," IGN .com, Sep. 13, 2000.

199 **"If I can speak":** M. Kodama, *Knowledge Integration Dynamics* (Singapore: World Scientific): 211.

199–200 **"simply innovated in a different way":** C. Christensen and S. C. Anthony, "What Should Sony Do Next?," *Forbes,* August 1, 2007, online ed.

200 **focused frogs and visionary birds:** F. Dyson, "Bird and Frogs," *Notices of the American Mathematical Society* 56, no. 2 (2009): 212–23. (Dyson may be a math frog, but he is also an excellent writer.)

201 **multilayer optical film:** M. F. Weber et al., "Giant Birefringent Optics in Multilayer Polymer Mirrors," *Science* 287 (2000): 2451–56; and R. F. Service, "Mirror Film Is the Fairest of Them All," *Science* 287 (2000): 2387–89.

202   **blue morpho:** R. Ahmed et al., "Morpho Butterfly-Inspired Optical Diffraction, Diffusion, and Bio-chemical Sensing," *RSC Advances* 8 (2018): 27111–18.

202   **"It's in front of you literally every day":** Ouderkirk's talk at TEDxHHL, October 14, 2016.

203   **set out to study inventors at 3M:** W. F. Boh, R. Evaristo, and A. Ouderkirk, "Balancing Breadth and Depth of Expertise for Innovation: A 3M Story," *Research Policy* 43 (2013): 349–66.

205   **"nobody ever told me":** Ouderkirk's talk at TEDxHHL, October 14, 2016.

205   **the state of Iowa alone:** G. D. Glenn and R. L. Poole, *The Opera Houses of Iowa* (Ames: Iowa State University Press, 1993). For a broader discussion of this phenomenon, see R. H. Frank, *Luxury Fever* (New York: The Free Press, 1999), ch. 3.

206   **relationship between R&D spending and performance:** B. Jaruzelski et al., "Proven Paths to Innovation Success," *Strategy+Business,* winter 2014, issue 77 preprint.

207   **They analyzed fifteen years of tech patents:** E. Melero and N. Palomeras, "The *Renaissance Man* Is Not Dead! The Role of Generalists in Teams of Inventors," *Research Policy* 44 (2015): 154–67.

208   **comic books:** A. Taylor and H. R. Greve, "Superman or the Fantastic Four? Knowledge Combination and Experience in Innovative Teams," *Academy of Management Journal* 49, no. 4 (2006): 723–40.

208   **Wertham manipulated:** C. L. Tilley, "Seducing the Innocent: Fredric Wertham and the Falsifications That Helped Condemn Comics," *Information and Culture* 47, no. 4 (2012):383-413.

210   **specialized surgeons get better outcomes:** M. Maruthappu et al., "The Influence of Volume and Experience on Individual Surgical Performance: A Systematic Review," *Annals of Surgery* 261, no. 4 (2015): 642–47; N. R. Sahni et al., "Surgeon Specialization and Operative Mortality in the United States: Retrospective Analysis," *BMJ* 354 (2016): i3571; A. Kurmann et al., "Impact of Team Familiarity in the Operating Room on Surgical Complications," *World Journal of Surgery* 38, no. 12 (2014): 3047–52; M. Maruthappu, "The Impact of Team Familiarity and Surgical Experience on Operative Efficiency," *Journal of the Royal Society of Medicine* 109, no. 4 (2016): 147–53.

211   **analyzed its database of major flight accidents:** "A Review of Flightcrew-Involved Major Accidents of U.S. Air Carriers, 1978 Through 1990," National Transportation Safety Board, Safety Study NTSB/SS-94/01, 1994.

211   **University of Utah professor Abbie Griffin:** A. Griffin, R. L. Price, and B. Vojak, *Serial Innovators: How Individuals Create and Deliver Breakthrough Innovations in Mature Firms* (Stanford, CA: Stanford Business Books, 2012 [Kindle ebook]).

212   **"could be considered a professional outsider":** D. K. Simonton, *Origins of Genius* (Oxford: Oxford University Press, 1999).

212   **"unwilling to spend more time on the subject"; Howard Gruber:** H. E. Gruber, *Darwin on Man: A Psychological Study of Scientific Creativity* (Chicago: University of Chicago Press, 1981).

212   **at least 231 scientific pen pals; experiments with seeds:** T. Veak, "Exploring Darwin's Correspondence," *Archives of Natural History* 30, no. 1 (2003): 118–38.

212   **"bewildering miscellany":** H. E. Gruber, "The Evolving Systems Approach to Creative Work," *Creativity Research Journal* 1, no.1 (1988): 27–51.

213   **"a lot of apps open in my brain":** R. Mead, "All About the Hamiltons," *The New Yorker*, February. 9, 2015.

CHAPTER 10: FOOLED BY EXPERTISE

215   **The bet was on:** Yale history professor Paul Sabin's book *The Bet* (New Haven, CT: Yale University Press, 2013) gives fascinating background and analysis. A shorter sample of that analysis is C. R. Sunstein, "The Battle of Two Hedgehogs," *New York Review of Books,* December 5, 2013.

215   **"population growth curve":** P. Ehrlich, *Eco-Catastrophe!* (San Francisco: City Lights Books, 1969).

216   **"green revolution":** G. S. Morson and M. Schapiro, *Cents and Sensibility* (Princeton, NJ: Princeton University Press, 2017 [Kindle ebook]).

217   **the food supply per person increased:** This and other statistics in the paragraph (share of undernourished citizens; death rate from famine; birth rates; population growth trajectory) come from the incredible online publication *Our World in Data,* founded by University of Oxford economist Max Roser. The supply of calories per person per day, for example, can be found here: https://slides.our world-indata.org/hunger-and-food-provision/#/kcalcapitaday-by-world-regions-mg-png.

217   **United Nations projects:** United Nations, Department of Economic and Social Affairs, Population Division, "World Population Prospects: The 2017 Revision, Key Findings and Advance Tables," Working Paper No. ESA/P/WP/248.

217   **"now the population bomb has detonated":** P. R. Ehrlich and A. H. Ehrlich, *The Population Explosion* (New York: Simon & Schuster, 1990).

217   **When economists later examined:** K. Kiel et al., "Luck or Skill? An Examination of the Ehrlich-Simon Bet," *Ecological Economics* 69, no. 7 (2010): 1365–67.

219   **Tetlock decided to put:** Tetlock gives the results of his work in great (and witty) detail in *Expert Political Judgment: How Good Is It? How Can We Know?* (Princeton, NJ: Princeton University Press, 2005).

220   **"curiously inverse relationship":** Tetlock, *Expert Political Judgment.*

225   **Superforecasters' online interactions:** P. E. Tetlock et al., "Bringing Probability Judgments into Policy Debates via Forecasting Tournaments," *Science* 355 (2017): 481–83.

226   **"Forecasts of dollar-euro exchange rates":** G. Gigerenzer, *Risk Savvy* (New York: Penguin, 2014).

227   **"active open-mindedness"; "myside" ideas:** J. Baron et al., "Reflective Thought and Actively Open-Minded Thinking," in *Individual Differences in Judgment*

and Decision Making, ed. M. E. Toplak and J. A. Weller (New York: Routledge, 2017 [Kindle ebook]).

227 **never mind seriously entertain them:** J. A. Frimer et al., "Liberals and Conservatives Are Similarly Motivated to Avoid Exposure to One Another's Opinions," *Journal of Experimental Social Psychology* 72 (2017): 1–12.

227 **study during the run-up to the Brexit vote:** Online Privacy Foundation, "Irrational Thinking and the EU Referendum Result" (2016).

228 **skin cream and gun control:** D. Kahan et al., "Motivated Numeracy and Enlightened Self-Government," *Behavioural Public Policy* 1, no. 1 (2017): 54–86.

228 **Not science knowledge, science *curiosity*:** D. M. Kahan et al., "Science Curiosity and Political Information Processing," *Advances in Political Psychology* 38, no. 51 (2017): 179–99.

228 **"Depth can be inadequate":** Baron et al., "Reflective Thought and Actively Open-Minded Thinking."

228 **first four models:** H. E. Gruber, *Darwin on Man: A Psychological Study of Scientific Creativity,* 127.

229 **"views therein advocated":** *The Autobiography of Charles Darwin.*

229 **"In one of the most remarkable interchanges":** J. Browne, *Charles Darwin: A Biography,* vol. 1, *Voyaging* (New York: Alfred A. Knopf, 1995), 186.

229 **Einstein was a hedgehog:** For one of many references to Einstein's hedgehoginess, see Morson and Schapiro, *Cents and Sensibility.*

229 **"A consensus seems to exist":** G. Mackie, "Einstein's Folly," *The Conversation,* November 29, 2015.

229 **Niels Bohr . . . replied:** C. P. Snow, *The Physicists,* (London: Little, Brown and Co., 1981). Einstein also expresses this idea in: H. Dukas and B. Hoffmann eds., *Albert Einstein, The Human Side: Glimpses from His Archives* (Princeton, NJ: Princeton University Press, 1979), 68.

230 **In four straight years:** W. Chang et al., "Developing Expert Political Judgment: The Impact of Training and Practice on Judgmental Accuracy in Geopolitical Forecasting Tournaments," *Judgment and Decision Making* 11, no. 5 (2016): 509–26.

CHAPTER 11: LEARNING TO DROP YOUR FAMILIAR TOOLS

233 **It was early afternoon in fall:** Professor Max Bazerman kindly allowed me to observe the Carter Racing case study at the Harvard Business School over the course of two days in October 2016. (The case study was created in 1986 by Jack W. Brittain and Sim B. Sitkin.)

240 **"professional weakness shared by all":** F. Lighthall, "Launching the Space Shuttle Challenger: Disciplinary Deficiencies in the Analysis of Engineering Data," *IEEE Transactions on Engineering Management* 38, no. 1 (1991): 63–74. Boisjoly's "away from goodness" quote is from transcripts of the Feb 25, 1986 hearing of the presidential commission.

243 **Boisjoly had personally inspected:** R. P. Boisjoly et al. "Roger Boisjoly and the Challenger Disaster," *Journal of Business Ethics* 8, no. 4 (1989): 217–230. Boisjoly's "away from goodness" quote is from transcripts of the Feb 25, 1986 hearing of the presidential commision.

244 **most complex machine ever built:** J. M. Logsdon, "Was the Space Shuttle a Mistake?," *MIT Technology Review,* July 6, 2011.

244 **McDonald and two Thiokol VPs:** Transcripts of presidential commission hearings, which provided information and quotes in this chapter are available at https://history.nasa.gov/rogersrep/genindex.htm. Allan McDonald also gives a fascinating account of the investigation and the return of the shuttle to flight in *Truth, Lies, and O-Rings* (Gainesville: University Press of Florida, 2009).

244 **"They said because they had flown":** From Diane Vaughan's book, which includes a fascinating exploration of "the normalization of deviance" in decision making: *The Challenger Launch Decision: Risky Technology, Culture, and Deviance at NASA* (Chicago: University of Chicago Press, 1996).

245 **"In God We Trust, All Others Bring Data":** A number of background interviews with current and former NASA managers and engineers—especially during a visit to NASA's Johnson Space Center in 2017—provided helpful context. NASA's own APPEL Knowledge Services portal was extremely helpful. It is an incredible repository of information that links to NASA's voluminous "Lessons Learned System."

245 **Karl Weick noticed something unusual:** K. E. Weick, "The Collapse of Sensemaking in Organizations: The Mann Gulch Disaster," *Administrative Science Quarterly* 38, no. 4 (1993): 628–52.; K. E. Weick, "Drop Your Tools: An Allegory for Organizational Studies," *Administrative Science Quarterly* 41, no. 2 (1996): 301–13; K. E. Weick, "Drop Your Tools: On Reconfiguring Management Education," *Journal of Management Education* 31, no. 1 (2007): 5–16.

245 **eleven feet per second:** R. C. Rothermel, "Mann Gulch Fire: A Race That Couldn't Be Won," Department of Agriculture, Forest Service, Intermountain Research Station, General Technical Report INT-299, May 1993.

246 **wildland firefighters continued to lose races with fires:** K. E. Weick, "Tool Retention and Fatalities in Wildland Fire Settings," in *Linking Expertise and Naturalistic Decision Making,* ed. E. Salas and G. A. Klein (New York: Psychology Press, 2001 [Kindle ebook]).

246 **"like a jet during take off":** USDA, USDI, and USDC, *South Canyon Fire Investigation* (Report of the South Canyon Fire Accident Investigation Team), U.S. Government Printing Office, Region 8, Report 573-183, 1994.

246 **"still wearing his backpack"; "then I realized I still had my saw"; twenty-three . . . perished beside them:** Weick, "Tool Retention and Fatalities in Wildland Fire Settings."

246–247 **grabbed it again in the air; "proxy for unlearning"; "regress to what they know best"; "existential crisis":** Weick, "Drop Your Tools: An Allegory for Organizational Studies."

248 **"a common pattern"**: J. Orasanu and L. Martin, "Errors in Aviation Decision Making," *Proceedings of the HESSD '98* (Workshop on Human Error, Safety and System Development) (1998): 100–107; J. Orasanu et al., "Errors in Aviation Decision Making," Fourth Conference on Naturalistic Decision Making, 1998.

248 **"If I make a decision"**: Weick, "Tool Retention and Fatalities in Wildland Fire Settings."

249 **"Between the lines, it suggested"**: M. Kohut, "Interview with Bryan O'Connor," NASA's *ASK* (*Academy Sharing Knowledge*) magazine, issue 45 (January 2012).

249 **"you have to use reason"**: transcript, Hearings of the Presidential Commission on the Space Shuttle Challenger Accident Vol. 4, February 25, 1986.

254 **"must have been really hard"**: Several members of the 48th Rescue Squadron provided invaluable background and corroboration.

255 **"live in the real world"**: C. Grupen, *Introduction to Radiation Protection* (Berlin: Springer, 2010), 90. Shafer's entire original message is preserved at https://yarchive.net/air/perfect_safety.html.

255 **But in the first study**: K. S. Cameron and S. J. Freeman, "Cultural Congruence, Strength, and Type: Relationships to Effectiveness," *Research in Organizational Change and Development* 5 (1991): 23–58.

255 **effective leaders and organizations had range**: K. S. Cameron and R. E. Quinn, *Diagnosing and Changing Organizational Culture*, 3rd Edition (San Francisco: Jossey-Bass, 2011).

256 **In one experiment**: S. V. Patil et al., "Accountability Systems and Group Norms: Balancing the Risks of Mindless Conformity and Reckless Deviation," *Journal of Behavioral Decision Making* 30 (2017): 282–303.

258 **Gene Kranz**: G. Kranz, *Failure Is Not an Option* (New York: Simon & Schuster, 2000). See also: M. Dunn, "Remaking NASA one step at a time," Associated Press, October 12, 2003.

258–259 **"Monday Notes"; William Lucas . . . "often grew angry"**: S. J. Dick, ed., *NASA's First 50 Years* (Washington, DC: NASA, 2011 [ebook]). Also, von Braun's weekly notes are archived at https://history.msfc.nasa.gov/vonbraun/vb_weekly_notes.html.

259 **"the quality of the notes fell"**: R. Launius, "Comments on a Very Effective Communications System: Marshall Space Flight Center's Monday Notes," *Roger Launius's Blog*, February 28, 2011.

260 **"proper channels"; "stringent and inhibiting"**: Columbia Accident Investigation Board, "History as Cause: *Columbia* and *Challenger*," in *Columbia Accident Investigation Board Report,* vol. 1, August 2003.

260 **Gravity Probe B**: Stanford University maintains an archive with copious information (both technical and written for the public) on GP-B, at einstein.stanford.edu. For a scientific deep dive, a special issue of the journal *Classical and Quantum Gravity* was devoted to GP-B (vol. 32, no. 22 [November 2015]).

261 **technology took twenty years:** T. Reichhardt, "Unstoppable Force," *Nature* 426 (2003): 380–81.

261 **"was confident that we could succeed":** NASA Case Study, "The Gravity Probe B Launch Decisions," NASA, Academy of Program/Project and Engineering Leadership.

262 **"a healthy tension in the system":** Geveden also discusses healthy tension in R. Wright et al., eds., *NASA at 50: Interviews with NASA's Senior Leadership* (Washington, DC: NASA, 2012).

263 **first direct test:** J. Overduin, "The Experimental Verdict on Spacetime from Gravity Probe B," in Vesselin Petkov, ed., *Space, Time, and Spacetime* (Berlin: Springer, 2010).

265 **Himalayan mountain climbers:** E.M. Anicich et al., "Hierarchical Cultural Values Predict Success and Mortality in High-Stakes Teams," *Proceedings of the National Academy of Sciences of the United States of America* 112, no. 5 (2015): 1338–43.

266 **"oculostenotic reflex":** Eric Topol is the cardiologist who coined that term. (For a patient who is actually having a heart attack, a stent can be lifesaving.)

266 **one in fifty patients:** K. Stergiopoulos and D. L. Brown, "Initial Coronary Stent Implantation With Medical Therapy vs Medical Therapy Alone for Stable Coronary Artery Disease: Meta-analysis of Randomized Controlled Trials," *Archives of Internal Medicine* 172, no. 4 (2012): 312–19.

266 **cannot believe that stenting:** G. A. Lin et al., "Cardiologists' Use of Percutaneous Coronary Interventions for Stable Coronary Artery Disease," *Archives of Internal Medicine* 167, no. 15 (2007):1604–09.

266 **were less likely to die:** A. B. Jena et al., "Mortality and Treatment Patterns among Patients Hospitalized with Acute Cardiovascular Conditions during Dates of National Cardiology Meetings," *JAMA Internal Medicine* 175, no. 2 (2015): 237–44. See also: A. B. Jena et al., "Acute Myocardial Infarction during Dates of National Interventional Cardiology Meetings," *Journal of the American Heart Association* 7, no. 6 (2018): e008230.

266 **"At large cardiology conventions":** R. F. Redberg, "Cardiac Patient Outcomes during National Cardiology Meetings," *JAMA Internal Medicine* 175, no. 2 (2015): 245.

267 **compared the surgery with "sham surgery":** R. Sihvonen et al., "Arthroscopic Partial Meniscectomy Versus Sham Surgery for a Degenerative Meniscal Tear," *New England Journal of Medicine* 369 (2013): 2515–24. Hyperlinks to several other studies with supporting findings can be found in: D. Epstein, "When Evidence Says No, But Doctors Say Yes," *ProPublica,* February 22, 2017.

CHAPTER 12: DELIBERATE AMATEURS

270 **"Very promising!":** Smithies discussed some of his work and notebook pages in his publicly available Nobel Lecture, "Turning Pages" (December 7, 2007). The

University of North Carolina maintains an extraordinary online archive of digitized versions of more than sixty years of Smithies's notebooks, along with audio recordings of Smithies himself going through them and providing commentary. (Smithies told me that one should always have a notebook, even on Saturday.) The archive was a wonderful resource for interview preparation, and can be found at smithies.lib.unc.edu/notebooks.

271 **A 2016 analysis of ten thousand researchers' careers:** A. Clauset et al., "Data-Driven Predictions in the Science of Science," *Science* 355 (2017): 477–80.

272 **had reportedly tested 240,000 compounds:** P. McKenna, "Nobel Prize Goes to Modest Woman Who Beat Malaria for China," *New Scientist,* November 9, 2011, online ed.

272 **a fourth-century Chinese alchemist:** Alchemist and herbalist Ge Hong wrote *A Handbook of Prescriptions for Emergencies* in the fourth century, during the Jin dynasty. Tu gives background in her Nobel Lecture: "Artemisinin—A Gift from Traditional Chinese Medicine to the World" (December 7, 2015). She shares a photo of a sixteenth-century copy of the handbook in: Y. Tu, "The Discovery of Artemisinin (Qinghaosu) and Gifts from Chinese Medicine," *Nature Medicine* 17, no. 10 (2011): 1217–20.

272 **A study on the decline of malaria:** Bhatt et al., "The Effect of Malaria Control on *Plasmodium falciparum* in Africa Between 2000 and 2015," *Nature* 526 (2015): 207–11.

273 **the label NBGBOKFO:** G. Watts, "Obituary: Oliver Smithies," *Lancet* 389 (2017): 1004.

273 **Scotch tape to rip thin layers of graphite:** Geim details the discovery in his aptly titled Nobel Lecture, "Random Walk to Graphene" (December 8, 2010). Among the cleverly titled lecture sections: "Zombie Management," "Better to Be Wrong Than Boring," and "Legend of Scotch Tape."

273 **stronger than steel:** C. Lee et al., "Measurement of the Elastic Properties and Intrinsic Strength of Monolayer Graphene," *Science* 321 (2008): 385–8.

273 **Spiders fed graphene:** E. Lepore et al., "Spider Silk Reinforced by Graphene or Carbon Nanotubes," *2D Materials* 4, no. 3 (2017): 031013.

273 **"sufficient scientific advance":** J. Colapinto, "Material Question," *The New Yorker,* December 2014, online ed.

274 **"deliberate amateur"; "paradox of innovation":** Sarah Lewis's fascinating book on creativity: *The Rise: Creativity, the Gift of Failure, and the Search for Mastery* (New York: Simon & Schuster, 2014).

274 **"It is rather unusual":** "U. Manchester's Andre Geim: Sticking with Graphene—For Now," *ScienceWatch* newsletter interview, August 2008.

274 **"never bother to ask":** Lewis, *The Rise.*

274 **"principle of limited sloppiness":** Max Delbrück interviews with Carolyn Harding in 1978, California Institute of Technology Oral History Project, 1979.

274 **"seems to be wasting his life,"; "this flexibility":** E. Pain, "Sharing a Nobel Prize at 36," *Science,* online ed. career profiles, February 25, 2011.

276 **"If this continues unabated":** A. Casadevall, "Crisis in Biomedical Sciences: Time for Reform?," Johns Hopkins Bloomberg School of Public Health Dean's Lecture Series, February 21, 2017, www.youtube.com/watch?v=05Sk-3u90Jo. See also: F. C. Fang et al., "Misconduct Accounts for the Majority of Retracted Scientific Publications," *Proceedings of the National Academy of Sciences of the USA* 109, no. 42 (2012): 17028–33.

276 **retraction-prone journal:** "Why High-Profile Journals Have More Retractions," *Nature,* online ed., September 17, 2014.

277 **If a test to detect a disease:** A. K. Manrai et al., "Medicine's Uncomfortable Relationship with Math," *JAMA Internal Medicine* 174, no. 6 (2014): 991–93.

278 **"The guild system in Europe arose"; growth industry of conferences:** A. Casadevall and F. C. Fang, "Specialized Science," *Infection and Immunity* 82, no. 4 (2014): 1355–60.

279 **biomedical research funding rose exponentially:** A. Bowen and A. Casadevall, "Increasing Disparities Between Resource Inputs and Outcome, as Measured by Certain Health Deliverables, in Biomedical Research," *Proceedings of the National Academy of Sciences of the USA* 112, no. 36 (2015): 11335–40.

279 **Life expectancy . . . recently declined:** J. Y. Ho and A. S. Hendi, "Recent Trends in Life Expectancy Across High Income Countries," *BMJ* (2018), 362:k2562.

280 **researchers analyzed the networks:** R. Guimerà et al., "Team Assembly Mechanisms Determine Collaboration Network Structure and Team Performance," *Science* 308 (2005): 697–702.

280 **"The entire network looks different":** "Dream Teams Thrive on Mix of Old and New Blood," *Northwestern Now,* May 3, 2005.

280 **The commercial fate of Broadway:** B. Uzzi and J. Spiro, "Collaboration and Creativity," *American Journal of Sociology* 111, no. 2 (2005): 447–504.

280 **"import/export business of ideas":** "Teaming Up to Drive Scientific Discovery," Brian Uzzi at TEDxNorthwesternU, June 2012.

281 **migrants' "arbitrage" opportunities:** C. Franzoni et al., "The Mover's Advantage: The Superior Performance of Migrant Scientists," *Economic Letters* 122, no. 1 (2014): 89–93; see also: A. M. Petersen, "Multiscale Impact of Researcher Mobility," *Journal of the Royal Society Interface* 15, no. 146 (2018): 20180580.

281 **Uzzi and a team analyzed:** B. Uzzi et al., "Atypical Combinations and Scientific Impact," *Science* 342 (2013): 468–72.

281 **classified a paper as "novel":** J. Wang et al., "Bias Against Novelty in Science," *Research Policy* 46, no. 8 (2017): 1416–36.

281 **history of innovation in Japan:** D. K. Simonton, "Foreign Influence and National Achievement: The Impact of Open Milieus on Japanese Civilization," *Journal of Personality and Social Psychology* 72, no. 1 (1997): 86–94.

282 **work that builds bridges:** K. J. Boudreau et al., "Looking Across and Looking Beyond the Knowledge Frontier: Intellectual Distance, Novelty, and Resource Allocation in Science," *Management Science* 62, no. 10 (2016): 2765–83.

283 **nourishing itself with radiation:** E. Dadachova et al., "Ionizing Radiation Changes the Electronic Properties of Melanin and Enhances the Growth of Melanized Fungi," *PLoS ONE* 2, no. 5 (2007): e457.

284 **I sat in on funding policy hearings:** For example: D. Epstein, "Senatorial Peer Review," *Inside Higher Ed,* May 3, 2006; and: D. Epstein, "Science Bill Advances," *Inside Higher Ed*, May 19, 2006. Interestingly, in those hearings, New Hampshire senator (and engineering PhD) John Sununu, normally a strident budget hawk, stood precisely opposite Hutchison and advocated funding research with no clear application. "If you can identify an economic benefit you shouldn't be funding it," he said. "That's what we have a venture capital community for."

285 **A curious phenomenon:** Clauset et al., "Data-Driven Predictions in the Science of Science."

286 **"these players performed":** M. Hornig et al., "Practice and Play in the Development of German Top-Level Professional Football Players," *European Journal of Sport Science* 16, no. 1 (2016): 96–105.

286 **"dabble time":** J. Gifford, *100 Great Business Leaders* (Singapore: Marshall Cavendish Business, 2013).

CONCLUSION: EXPANDING YOUR RANGE

288 **the more work eminent creators produced:** There is an excellent discussion of this research (including Edison's patents) in chapter 10 of S. B. Kaufman and C. Gregoire, *Wired to Create* (New York: Perigee, 2015). An interesting analysis of Shakespeare's plays based on "popularity" scores is D. K. Simonton, "Popularity, Content, and Context in 37 Shakespeare Plays," *Poetics* 15 (1986): 493–510.

288 **Rachel Whiteread achieved a feat:** W. Osgerby, "Young British Artists," in *ART: The Whole Story,* ed. S. Farthing (London: Thames & Hudson, 2010).

289 **"Baseball has a truncated outcome distribution":** M. Simmons, "Forget the 10,000-Hour Rule," *Medium,* October 26, 2017.

289 **started formal lessons at twenty-two:** W. Moskalew et al., *Svetik: A Family Memoir of Sviatoslav Richter* (London: Toccata Press, 2015).

289 **did not get a basketball until he was thirteen years old:** "My Amazing Journey—Steve Nash," NBA.com, 2007–08 Season Preview.

290 **Julius Caesar:** C. Pelling, *Plutarch and History* (Swansea: Classical Press of Wales, 2002).

291 **"It is an experiment":** Abrams v. United States, 250 U.S. 616 (1919) (Holmes dissenting opinion).

Expanding Your Range

WHEN I BEGAN to write and speak about data indicating that athletes who go on to become elite are usually *not* early specializers, the reactions (particularly from parents) reliably fell into two categories: (1) Simple disbelief, can't be true; and (2) "So, in one sentence, what is the advice?" What one sentence of advice can encapsulate the embrace of breadth and the journey of experimentation that is necessary if you want, like Van Gogh or Andre Geim or Frances Hesselbein, to arrive at a place optimized for you alone? Like the paths of those individuals, my exploration of breadth and specialization was inefficient, and what began as a search for one sentence of advice ended in this book.

Told in retrospect for popular media, stories of innovation and self-discovery can look like orderly journeys from A to B. Sort of like how inspirational-snippet accounts of the journeys of elite athletes appear straightforward, but the stories usually get murkier when examined in depth or over time. The popular notion of the Tiger path minimizes the role of detours, breadth, and experimentation. It is attractive because it is a tidy prescription, low on uncertainty and high on efficiency. After all, who doesn't like a head start? Experimentation is not a tidy prescription, but it is common, and it has advantages, and it requires more